D1165656

Consumer Credit Fundamentals

Also by Steven Finlay

THE MANAGEMENT OF CONSUMER CREDIT
Theory & Practice

Consumer Credit Fundamentals

Second Edition

Steven Finlay

First edition published 2005
Second edition published 2009 by
PALGRAVE MACMILLAN

Palgrave Macmillan in the UK is an imprint of Macmillan Publishers Limited, registered in England, company number 785998, of Houndmills, Basingstoke, Hampshire RG21 6XS.

Palgrave Macmillan in the US is a division of St Martin's Press LLC, 175 Fifth Avenue, New York, NY 10010.

Palgrave Macmillan is the global academic imprint of the above companies and has companies and representatives throughout the world.

Palgrave® and Macmillan® are registered trademarks in the United States, the United Kingdom, Europe and other countries

ISBN-13: 978-0-230-22015-7   hardback
ISBN-10: 0-230-22015-0   hardback

This book is printed on paper suitable for recycling and made from fully managed and sustained forest sources. Logging, pulping and manufacturing processes are expected to conform to the environmental regulations of the country of origin.

A catalogue record for this book is available from the British Library.

A catalogue record for this book is available from the Library of Congress.

10   9   8   7   6   5   4   3   2   1
18 17 16 15 14 13 12 11 10 09

Printed and bound in Great Britain by
CPI Antony Rowe, Chippenham and Eastbourne

To Sam and Ruby

Contents

List of Tables and Figures

Tables

Figures

Preface

Like many people I have a mortgage. I recently bought a new dish-washer and it made sense to take the interest-free repayment option and leave the money earning interest in the bank, rather than paying for it there and then. The last time I bought a car there was no discount for cash like the good old days, but if I had taken the company's motor finance plan then they would have cut me a deal. When I do my grocery shopping I use the credit card supplied by the supermarket to gain loyalty points, and I'll even use my credit card to buy a newspaper if I go to the local store and don't have any cash. I'm a typical individual living in a world where credit is prevalent across almost every aspect of consumer society.

Was credit always so pervasive? Between the early 1980s and the late 2000s the amount of personal debt more than quadrupled in real terms in the US, UK and many other countries, and today more people use more credit in more ways than ever before. Yet credit is not just a modern phenomenon, and the nature of the credit we use today is little different in principle from that used by the Babylonians, Greeks and Romans thousands of years ago. What has changed is the speed, sophistication and convenience of the credit experience brought about through the application of modern technology.

Is credit a good thing? Arguments about the pros and cons of credit have raged since antiquity, with references to its use and misuse in many ancient texts including the Bible, the Qu'ran and the Torah. Aristotle argued against the unnatural nature of interest-bearing credit while others, such as the eighteenth-century philosopher and social commentator Jeremy Bentham, argued for the right of each person of sound mind to borrow under whatever terms they saw fit, without undue restriction or legislation – an argument widely accepted by modern economists.

Today, there is often an undercurrent of 'us versus them'. The consumer is represented by the media as the underdog, enslaved to debt by the financial services industry in its never ending drive for profit. Yet it is difficult to see how western societies, particularly the UK and US, could manage without consumer credit in something resembling its current form. We live in a state of tension. On one hand credit provides the ability to buy goods and services when we want them, and provides a cushioning effect against short term economic downturns, allowing spending to continue until conditions improve. On the other hand debt has caused a huge amount of misery and unhappiness. Between 5 and 10 percent of the UK adult population has been taken to court at some point in their lives because of unpaid debts. Millions of Americans lost their homes in the aftermath of the sub-prime mortgage fiasco of 2006/7 and the subsequent weakening of the US housing market – with the effects of the credit crunch that followed felt throughout the world. The issue we need to address as a society lies in balancing these opposing forces. The benefits of a liberal financial services framework need to be weighed against the protections required to safeguard the wellbeing and livelihoods of the populace in a manner we have come to expect in modern civilized societies.

Despite widespread use of credit and almost daily coverage in the media, the literature relating to consumer credit issues is fragmented, and there is much ignorance about one of the world's largest industries. What material does exist is often specialized and focused towards specific aspects of the subject. There is very little that comprehensively introduces consumer credit in something approaching its entirety. Therefore, this book has been written to fill what I perceive as a gap. My objective has been to provide a broad contextual and cross-disciplinary introduction to consumer credit, covering its history, the types of credit available, how credit is granted and managed, the legal frameworks within which commercial lenders must operate, as well as consumer and ethical issues. I have also tried to provide a text that is relevant to consumer credit markets around the world. This is a tall order, but I hope I have been able to provide sufficient information for it to be of worth to anyone with an interest in the subject.

Steven Finlay, December 2008

Acknowledgements

First and foremost I would like to thank my wife Sam, and my parents, Ann and Paul, all of whom contributed from their own areas of expertise and devoted much of their time towards reading early drafts of the manuscript. My thanks also to Professor Robert Fildes of Lancaster University for his comments, input and guidance. I would also like to thank Dr Ian Glover of Experian, Dr Mohammed Salisu of Lancaster University, Professor John Presley and Dr Keith Pond of Loughborough University, Nathen Finch of the National Pawnbrokers Association and Mark Rowe of Pentest Limited for their help. Finally, there are numerous others to whom I am indebted in one way or another for their help and support, and my thanks goes to all of you.

1
Introduction

This book provides an introduction to a range of topics concerning consumer credit. The objective is to describe the nature of credit-debt relationships and the way in which commercial lending institutions manage the credit-debt relationships they have with their customers. These relationships are then placed within a historical, ethical and legal context.

The book is suitable for anyone interested in consumer credit, whatever their background. The reader may be a student of economics, banking and finance, business studies, marketing, history, sociology or some similar course of study, a university researcher or a professional working within the financial services industry. The book is also suitable as a reference text for people who already have some knowledge of the consumer credit industry, but who are looking to expand their knowledge beyond their immediate domain of expertise; for example, financial journalists, social scientists, civil servants, debt advisors and members of the legal profession.

The US and UK have the largest and most developed consumer credit markets in the world. Together they account for over half of the entire worldwide consumer credit market. Therefore, much of the material for this book is drawn from the experiences of these two countries. For purposes of convenience all financial values are quoted in US dollars, with an exchange rate of \$2 to £1 used for UK source material. However, concepts of credit and debt are largely universal, as are the practices employed by lenders to provide credit products to their customers, and where the US and UK led many others now follow. Therefore, the overwhelming majority of material is applicable to credit markets around the world.

The first two chapters are introductory. In this chapter we discuss the nature of consumer credit and its increasing prevalence in modern society. In Chapter 2 the different types of consumer credit are introduced together with the different sorts of institution that provide credit. Chapters 3, 4 and 5 focus on historical, social, ethical and legal aspects of debt. Chapter 3 provides a history of consumer credit, charting its use from ancient times to the present day. Chapter 4 discusses ethics and the arguments that have been put forward about what constitutes an ethical credit-debt relationship. Chapter 5 introduces the main consumer credit legislation in the UK and US.

Chapters 6 through 9 cover the mechanics of credit granting and credit management as undertaken by the major providers of consumer credit such as retail banks, credit unions and saving and loan companies (building societies). In Chapter 6 the economics and marketing of credit are discussed in relation to the costs of credit provision and revenue streams that are generated from customers. Provision, capital requirements and securitization are also covered in this chapter. Chapter 7 looks at how credit granting decisions are made, and in particular how credit scoring systems are used to make the vast majority of consumer lending decisions without any human involvement in the decision making process. In Chapter 8 we look at credit reference agencies and their role in facilitating information sharing between financial institutions. Chapter 9 provides an introduction to credit management; that is, the operational systems and decision processes employed by financial services organization to manage customer enquiries, make lending decisions, open new accounts and manage customer relationships on an ongoing basis. Debt recovery and fraud are also discussed in this chapter. Appendix A explains how interest and APR are calculated.

1.1   The rise and rise of consumer credit

For many people in modern society credit has become an integral part of everyday life. Every day dozens of credit advertisements appear in the media and millions of mail shots are delivered to our doors. Almost every newspaper has its 'best buy' credit tables and reports on credit issues on a frequent basis. Today there are very few goods or services that can't be bought on credit terms or retailers who don't cater for credit facilities. Towards the end of the 2000s, the American public had a combined debt of more than $13 trillion. Of this, about $10.5 trillion was accounted for by mortgages and other lending secured against residential property. The remaining $2.5 trillion was mainly in the form of credit cards, personal loans and hire-purchase agreements (The

Federal Reserve Board 2008, p.102). To put these figures in perspective, the entire gross domestic product of the US in 2007 was \$14.1 trillion (The Federal Reserve Board 2008, p.13). Personal debt in the US rose steadily in real terms between the early-1980s and the late-2000s. At the start of the 1980s the average American had total debts equal to around half their annual income. By the late-2000s this had risen to almost twice annual income. A similar pattern of growth in personal debt has also occurred in the UK, parts of Europe and many other regions. However, the consumer credit phenomena has not been entirely global. In many developed countries, including parts of Europe, the growth in the use of consumer credit has been less pronounced – particularly in the credit card market. For the estimated one and a half billion members of the Islamic community, while credit is permitted, the charging of interest is forbidden. Consequently, the products available and the patterns of credit usage within this population differ from those of the typical western consumer.

1.2   Consumer credit defined

A credit-debt relationship is defined as *'that which is owed by one entity to another'*. An entity may be an individual, company, government or any other type of institution or organization. Credit and debt represent flip sides of the same coin. Credit is that which is provided, debt is that which is owed. Credit-debt relationships are distinguished from other types of relationship by two key features. The first is time. If money is viewed as a medium of exchange, facilitating trade in goods and services at a point in time, then a monetary credit-debt relationship can be viewed as money across time. Credit is future money made available in the present; debt is past money to be repaid in the future. The effort (cost) required to transport money through time is incorporated into the cost of credit provision, represented in the form of interest rates and other charges made by credit providers. The longer the time required to repay a debt the further into the future one must go to obtain funds, and hence the greater the cost involved. The second differentiating feature of credit-debt relationships is risk. Risk is the expected loss associated with a debt should the borrower default, and this must also be factored into the cost of credit provision. The greater the risk, the greater the cost, and hence, the higher the price someone must pay for the credit they require.

Credit need not necessarily be based on formal monetary systems. The credit concept can be applied in barter economies based on the direct exchange of goods and services, and some would go so far as to suggest that the true nature of money is best described as a representation of the credit-debt relationships that exist in society, rather than as a medium of exchange or 'neutral veil' across trading relationships, as is commonly accepted by many economists (Ingham 2004, pp.12–19). As Ingham points out, all modern currencies are based on a guarantee of repayment (a debt) made by the currency issuer and one is reminded of this relationship by the phrase printed on UK banknotes: 'I promise to pay the bearer on demand the sum of.....'

Consumer credit represents one area in which credit-debt relationships exist and can be defined as '*money, goods or services provided to an individual in lieu of payment*'. Lending to individuals in the form of credit cards, loans, mortgages and so on are the most obvious forms of consumer credit and the ones that are the primary focus of this book, but consumer credit in its broadest sense also encompasses government, not-for-profit and informal credit-debt relationships. For example, government lending to people receiving state benefits, student loans and money lent between friends and relatives. Many people pay utility and telecoms bills in arrears and these too can be considered forms of consumer credit.

Institutional borrowing is not considered in this book, but a grey area is that occupied by sole traders and small business. Is someone self-employed who borrows to fund their livelihood a commercial or personal borrower? One might consider the amount borrowed, with commercial lending defined by larger amounts, but this is quickly seen as untenable once some typical lending situations are considered. A $500,000 residential mortgage is not uncommon, but a $500,000 overdraft facility would be considered substantial for many companies with six, or even seven figure turnovers. The purpose for which credit has been obtained can also be considered, but again it can be demonstrated that this is not ideal. Consider the self-employed consultant who obtains a loan to purchase a laptop and a car, but also uses the equipment for domestic purposes such as surfing the internet and taking the kids to school. Is this a commercial or personal transaction?

A better approach is to consider where responsibility for the debt lies. For the consultant, if the loan is taken out in their own name and they are responsible for making repayments, then this is consumer credit. If however, the consultant creates a limited company (a common practice that costs only a few hundred dollars) and borrows in the company name, then the company is liable and not the consultant. So, if an individual is personally liable for debt,[1] the debt can be classified as consumer credit regardless of purpose or value. If the responsibility lies with an organization such as a limited company, public utility, cooperative or charity, then this is institutional borrowing, and therefore not consumer credit.

This book adopts a broad definition of consumer credit, but it is worth noting that 'consumer credit' is sometimes used in a narrower context. Residential mortgage lending in particular, is often treated as a separate category of individual borrowing. This is because credit provided for a house purchase is viewed as a long term investment with the potential to yield a return for the borrower, rather than credit acquired to support immediate consumption. While it is often sensible to distinguish between mortgages and other types of individual borrowing due to the size, nature and the peculiarities of the mortgage market, it is included within the definition presented here for a number of reasons. First, many of the issues and problems relating to credit and debt, and the mechanics of credit operations are similar (although not identical) regardless of the form in which credit is provided. Second, equity withdrawal – where an individual extends the mortgage secured against their home to acquire funds for immediate consumptive purposes – is common. This was a particularly pronounced feature of the US/UK mortgage market in the early/mid-2000s when house prices rose rapidly and equity withdrawal was responsible for a considerable proportion of the growth in retail spending that occurred during this period. Third, there are a range of financial products available, such as Home Equity Lines of Credit (HELOC), that combine different kinds of saving and borrowing into a single financial package providing banking and short term credit facilities in conjunction with mortgage borrowing. It therefore makes sense to consider these components together rather than separately.

As the remainder of the book deals primarily with consumer credit the terms 'credit' and 'consumer credit' will be used interchangeably from now on.

1.3   Boon or bane?

Credit is generally viewed as beneficial to economic growth and empirical evidence supports this view. In economies where credit has been widely utilized, such as in the UK and US, economic growth has traditionally been strong in comparison to many other first world economies where credit is less prevalent. From an economic perspective it can be argued that credit allows goods and services to be purchased in times when the economy is weak to be repaid when the economy is strong, thus damping the potentially damaging effects of the economic cycle. Other reasons for the relationship between economic growth and credit may be psychological, with people who borrow believing they are borrowing against a better future and are driven to realize their ambitions – the very embodiment of the American dream.

Credit can mean flexibility and choice. In the short term it enables people to purchase essential items if they run short of funds before payday and it allows flexibility in household budget planning as expenditure in one week or month can be offset against income in another. Longer term it means that if an unexpected event occurs, such as the car breaking down or the roof starts to leak, these can be dealt with quickly, whereas if someone has no ready cash it could be a considerable period of time before they could afford the repair. The growth in the volume and diversity of consumer credit products has also resulted in a thriving consumer credit industry providing employment for millions of people around the world.

Like most things credit also has its negative aspects which should not be forgotten or understated. A survey undertaken on behalf of the UK Government Taskforce on over-indebtedness reported that 18 percent of households had experienced some type of financial difficulty within the previous 12 months, with 10 percent in arrears with one or more credit commitments (Kempson 2002, p.28). Independent estimates based on the UK government's annual Expenditure and Food Survey estimated that 20 percent of households could be classified as over-indebted (Finlay 2006a). These figures are not from a period of economic recession, but a time when the UK economy had grown consistently for several years, with interest rates and unemployment low by modern standards. Every year in the UK, hundreds of thousands of court orders are made against individuals for unpaid debts and many tens of thousands of families have their homes repossessed or are declared bankrupt (personally insolvent) because they are unable to maintain debt repayments. Research evidence suggests that the burden of debt can cause physiological stress and depression (Nettleton and Burrows 1998; Drentea and Lavrakas 2000; Reading and Reynolds 2001). There is also evidence of a link between physical illness and debt (Jacoby 2002; Balmer *et al.* 2005). However, the reasons why debt should cause people to become physically ill have yet to be fully established.

As Burton (2007, pp.66–70) describes, since the 1970s the nature of the credit-debt relationships between lenders and borrowers, and the perception of credit within society, has changed significantly. Legislative changes opened up the credit market to new entrants and relaxed credit controls. At the same time technological developments made credit more cheaply and easily accessible to more people than ever before. Debt has also become more socially acceptable. Not that long ago debt had almost entirely negative connotations. Those who borrowed were considered frivolous and their behaviour morally questionable, but today debt is an accepted part of everyday life in many societies. While many have benefited from increased access to easy credit, there have been side effects. One is the relative ease with which it is possible build up massive unaffordable debt by making use of equity withdrawal and balance transfer facilities using credit cards, consolidation loans and home equity lines of credit. Debt is repeatedly transferred between an ever-increasing number of lenders, all of whom are eager for new customers in a highly competitive market. It is only the lender at the end of the line, when all credit facilities have been used to their full, who will be left holding the debt. Many examples of this type of behaviour have been reported in the press. An individual will find themselves with unsecured debts equal to many times their salaries and repayment burdens beyond all hope of ever being met, but which were sustained for a considerable period of time, often many years, before coming to light. See Carter (2004) and Knight (2004) for some typical examples of this type of behaviour. Another downside of greater access to credit is that it can fuel certain psychological disorders. One example is compulsive shopping. It is estimated that anything up to ten million Americans and two million Britons are shopaholics (Burton 2007, p.39). Another problem is compensatory consumption, where people consume products or services to compensate for something missing in their lives. Examples include gambling, alcohol and drug addition. This is not to say that credit is the root cause of these behaviours, but that easy access to credit allows them to be engaged in more easily and to a greater extent than would otherwise be possible.

While for some people the problem is an inability to control their spending or service their debts, for many the problem is obtaining affordable credit in the first place – standard credit facilities are simply not available because the major credit granting institutions are unwilling to provide them. There is no 'right to credit' and if a credit provider does not wish to deal with an individual for whatever reason, there is no compulsion for them to do so. A study undertaken on behalf of the National Consumer Council in the UK reported on research that found that almost 20 percent of the UK population were denied access to credit from standard credit providers such as the major high street banks and building societies (Whyley and Brooker 2004, p.10). However, as previous studies have noted, the number of people who technically do not have access to any type of credit whatsoever is probably very small (Kempson *et al.* 2000, p.42). This can be attributed to the willingness of some lenders, such as pawnbrokers, to lend against property which is kept in their possession for the duration of the loan, and lenders charging rates of interest that could be considered extortionate. For example, Provident Financial, one of the 250 largest UK companies, advertises $1,000 cash loans on its website with an APR in excess of 360 percent (Provident Personal Credit 2008).

1.4 Working with credit

The credit industry is large, forming a significant part of the wider financial services industry that also covers savings, investment and insurance. Large numbers of people are employed in customer contact centres (call centres) to process applications, deal with customer account queries and to promote products and services to existing and prospective customers. At every branch of every bank there will be at least one trained financial advisor who can advise potential customers about the benefits, terms and conditions of the credit products offered by their organization. In the UK for example, the credit industry is estimated to be responsible for around 5 percent of GDP and provides employment for over one million people (Leenders 2005).

For graduates and members of the professional community, consumer credit represents a significant employment area, offering careers in marketing, accounting and finance, IT, law, credit management, data analysis and operations management, with many of these roles associated with strategically important head office functions. Marketing departments formulate branding strategies, develop marketing plans and design customer acquisition and retention strategies. Credit risk functions make decisions about which credit applications to accept, on what terms and how accounts are managed on an ongoing basis. The operational and IT areas are concerned with the physical processes and information flows required to ensure smooth and efficient systems for customer enquiries, account set-up, account management, collections activity and the production of management information required by other groups within the organization. Finance departments deal with the higher level accounting functions and the strategic flow of funds;

for example, ensuring funds are available in support of the customer demand generated from the operational strategies implemented by the marketing and credit functions. Considerable legal expertise is required to deal with an array of consumer and corporate issues covering credit and credit related legislation.

For external agencies working in conjunction with the financial services industry, advertising is a key field. For example, the major credit granting institutions, such as banks and building societies, account for more than 10 percent of all UK advertising expenditure (The Advertising Association 2007). There are also numerous third party suppliers providing the credit industry with services such as database marketing, statistical analysis, management consultancy, computer hardware and software, legal services, and outsourcing of customer services and IT functions.

Paralleling the growth of the credit industry there have been increasing concerns about debt and over-commitment. Social scientists, politicians, civil servants and journalists have expressed growing levels of interest and concern over credit issues and the psychology and social impact of debt. Consequently, there has been increased demand for people with knowledge of consumer credit issues to work for advice centres, the media, academia and various government agencies.

1.5 Chapter summary

Consumer credit covers the provision of goods and services, provided to individuals in lieu of payment. For many credit is an integral part of modern life, provided by a large and established credit industry, employing significant numbers of people from a variety of backgrounds and with a wide range of expertise. However, while credit is widely perceived as bringing benefit to consumers and the wider economy, the pressures of debt affect a significant proportion of the population. There are a considerable number of households struggling financially and in arrears with their credit commitments, and every year millions of people are taken to court, are declared bankrupt or have their homes repossessed as a direct consequence of their debt situation. There is also evidence that the effects of debt are not just material, but that the psychological effects can have a serious impact on an individual's mental and physical health.

Access to credit is not a right. In many countries a significant proportion of the population do not have access to standard forms of credit that most people take for granted, such as a credit card, mortgage, overdraft or a personal loan. In the UK about a fifth of the population fall into this category. If these people need credit they are generally forced to seek it on unfavourable terms, from sources that demand considerably higher interest rates and/or fees for the privilege of borrowing.

There are two main issues about the availability and use of credit. On one hand there is the fear that we are an over-indebted society and current levels of debt are unsustainable and must be controlled. On the other hand there is concern that affordable credit facilities, such as those offered by the main high street banks and building societies, are simply not available to a large number of people and that efforts should be made to widen access to as much of the population as possible. These two positions are not entirely contradictory, but providing a framework that encompasses both of them is a challenge for both the credit industry and society.

1.6   Suggested sources of further information

Ingham, G. (2004). *The Nature of Money*. Polity Press. Ingham writes from a viewpoint straddling the social sciences, challenging the conventional economic orthodoxy of money as a medium of exchange. He argues for an alternative model for the operation of monetary systems, describing money in terms of the credit-debt relationships that exist between individuals, institutions and other organizational entities that constitute society.

Burton, D. (2007). *Credit and Consumer Society*. Routledge. This book draws together research findings from across a number of disciplines to provide a comprehensive view of the role of consumer credit within modern society.

2
Products and Providers

There are many forms of credit consumers can obtain and use, and many types of organization that provide credit. The goal in this chapter is to introduce each type of credit and describe the nature and objectives of credit providers. The chapter begins with a discussion of the features that can be used to define each type of consumer credit. The central part of the chapter then presents the different types of credit available in the market today, such as credit cards, mortgages and pawn loans, in terms of these features. The final part of the chapter discusses the institutions that provide consumer credit and the characteristics that differentiate one type of lending institution from another.

2.1   The features of credit agreements

As we shall see later in the chapter, there are many different types of consumer credit, each of which has its own particular characteristics. However, each type of credit product can be described in terms of one or more of the following features:

- Secured or unsecured credit: Credit is secured if, when the customer breaks the terms of the credit agreement, specific assets named in the agreement can be possessed by the lender in lieu of the debt; for example, the borrower's home or car. Credit that is not secured against a specific asset is said to be unsecured.
- Amortized or balloon: Credit is amortized if the debt is repaid gradually over time. Repayments cover both interest and capital so that by the end of the agreement the debt has been repaid. With balloon credit a loan is provided for a fixed period of time and then repaid

in full. Interest may be paid at regular intervals or as a single payment at the end of the agreement. Balloon is also used to describe agreements where irregular repayments are made as and when funds become available (Butler *et al.* 1997, p.25) or where individual repayments include repayment of some of the loan capital, but the final payment is larger than all other payments (Collin 2003, p.28).

- Fixed sum or running account: A fixed sum agreement is where an amount is borrowed for a fixed period of time (the term of the agreement). When the repayment schedule is complete the agreement is terminated. Where the amount to be borrowed is unknown, but a credit facility is created, a running account credit agreement exists. The size of the debt is allowed to fluctuate as new credit is advanced and repayments made. Running account credit agreements usually have a maximum stated spending limit, termed the credit limit or credit line, against which funds can be drawn. Running account agreements are also known as open ended credit agreements or revolving credit agreements.

- Unrestricted or restricted: Unrestricted credit is where the borrower decides how the credit will be used. This usually means funds are provided as cash, a cheque or paid directly into a bank account. Restricted credit is where the credit can only be used to buy certain goods or services. In this case no money passes through the hands of the borrower.

- Credit sale, conditional sale or hire-purchase. These features apply only to restricted credit agreements. If a customer buys goods on a credit sale basis, then the goods become the immediate property of the customer. The merchant is not permitted to reclaim/seize the goods if the customer then fails to pay for them. With a conditional sale, ownership transfers to the borrower only when the terms of the agreement have been complied with.[1] This means that if the terms of the agreement are broken the lender can repossesses the goods. Hire-purchase is similar to conditional sale, but the crucial difference is that the customer is hiring the goods with an option to buy at the end of the agreement.[2] The hirer can therefore, decide not to exercise their option to buy and return the goods. With a conditional sale the borrower is committed to the purchase; the goods can not be returned once the agreement has been signed.

- Two party or three party credit agreement: A two party agreement (known as a Debtor-Creditor or DC agreement) exists where only the debtor and the creditor are parties to the agreement. A three party agreement (known as a Debtor-Creditor-Supplier or DCS agreement) exists when someone purchases goods or services from a merchant,[3] with credit provided by a third party. The person is indebted to the third party not the merchant. In many countries, including the US and EU member states, the distinction between a DC and DCS agreement is important when there is a dispute about the purchase. With a DCS agreement the credit provider has joint liability with the merchant for the items that have been purchased. If you buy a holiday using your credit card a DCS agreement exists because the card issuer, not the travel agent, provides the credit. If you subsequently can't go on holiday because the travel agent goes bust, the credit card company will be liable to compensate you for your loss. In the UK, all restricted credit agreements regulated by the Consumer Credit Act 1974 are defined as DCS agreements in law, even if the credit provider and the supplier of the goods are one and the same (Dobson 1996, p.285).

2.2 The cost of credit

The cost of credit is the additional amount over and above the amount borrowed that the borrower has to pay. It includes interest, arrangement fees and any other charges. Some costs are mandatory, required by the lender as an integral part of the credit agreement. Other costs, such as those for credit insurance, may be optional, with the borrower choosing whether or not they are included as part of the agreement. Interest is a charge made in proportion to the amount and term of the loan, expressed as a percentage of the total sum borrowed per unit time. The unit of time may be a day, month, year or some other period. For example, for a sum of $1,000 borrowed for five years and then repaid in full, if the interest charge is 7 percent per annum, the interest payable would be $350 ($1,000 * 7% * 5).[4]

In some circumstances, charges are made to carry out certain tasks or in response to customer behaviour. Arrangement fees are common for some types of lending, and many lenders charge penalty fees if a loan repayment is missed or late.

Interest and other charges are presented in a variety of different ways, but under many legislative regimes lenders are required to quote all mandatory charges in the form of an Annual Percentage Rate of Charge (APR). The goal of the APR calculation is to promote 'truth in lending', to give potential borrowers a clear measure of the true cost of borrowing and to allow a comparison to be made between competing products. The APR is derived from the pattern of advances and repayments made during the agreement. Optional charges are not included in the APR calculation. So if there is a tick box on the application form asking if the borrower would like to take out payment insurance, then insurance costs will not be included in the APR calculation. The following is a simple example illustrating how the APR reflects charges other than just interest.

Consider a $10,000 balloon loan with a one year term and interest charged at 6 percent per annum. At the end of the year the loan is repaid in full, together with the $600 interest that has accrued. The lender also charges an arrangement fee of $120 to cover administrative charges, and this is paid by the borrower when the loan is advanced. This means that the total charge for credit is $720 ($600 + $120). $720 as a percentage of $10,000 is 7.2 percent. Therefore, the lender would be legally obliged to state that the APR for the loan is 7.2 percent.

One problem with the use of APR is that it is intended to give a standardized measure of the cost of credit, but in practice it is possible to make certain assumptions and calculate credit charges in different ways. The result is that two lenders who charge the same amount could quote different APRs. Conversely, they could quote the same APR, but charge very different amounts. This does not tend to result in large differences in the APR calculation for fixed sum credit, but for revolving credit where the concept of a repayment schedule is somewhat arbitrary and the actual term and amount borrowed is not known at the outset, large discrepancies can result. A report by the UK Government noted that up to ten different methods of calculating interest (and hence the APR) were employed by UK credit card providers and the actual charges levied by lenders quoting identical APRs varied by as much as 76 percent (House of Commons Treasury Committee 2003, p.24).

Details of the methods for calculating interest and the APR, and the reasons why the interest (and hence APR) calculation for revolving credit products can vary so much between different lenders, are discussed in Appendix A.

2.3 Credit products

2.3.1 Mortgages

A mortgage is a loan used to purchase a fixed asset such as land or buildings, with the loan secured against the asset. In most cases this will be the borrower's home. A standard mortgage is offered as a fixed term agreement. In the UK this is commonly 20 or 25 years and in the

US 15 or 30 years. In Japan, terms as long as 50 years are not unusual, with the debt being passed on to the next of kin if the original borrower dies. When a mortgage has been fully repaid it is said to have been redeemed.

With a repayment mortgage the borrower makes fixed repayments at regular intervals, usually each month or year. Repayments cover both interest and capital, resulting in the debt being paid off by the end of the agreement. In banking circles a repayment mortgage is often referred to as an amortizing mortgage. With an interest only mortgage (sometimes referred to as a non-amortizing or balloon mortgage) payments only cover interest. At the end of the agreement the borrower must repay the original debt in full. This is usually via an investment trust or endowment policy that runs in parallel with the mortgage, but which is technically a separate financial product and can be cashed in or sold independently. Although some mortgage providers will advance up to 100 percent of the value of the property (and a few even more than that), most will limit their exposure to mortgages secured against 90 or 95 percent of the property value. The borrower is required to fund the difference via a deposit. If the value of the property is less than the value of the loan secured against it, then a state of negative equity exists.

In the US fixed rate mortgages are the norm, with a single interest rate applying for a period of ten years or more, and possibly for the entire life of the mortgage. In the UK variable rate mortgages and short term fixed rate mortgages, of between two and seven years, are prevalent. A variable rate means that the interest rate can vary over the life of the loan, resulting in changes to the payments made by the borrower. There are no fixed criteria as to when or how a lender varies their interest rates, but most changes track the base rate set by the central bank of the country in which the mortgage is granted. For example, most UK mortgage rates remain between 1 and 2 percent above the base rate set by The Bank of England. In the US the equivalent body is The Federal Reserve Board and within the Euro zone, The Central European Bank.

A re-mortgage (re-financing) is where the borrower renegotiates the mortgage or switches to a different lender. This occurs either to secure more attractive repayment terms or for equity withdrawal to obtain funds that can be used for purposes such as debt consolidation, buying a new car, or general consumer expenditure.

When someone with a mortgage moves home, the mortgage on their existing property is redeemed at the same time as a new mortgage agreement is created for the new property. A bridging (bridge) loan is used when a buyer is ready to proceed with a property purchase but has not yet sold their existing property. The bridging loan is a short term loan to cover the purchase of the new property before the mortgage on the old property is redeemed.

There are a number of variations on the standard mortgage. A flexible mortgage allows the borrower to make variable repayments, thus allowing reduced payments when household budgets are stretched or overpayments when spare funds are available. Given that repayments can vary, this type of mortgage agreement does not necessarily have a fixed repayment period. The most sophisticated types of mortgage on the market today are offset or account based mortgages, combining the mortgage with a current account, savings and other credit facilities. Each month the borrower's salary is paid into their account, offsetting a proportion of their mortgage debt. Over the course of the month the debt rises as interest accrues and the customer spends to cover things such as household bills, travel and entertainment. The borrower is also permitted to draw new funds from the account up to an agreed limit; for example, to fund the purchase of a new car or a holiday. In the US, a Home Equity Line of Credit (HELOC) can be considered broadly equivalent to an offset mortgage offered in the UK.

Given their size, term and security, mortgages usually represent the cheapest form of credit available to an individual.

2.3.2   Personal loans (installment loans)

An unsecured personal loan (signature loan) is a loan advanced with no guaranteed security in the case of default. However, as with other forms of borrowing, the lender may be able to recover unpaid debts via a court order, possibly leading to possession of the borrower's assets. The purpose to which a personal loan is put is generally unrestricted,[5] and although a lender will sometimes enquire as to the purpose of the loan during the application process, the borrower is not usually required to guarantee that funds will be spent for the purpose specified. A student loan is a specific type of unsecured personal loan where repayments are deferred until sometime after the period of study has been completed.

A secured personal loan is secured against the borrower's assets, most commonly their home. Therefore, it is little different in principle to a mortgage and an individual may have both a mortgage and one or more other loans secured against their home. In the US there are examples of these types of loan being secured against insurance policies, motor vehicles or other property and are these are commonly referred to as title loans.

A consolidation loan is a secured or unsecured personal loan that is used to repay existing debts – the rationale being that the repayment terms of the consolidation loan are better for the borrower than those of their existing credit agreements.

Personal loans are usually (but not always) amortizing in nature. Repayments cover both capital and interest, with the debt having been repaid in full by the end of the agreement. While personal loan is the common term in the UK, installment loan is more widely used in the US.

2.3.3   Retail credit (retail loans)

A retail credit agreement (sometimes referred to as a retail loan) is taken out to cover the purchase of specific consumer durable(s) such as a sofa, washing machine or a television. The key difference from a personal loan is that no cash is advanced to the customer – the credit is restricted. The customer signs an agreement, receives the goods and then makes regular repayments until the debt is satisfied. In some cases a deposit will be required in order to limit the overall exposure of the lender, with 10 or 20 percent a common amount. In the UK most retail credit agreements are undertaken on a credit sale basis – with the goods becoming the immediate property of the customer. In the US it is more common for retail credit to be provided on a conditional sale basis.

In the US retail loans are often referred to as retail installment loans or retail installment credit.

2.3.4   Hire-purchase

From a customer's perspective, a hire-purchase (HP) agreement operates in an almost identical manner to a retail loan made on a conditional sale basis – the credit is restricted and the goods legally remain the property of the loan company until all, or an agreed proportion of the loan, has been repaid. The key difference is that until transfer of ownership occurs, the borrower is technically hiring the goods, not purchasing them. In order to qualify as a hire-purchase agreement the borrower must have the *option* to buy the goods at some point (or to return the goods and terminate the agreement). With most hire-purchase agreements the option to buy is exercised automatically when the final repayment is made. To put it another way, if the borrower decides to terminate the agreement before they have paid all of the installments then it is taken that the option to buy has not been exercised and the goods remain the property of the lender. With a conditional sale, the borrower agrees when the agreement is made to purchase the goods – there is no option for them to change their mind at a later date. Since the goods remain the property of the lender, they can repossess the goods should the terms of the agreement be breached.

A personal contract purchase is a form of hire-purchase that is partly amortized and partly balloon in nature, and is generally associated with motor finance. Over the term of the agreement the borrower pays regular installments covering interest and some of the capital, so that when the agreement ends a proportion of the original debt remains outstanding. The borrower then has the option to purchase the car by paying the outstanding amount in full or returning the car to the credit provider. These types of agreement enable a consumer to obtain a new car at regular intervals without the need to bother about disposing of their old car. When one credit agreement ends, they return the old car and take out another agreement for a new one.

2.3.5   Card accounts

A credit card account allows a customer to purchase goods and services from any merchant who has entered into an arrangement with the card issuer. The card issuer acts as a third party, guaranteeing payment to the merchant and recovering the resulting debt directly from the borrower. In return for this payment guarantee, the merchant pays a fee, usually between 1 and 4 percent of the value of the goods. The card issuer allocates each borrower a maximum credit facility, or credit line, up to which they can spend without the need for further negotiation.

Credit card accounts represent one of the most complex forms of consumer credit agreement, and the detail of their operation is not well understood by a large proportion of users. This is mainly because of subtle differences in the way different lenders calculate interest and apply charges, with different rates and charges applied to different parts of the balance depending on whether it originated from a balance transfer, retail purchase, cash withdrawal or some other type of transaction (see Appendix A for more details of the different ways in which interest can be calculated and applied). However, one of the most popular models applied by card issuers to the operation of credit card accounts is as follows.

On a regular, usually monthly, basis the borrower will receive a statement of account detailing any outstanding balance carried forward from the previous statement and all purchases, payments and other transactions that have occurred since the previous statement was issued. This period is termed the statement period. The date of issue of the statement is called the statement date or the account cycle point. The borrower then has a fixed time after the statement date to repay some or all of the outstanding balance by the due date. If only a portion of the balance is paid by the due date, interest is charged on the entire statement balance. For example, if the borrower receives a statement showing an account balance of $500 and pays $499, interest will be charged on the $500, not on the outstanding $1. Any resulting interest charge will then appear as a transaction on the next statement. The interest-free period is the time between a transaction occurring and the due date quoted on the statement on which the transaction appears, and only applies if the outstanding balance is paid in full. The maximum interest-free period, which is commonly quoted in promotional literature, is equal to the time between the statement date of the current statement and the due date on the next statement. Figure 2.1 illustrates the relationship between statement dates, due dates and the interest-free period.

Account providers usually specify the minimum repayment to be made by the due date as the larger of a fixed minimum amount or a percentage of the outstanding balance. Common minimum payment terms are the larger of $5 or 5 percent, or $5 or 3 percent. Any outstanding balance that is not paid by the due date is said to revolve and is carried over to the next statement. It is from this principle the term 'revolving credit' originates.

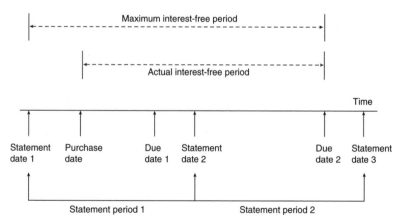

Figure 2.1   Key dates for credit card accounts

Most credit cards permit cash withdrawals via automated teller machines (ATMs). In the UK cash withdrawals incur a fee, usually between 1.5 and 3 percent of the amount withdrawn. In the US fees of between 3 and 4 percent are more common. Cash withdrawals also differ from retail purchases in that there is no interest-free period. Interest begins to accrue as soon as a cash withdrawal occurs, regardless of whether or not the balance is paid in full by the due date.

A credit card is an example of a multiple credit agreement, providing both restricted and unrestricted use credit. Credit cards provide restricted credit because only a limited number of merchants accept credit cards (even though the number of merchants is very large). However, most credit cards can also be used to make cash withdrawals – an unrestricted form of credit (Dobson 1996, p.285).

Credit card cheques are a marketing tool used to encourage large expenditures to be made against an account. The cheques are similar in appearance to those offered as part of a standard bank chequing facility. They are attractive in some situations because they can be paid directly into a bank account, which means that whoever receives the cheque does not need to have any prior agreement with the card provider or to have the facilities necessary to process credit card transactions. Like cash withdrawals, there is usually a fee of between 1.5 and 3 percent and there is no interest-free period, with interest beginning to accrue as soon as a cheque is used.

The actual card carried by the account holder is a credit token, acting primarily as a means by which they can be identified by a merchant when making a transaction. The physical card is not an intrinsic requirement for the operation of a card account, which is demonstrated by the fact that customers can use their account to purchase goods or services remotely via the phone or the internet.

The majority of credit card transactions are processed by one of the two main networks, VISA and MasterCard. The relationship between individual card issuers and merchants is managed via a third party organization known as a merchant acquirer. This frees merchants from having to deal with each card issuer on an individual basis. The relationships between these organizations are discussed in more detail in Chapter 6. Own brand cards such as American Express and Discover operate their own card processing networks.

Most credit card accounts represent an unsecured form of credit. However, some lenders, particularly in the US, will offer high risk customers credit cards secured against cash deposited in an account controlled by the credit card issuer. The credit line on the card is then set to be equal to the value of the deposited funds. After the customer has demonstrated good repayment behaviour for a period of time, the issuer may allow the account to transfer to an unsecured status with the credit limit increased beyond the value of the secured funds.

A store card is very similar to a credit card in principle, but is generally issued by a single merchant (or sometimes a group of merchants). Use of a store card is restricted to the issuing merchant's stores and in general does not permit cash withdrawals, which means that all credit is provided on a restricted basis. The credit account is sometimes managed directly by the store itself, but more commonly the credit operation is contracted out to a third party.

In the US, the term 'credit card' is generally used to refer to both credit cards and store cards. The term 'bank card' or 'universal credit card' is used to refer explicitly to what in the UK would be termed a credit card.

A charge card is a credit token used in conjunction with a charge account (see section 2.3.6) and operates in a similar manner to a credit or store card. However, a charge account requires the balance to be paid in full by the due date. Therefore, there is no facility for the balance to revolve from one statement to the next.

2.3.6   Charge accounts

A charge account is where credit is granted, usually interest-free, for a fixed period of time, after which the full amount owing becomes due. At one time this type of credit was common in convenience and grocery stores with people settling their bills at the end of the week or month. Where charge accounts are still used in a retail environment they are usually managed via the use of a charge card, as discussed previously.

Today, charge accounts are most widely found in the telecoms and household utility sectors with people billed for their gas, water, electricity and phone bills on a monthly or quarterly basis.

2.3.7   Revolving loans

A revolving loan, sometimes called a flexiloan or a budget account, is a form of revolving credit. A borrower agrees to make a fixed monthly payment and in return has the ability to draw cash up to a maximum limit, which is a multiple of the monthly payment amount. For example, an account with a 15 times multiplier will allow a customer who agrees to pay $200 a month to draw funds up to a maximum of $3,000. In the UK, this type of credit is most commonly offered by credit unions operating on a not-for-profit basis, although a few banks and building societies also offer these types of loan. There are also a number of store card providers who operate their card accounts on this basis, with the customer making a fixed payment each month rather than a percentage of the outstanding balance.

2.3.8 Mail order catalogue accounts

Mail order catalogue accounts operate on the basis of the borrower selecting goods from the company's catalogue and then paying for them over a number of weeks or months. Traditionally, goods were paid for on a weekly basis and many UK catalogue companies still quote weekly repayment terms. However, customers today usually manage their accounts on a monthly or four-weekly basis.

Once an account has been opened, the customer is given a credit limit up to which they can make further purchases from the catalogue and receives regular statements detailing the transactions that have occurred, the outstanding balance and the minimum payment which must be made by the due date. In this respect, the operation of the account is almost identical to that of a store card. Some mail order accounts operate on an interest-bearing basis, with interest accruing on unpaid balances at the due date. Others operate a principle of bundling interest, offering interest-free payment terms for goods sold at prices that are not competitive with general retailers. The cost of providing credit is factored into the retail price of the goods (this is also a feature of zero interest retail credit offers).

There have traditionally been two types of mail order credit account – direct and agency. With a direct mail order account there is a straight forward one-to-one relationship between the customer and the retailer. With an agency account, the customer, termed an 'agent,' has the option to buy goods on behalf of friends, relatives and neighbours, with the agent receiving a commission of around 10 percent for their trouble. Therefore, the agent can effectively operate as a small business, generating income from the purchases of their customers. The agent is solely responsible for managing the account and in most cases the mail order company knows little or nothing about the agent's customers. Although in decline, a significant proportion of UK mail order credit sales are still based on the agency account model.

2.3.9 Overdrafts

A current account that permits a borrower to spend beyond the funds in their account is said to provide an overdraft facility. When the overdraft facility is used, resulting in a negative account balance, the account is said to be overdrawn. Overdrafts operate in one of two modes. An authorized overdraft is where the overdraft facility has been agreed with the lender in advance. An unauthorized overdraft is where the lender permits the account to become overdrawn without a formal agreement to do so. Unauthorized overdrafts usually incur penalty fees and/or higher interest charges than other popular forms of credit. Overdrafts are usually associated with short term lending, particularly at month-end prior to a salary being paid into an individual's account.

2.3.10   Pawning (pledging)

The pawning (pledging) of goods is where a cash loan is secured against property, with the property retained by the lender until the loan is repaid. An individual will deposit item(s) they own, often jewellery, with the pawnbroker. The pawnbroker will then provide a cash loan based on a discounted value of the item(s). The borrower then has a fixed period within which to redeem the items upon repayment of the original loan plus interest. If by the end of the agreement the borrower has not returned and redeemed the goods, the pawnbroker is permitted to sell the items in order to satisfy the debt. Pawning is therefore a form of secured credit that is balloon in nature.

The APRs charged on pawn loans tend to be significantly higher than many other forms of borrowing, often in the region of 40–85 percent per annum (Kempson and Whyley 1999, p.11).[6] This can mainly be attributed to the overheads associated with small scale lending operations, the cost of secure storage of items during the loan period and the relatively short term and low value of a typical pawn agreement.

Pawning is sometimes frowned upon as a socially undesirable activity, due to the technically high APR and the traditional association with the poor and working classes. However, there a number of features of pawn credit which can make it attractive in some circumstances, particularly when the borrower is seeking a low value, short term credit facility. Unlike many forms of credit, such as a credit card or personal loan, the customer's financial exposure is limited to the goods against which the pledge is secured. There is no danger of interest spiralling out of control or court action if the debt remains unpaid.

Typical pawn loans are for a few hundred dollars, but many pawnbrokers will lend sums as small as $10. For small sums borrowed over a period of a few days or weeks, the fees can be comparable to those charged by some banks for overdrafts, or the cash withdrawal fees of some credit cards. Pawn agreements are also comparatively transparent;

there is little small print and no hidden charges, with all costs clearly stated when the agreement is made. A further advantage is that there is no requirement for individuals to undergo credit vetting procedures, which are undertaken by most high street lenders. Consequently, there are very few circumstances where a pawnbroker will decline to offer credit.

2.3.11   Payday loans and cheque cashing services

A payday loan is a short term loan to cover a borrower until they receive their next pay cheque, at which time the loan is repaid in full with interest. The term of the loan is usually no longer than a few days or weeks. This type of lending is often associated with cheque cashing services where funds are advanced on a post-dated cheque. The borrower will write a cheque payable to the cheque cashing company and receive cash for the value of the cheque, less the fee charged by the company. Payday loans and cheque cashing are generally associated with sections of the market where credit is sought to cover immediate personal need by individuals who cannot obtain credit elsewhere.

2.4   Productive and consumptive credit

Credit is often described as productive or consumptive in nature. Productive credit is where the money lent is invested in some way, providing the *potential* to generate a return for the borrower, although if the investment is a poor one the investor may be left with less than they started with. Consumptive credit is where the money borrowed is used for immediate personal need or gratification. The differentiation between consumptive and productive credit is not always as clear cut as it might seem, and it cannot be assumed that any single type of credit is inherently productive or consumptive. As noted in Chapter 1, just because credit is secured against an asset, such as mortgage secured on a home, it does not mean that these funds are then used in a productive manner. Most consolidation loans are secured against property, but are then used to re-finance consumptive expenditures incurred using credit cards, mail order accounts, personal loans and so forth. Alternatively, a holiday bought using a credit card would normally be considered consumptive with no productive potential. Yet it could be argued that in taking a holiday and getting away from their work for a while, an individual comes back refreshed and energized and so therefore, more productive in their employment.

2.5 Prime and sub-prime (mainstream and non-mainstream) lending

The terms 'prime' and 'sub-prime' are widely used within the financial services industry. The prime market represents those sections of the population where the risk of defaulting on a credit agreement is low and hence these people have access to the best credit deals on offer from mainstream credit providers such as the major banks and saving and loan companies.

Sub-prime (non-status) refers to the rest of the population. People typically fall into this category because of previous repayment problems that indicates a high likelihood of future default, or because of their current socio-economic profile, such as being unemployed or having a low income. Consequently, these people experience difficulty obtaining credit on standard terms from mainstream credit providers.

There are no widely accepted definitions of prime and sub-prime, and there are many gradations between those the industry identifies as the 'best' and 'worst' segments of the population. However, the prime market probably consists of between 60 and 70 percent of the population in most developed countries.

Traditionally, the sub-prime market has been serviced by organizations that are collectively referred to as non-mainstream, sub-prime or non-status lenders. The credit facilities provided by these organizations are relatively expensive and in some cases extortionate. Arrangement fees are common and interest rates of well over 100 percent per annum are legally charged for certain types of credit. In the late-1990s and early–mid-2000s many mainstream lending organizations entered the upper end of the sub-prime market, driven by a desire to expand market share in a saturated market. However, after the problems in the US sub-prime housing market in 2006–7 and the subsequent credit crunch, many lenders retreated from the sub-prime market after suffering significant losses due to much higher than expected write-off from defaulting customers.

At the extreme end of the scale, the sub-prime market is serviced by pawnbrokers, payday lenders, home credit companies and unlicenced loan sharks.

2.6 Credit products permitted under Islamic (Shari'ah) law

An underlying principle of Islamic finance is that money is not a commodity that can be traded, but is merely a mechanism by which goods and services are exchanged. Money has no inherent use or utility in itself and therefore, there is no rationale for making a profit from the exchange of money (Usmani 2002, pp.xiv–xv). This does not mean that credit cannot be provided with the intent of generating a profit for the lender, but that the charging mechanism must be such that it reflects a tangible product or service which is sold to a purchaser. Charging interest (or riba as it is traditionally known) on a credit transaction is forbidden because it explicitly implies the generation of money from money.

Trade and commerce on the other hand are encouraged as activities which benefit the community. Therefore, selling a product or service at a profit is acceptable. It is also acceptable to sell an item on a deferred payment basis, with the borrower making one or more payments over a period of time as long as no interest is charged. One way the lender can be compensated for agreeing to a deferred payment agreement is through charging a higher price for the item than would otherwise have been paid if it had been purchased outright when the sale was agreed (which is termed *murabahah* meaning 'mark-up'). Therefore, a retailer selling a washing machine for say $800, may agree to sell it for $900 if the buyer pays for it in ten monthly installments of $90. From a practical perspective, this might seem very similar to an interest-bearing credit agreement, but from an Islamic perspective the distinction between an agreement made on the basis of a trading relationship and one based on interest is an important one.

So what type of credit is available to those wishing to comply with Islamic (*Shari'ah*) law? It can be argued that traditional credit cards and store cards are permissible if balances are paid in full by the due date so that no interest is paid. However, most credit card providers will insist on a signed credit agreement in which the borrower agrees to pay interest if the balance is not paid in full. Therefore, the validity of these products is questionable. A better alternative is a charge card because interest does not form an inherent part of the product and the charging of a fixed annual fee to pay for the services provided by the card is acceptable. There also exists a range of card products, such as the Bank Islam MasterCard, designed especially for the Islamic market. These can be used in the same way as a standard MasterCard credit card and include a revolving credit facility, but charge no interest. The bank earns an income by charging an annual fee and a transaction charge each time the customer uses the card. Fees are also charged if a borrower is late with a payment or otherwise breaches the terms of the account, but on the understanding that charges reflect the extra cost incurred by the card issuer and that no profit results. The borrower is effectively paying for the simplicity and security provided by the card rather than the credit the card makes available.

Personal loans are acceptable, as long as no increase (interest) results from the agreement. This means that in most cases personal loans are only provided on a charitable basis as they make no profit for the lender. An overdraft as part of a bank account is also acceptable if the overdraft is interest-free, and the charging of a fixed regular (monthly or annual) fee for providing the service is permissible. Retail loans and mail order accounts are generally acceptable, if arranged in a *murabahah* compliant fashion.

The financing of larger assets such as a house or a car, are usually undertaken using a form of hire-purchase or rent/buy agreement, termed '*Ijara* with diminishing *musharakah*'.[7] This is a form of lease (*ijara*) with the decreasing participation/ownership (*musharakah*) of the credit provider. The asset is initially purchased and owned outright by the organization providing the finance (or an approved agent) who divides the asset into a number of shares. The client then agrees to makes regular payments – part of which is a rent or leasing charge for use of the asset, and the rest is used to purchase shares in the asset. As the agreement progresses the client owns an increasing share of the asset and rents a decreasing proportion of it from the finance company. The agreement ends when the asset is entirely owned by the client.

2.7 Credit providers

The majority of consumer credit is provided by the following four types of institution:

- Banks. A bank is an organization licenced to take deposits and extend loans. Banks that provide personal banking and consumer credit services, and which typically maintain branch networks, are described as commercial or retail banks. This contrasts with merchant banks which are primarily involved with corporate and international finance. Traditionally, retail banks obtained funds via deposits and current accounts that were then used to fund commercial lending to business. The granting of personal loans and overdrafts did occur, but was not common (Cole and Mishler 1998, p.82). Since the 1980s many banks have expanded their commercial operations to cover a broader spectrum of lending activities. Many banks now offer mortgages, secured and unsecured personal loans and credit cards as a central part of their banking operations.

- Saving and loan companies (building societies in the UK, Australia and Ireland). These are profit-making organizations owned by their members, who are the individuals who have savings accounts and/or loan agreements with the organization. Traditionally, saving and loan companies funded mortgage lending via the savings deposited by their members, but in recent years they have expanded to provide a broad range of financial services, very similar to those provided by retail banks.

- Finance houses. Finance house is a general term used to describe lending institutions licenced to provide consumer credit. Finance houses do not provide savings or deposit accounts; instead they obtain funds to support their lending activities through commercial loans obtained from merchant banks or other large financial institutions. Finance houses mainly provide credit in the form of secured and unsecured personal loans, hire-purchase agreements and card accounts. They are not generally involved in mortgage lending, although some do provide mortgage products. Large finance houses commonly act as third party credit providers, acting on behalf of retailers and merchants for the provision of store cards and retail credit.

- Credit unions. Credit unions are mutually owned financial cooperatives that first appeared in Germany in 1849. Like saving and loan companies the funds contributed by members are used to supply credit to other members.[8] Credit unions exist to service specific interest groups sharing some 'common bond'. For example, members of a trade union or residents of a town or city. Consequently, many credit unions operate on a small scale compared to the major banks and saving and loan companies. However, some American credit unions have hundreds of thousands of members and billions of dollars worth of assets. American credit unions offer a wide range of credit products including mortgages, personal loans and credit cards. They are able to provide very competitive terms for the credit they provide because they are run on a not-for-profit basis and enjoy a tax exempt status. In other countries the popularity of credit unions varies greatly in terms of the number of members, the average size of unions, and in the range of products they offer. In Ireland for example, about 45 percent of adults are members of credit unions. In the UK the figure is only around 1 percent (Goth *et al.* 2006, p. 1).

For the consumer there is little difference between the financial products offered by banks, saving and loan companies, finance houses and credit unions. What differentiates them is ownership, the objectives that drive their activities and the legislation under which they operate. Banks and finance houses are almost always driven by the profit motive, aiming to maximize shareholder return. Saving and loan associations are profit making organizations, but seek to maximize the benefits to their members. Credit unions are also member owned but non-profit making. Banks, saving and loan associations and credit unions are all categorized as deposit taking institutions. This means that as well as providing credit, they also provide current accounts and/or savings accounts. This puts a number of legal obligations on them to ensure that they can maintain their liquidity so that depositors' funds are protected. Finance houses do not offer such services, and therefore tend to be subject to less stringent regulatory requirements than deposit taking institutions (Finlay, S. 2008, p.6).

Between them banks, saving and loan companies, credit unions and finance houses are responsible for providing the vast majority of consumer credit throughout the world. In the UK for example, they account for around 98 percent of all consumer credit (by value) (Finlay 2005, p.55). However, credit is also provided by a number of other types of organization. These include:

- Utility companies: Many utility supplies (water, gas, electricity and telecoms) are provided on a credit basis. Bills are issued in arrears, usually monthly or quarterly.
- Pawnbrokers: Pawnbrokers have existed since ancient times, offering short term credit secured against the borrower's possessions. In recent years many pawnbroking operations have diversified into payday lending and cheque cashing services. Pawnbroking is much less prevalent than it once was, but there has been something of a revival since the 1980s. In the US the number of pawnbrokers rose from around 5,000 in 1985 to about 14,000 by the end of the millennium (Burton 2007, p.78). In the UK the pawnbroking industry had almost died out completely by the 1970s, but by 2007 the number of pawnbrokers had risen to around 850 (Haurant 2007), with a customer base numbering several hundred thousand.[9]
- Government agencies: Many governments provide credit in various forms. In the UK this includes student loans, and for those in receipt of certain state benefits, cash loans via the social fund. Social fund loans are unsecured and interest-free, and are provided for the

purchase of essential items, such as a bed, cooker or children's clothing. Loan repayments are deducted directly from future benefit payments.

- Licenced moneylenders (home credit companies or doorstep lenders): Any individual or organization legally permitted to provide credit can be described as a licenced moneylender. However, the term is usually applied to those specializing in providing small unsecured cash loans and/or payday lending/cheque cashing services. Some moneylenders maintain branch networks, but most operate on a door-to-door basis visiting households weekly to collect repayments. Loans are usually for no more than a few hundred dollars repaid over a few weeks or months. Interest rates depend upon the amount and term of the loan, but are typically in excess of 100 percent per annum. Most moneylenders operate on a relatively small scale, but the largest companies, such as Provident Financial and Cattles in the UK, have annual turnovers of hundreds of millions dollars. It has been estimated that about 10 percent of the UK population have borrowed from a moneylender at some point in their lives and that about 5 percent have done so within the last 12 months (Whyley and Brooker 2004, p.16).

- Unlicenced moneylenders (loan sharks): Unlicenced moneylenders have been around for as long as regulated credit markets have existed, with references to loan sharking to be found in Greek texts dating to the second and third centuries B.C. (Homer and Sylla 1996, p.38). Loans of less than $250 are common with annualized rates of interest of 100 percent the norm and 1,000 percent not unheard of. Given its illegal or semi-legal status, the exact size of this market is difficult to ascertain. However, research by Ellison *et al.* (2006, p.5) estimated that in the UK around 165,000 households, representing 0.44 percent of UK adults, were users of illegal money lenders.

2.8 Chapter summary

Credit comes in a variety of forms and can characterized by six key characteristics:

- Whether credit is provided on a secured or unsecured basis. Credit is secured if there are specific items named in the agreement that can be claimed by the lender should the terms of the agreement be breached.

- Whether credit is amortizing or balloon in nature; that is, whether debt is repaid gradually over the course of the agreement or as a lump sum at the end.
- Whether the credit agreement is fixed sum or running account.
- Whether the purpose for which credit is obtained is restricted or unrestricted.
- If credit is restricted, then whether credit is provided on a credit sale, conditional sale or hire purchase basis.
- Whether there is a two party (creditor-debtor) or three party (creditor-debtor-supplier) relationship.

The APR is a standardized way of representing mandatory charges that are applied to a credit agreement. A key point to note is that conceptually the APR is not the same as the interest rate charged by a lender. The APR is a representation of the total cost of credit presented in the form of an interest rate. It includes interest and other mandatory charges such as arrangement fees, valuation charges, product guarantees and brokers' fees. Optional charges, that the borrower can choose not to pay, are not included in the APR calculation. The main types of credit that individuals can obtain are:

- Mortgages
- Personal loans
- Retail loans
- Hire-purchase agreements
- Card accounts
- Charge accounts
- Revolving loans
- Mail order accounts
- Payday loans
- Pawn loans

The different organizations that provide credit include:

- Banks
- Saving and loan companies (building societies)
- Finance houses
- Credit unions
- Mail order catalogue companies
- Utility companies
- Governments

- Pawnbrokers
- Licenced moneylenders
- Unlicenced moneylenders

The vast majority of credit is supplied by banks, saving and loan companies, credit unions and finance houses. Mail order companies, pawnbrokers and moneylenders represent only a very small sector of the market – one that tends to be utilized by people who have difficulty obtaining credit on standard terms from mainstream providers.

2.9   Suggested sources of further information

Smullen, J. and Hand, N. (eds) (2008). *Oxford Dictionary of Finance and Banking.* Bloomsbury. This provides clear explanations of common terms used in the credit industry as well as other areas of banking and finance.

Evans, D. and Schmalensee, R. (2005). *Paying With Plastic. The Digital Revolution in Buying and Borrowing.* The MIT Press. Details the workings of the credit card and charge card market. While the book has a mainly US focus, much of the material is relevant to card operations around the world.

Usmani, M. T. (2002). *An Introduction to Islamic Finance.* Kluwer Law International. This book provides a comprehensive introduction to the principles of Islamic Finance. It is particularly useful for those wishing to contrast traditional western and Islamic views on the role of monetary credit in trade and commerce.

Collard, S. and Kempson, E. (2005). *Affordable credit. The way forward.* The Policy Press. This report describes the types of credit available to those who are unable to secure credit from mainstream sources in the UK. It also discusses a number of ways in which affordable credit could be made more available to people on low incomes, or who are otherwise unable to obtain credit on reasonable terms.

3
The History of Credit

3.1 Ancient origins

It is easy to think of credit as a modern phenomena based around a culture of mortgages, credit cards, personal loans and so on, but credit granting has existed since prehistoric times. It ranks alongside prostitution and brewing as one of the 'oldest professions' and over the ages has probably generated as much controversy and debate as either. It is easy to imagine the concept of 'I'll pay you tomorrow!' developing almost as soon as barter and trade evolved and it is likely that credit in a rudimentary form existed prior to the introduction of formal monetary systems. It has even been suggested that an understanding of debt and obligation may have been one factor that enabled early human societies to flourish (Horan *et al.* 2005). People began helping each other to hunt, lending tools and food to one another, caring for one another when they were sick and so on. These tasks were undertaken on the understanding that they created an obligation which would be reciprocated at some time in the future. This meant people were better able to overcome short term hardship, leading to greater survival rates and an increased population. It is also probable that one factor in the development of currency was a need to express debt in a standardized form (Einzig 1966, pp.362–6). The idea of lending on interest or usury[1] as it was traditionally known has origins of a similar age. Loans would be granted in the form of grain or livestock which had a propensity to reproduce and increase over time, and the lender naturally came to expect some share of the increase when the loan was repaid.

The earliest documentary evidence of interest-bearing credit agreements is to be found in Sumerian documents dating from the third millennium B.C. (Homer and Sylla 1996, p.17). The first comprehensive legislation concerning the management of credit agreements was issued in the Mesopotamian city of Babylon within the Code of Hammurabi circa 1750 B.C., a copy of which is inscribed on a black stone monolith more than two meters tall, preserved at the Louvre in Paris. It contains 282 rulings concerning issues of governance and trade, a number of which deal with credit and the charging of interest (Gelpi and Julien-Labruyere 2000, p.3). The code included the interest rates that could be charged for various goods, and the penalties for lenders who exceeded these amounts. For example, the maximum permissible interest rate for loans of silver was 20 percent, and 33.3 percent for loans of barley. The code required loan agreements to be formalized in writing and witnessed by an official, and as with credit agreements today, without a formal record of the agreement the loan was void and could not be enforced. Women were often required as joint signatories and a woman's property rights were protected so that her husband could not pledge her assets against the loan without her consent. Other strictures protected peasant borrowers, requiring creditors not to press for payment until the harvest had been gathered and allowing relief from capital and interest payments in times of hardship, such as drought or famine. The code also dictated the action lenders could take in order to recover debts from borrowers who had defaulted on their repayments. It was, for example, allowable to take a man or a member of his family into slavery for unpaid debts, but the code limited the period of slavery to three years and forbade the mistreatment of the debtor during this period (Homer and Sylla 1996, pp.26–7).

Law of such a detailed nature does not arise on a whim. It is constructed to address some specific need, concern, injustice or threat, either to the populace to which it is applied or the authority that decrees it. The existence of the code suggests that the misuse of credit and/or abuse of borrowers by creditors prior to 1750 B.C. was a significant problem within Babylonian society.

3.2   The Greek experience

By the seventh century B.C. the Greeks had developed a commercial economic system where there was extensive borrowing on interest, particularly to fund maritime merchant ventures (Homer and Sylla 1996, p.34). Mortgages were commonplace with loans secured against land or property. Many of the Greek temples acted as moneylenders, obtaining a considerable share of their income from their lending activities. Yet the penalties for non-payment of debts were severe, with it being accepted that unpaid debt invariably led to the debtor, their family and property becoming forfeit in lieu of payment. Thus unpaid debt could lead to poverty and slavery and this was a common fate for many Greeks. With such severe penalties for defaulters, it can be imagined that borrowing was not entered into lightly, but for many there was probably little choice when crops failed or some other emergency arose. By the end of the sixth century B.C. debt was causing major problems within Greek society and the pawning of goods and the mortgaging of land was widespread. Thankfully for the indebted Greek, relief came in the form of progressive new legislation introduced by the poet-magistrate Solon in 594 B.C., redefining the relationship between lender and borrower. Solon's reforms were revolutionary and wide-reaching. Those who had been enslaved for debts were pardoned and it became illegal to secure debt against one's own person, thus protecting individuals from the threat of slavery. The state even went so far as to buy back debtors sold abroad for their debts. However, Solon recognized the importance of credit within Greek society and he also relaxed existing lending laws, including the removal of interest rate ceilings. This more lenient and civilized attitude contributed to the growth in the use of commercial credit, used in support of the expanding merchant empire of the fourth and fifth centuries B.C.

Despite Solon's reforms, the provision of credit on interest was not without its objectors. In the fourth century B.C. both Plato and Aristotle argued vehemently against the use of credit, believing it to be a major source of society's ills which, given past experience, was not without some justification. Aristotle's argument, presented in 'The Politics' (Everson 1988, p.15) was particularly important because it was used as a core tenet by those who opposed the concept of usury for over 2,000 years. It was based on the idea of natural law, in which only things from the natural world should reproduce themselves. That which was man-made, either physical items, ideas, philosophies or the rule of law, by their very nature were sterile and therefore should not reproduce.[2] Money fell within this definition, being nothing more than a man-made convention by which goods and services were exchanged. This is perhaps not an unreasonable position to take; even today in this age of technological marvels, there are few human originated things, thoughts or processes which can be said to reproduce themselves in a lifelike manner. Therefore, as Aristotle might have argued, while it was natural for two pigs to breed to make a third, the idea that someone could earn a living by lending money to someone else and then 'reaping' the interest that resulted from the transaction went against the natural order of things.

3.3   The Romans

Like the Greeks, the Romans made extensive use of credit, but unlike the Greeks they legislated to limit interest rates. For most of the Roman era prior to 88 B.C. the legal maximum was around 8.3 percent, although at certain periods this was largely unenforced. Two years following state bankruptcy in 90 B.C. the rate was raised to 12 percent and more rigorously enforced for a time. This limit remained in place until 325 A.D., although actual market rates dropped as low as 4 percent at times. For many Romans debt was an accepted feature of everyday life, for senators and plebs alike. For the upper echelons of society money lending was a major source of income alongside other revenue generating assets such as land, slaves and other tradable commodities (Andreau 1999, p.12).

In the first and second centuries B.C., towards the end of the republican era, those who wished political success, particularly in the Senate, would spend enormous sums on bribery, coercion and public displays. The sponsoring of sporting events and great feasts were seen as routine and necessary items of expenditure to ensure public support. Although many were rich in terms of land and property, few had the available assets required to fund such activities and thus resorted to borrowing to support their political manoeuvrings (Finley 1973, p.53). The prevalence of assets in the form of land rather than ready cash is perhaps no surprise given that much of Roman wealth and power was founded on the spoils of conquest rather than the pursuit of commerce or industry, which had been more common amongst the Babylonians and Greeks. Debt was even used by representatives of the state to extract revenues from those whom Rome had conquered. Loans were deliberately advanced at high rates of interest to drain them of their wealth, leading to their eventual ruin and sale into slavery (Holland 2004, p.41). Set such examples by their leaders, it is no surprise that the average Roman felt borrowing to be a normal and acceptable part of life, even though it was not without its darker side should one fail to repay what was owed.

Apart from the sheer scale of borrowing within Roman society, two things stand out. First, the Romans made a clear distinction between productive credit, used to fund commercial or state ventures, and consumptive credit to support one's living and lifestyle (Mandell 1990, p.13). Second, from the second century B.C., they recognized the concept of limited liability. This was in the form of joint stock companies, which were accepted as being distinctly separate entities from the individuals that controlled them. This is very similar to what we would understand as a limited company today, with a board of directors who do not have any personal liability for the debts incurred by the company. However, such organizations were generally discouraged by Roman law from engaging in commercial ventures and were more widely associated with the finance and management of public projects, and these companies were at times contracted to undertake the construction of public works and tax collecting activities on behalf of the state (Homer and Sylla 1996, pp.46–7).

3.4 The early Church to late middle ages

In examining the usury practices of the first two millennium A.D. it is important to appreciate the religious context within which individuals and governments operated. From the fifth century A.D. until after the Protestant reformation of the sixteenth century, the teachings of the Roman Catholic Church were the dominant moral and political force in European politics. The power of the Church and individual nation states were often intertwined. Church law affected every aspect of secular life and few dared to openly challenge the edicts of the Church. Consequently, the Church's attitude to usury strongly influenced European lending practices for a period of well over a thousand years.

The early Church emerged in contradiction to the excesses of a declining Roman Empire in which usury was rife, as was the misery and ruin that often accompanied it. By the fourth century A.D. the Church had a well-established position against usury practices. What was to change over the coming millennium was the definition of usury and the severity with which transgressors would be dealt.

In support of their condemnation of usury the Church fathers had recourse to several biblical sources, as well as the arguments of the ancient scholars, in particular that of Aristotle as to the sterility of money. In the Old Testament the book of Exodus, chapter 22, verse 25 states: 'If you lend money to any of my people, to any poor man among you, you must not play the usurer with him: You must not demand interest from him.' And the book of Deuteronomy, chapter 23, verse 19 states: 'You must not lend on interest to your brother, whether the loan be of money or food or anything else that may earn interest.' Although no fixed date exists for the creation of these texts, they are thought to have their origins in an oral tradition dating from between the thirteenth and eleventh centuries B.C. Their written forms are thought to have been completed around 400 B.C. (Brown and Collins 1995, p.1038). There are also a number of other references to credit in the Old Testament including the books of Leviticus, Psalms and Proverbs.

From the New Testament, some took the Lord's Prayer in Matthew's Gospel (Matthew, chapter 6, verse 12) to be translated literally as: 'Forgive us our debts as we forgive our debtors' (Gelpi and Julien-Labruyere 2000, p.19) and indeed many modern translations from the original Greek, in which it was first recorded in written form, use 'debt', not trespass or sin. However, regarding this verse, there is broad agreement among modern biblical scholars that debt is a metaphor for sin, and that the central meaning of the verse is not to do with debt as such, but with forgiveness of sin in general (Houlden 1992, p.361; Viviano 1995). Chilton (2000, pp.79–80) claims that for Jesus, debt as metaphor for sin, had its roots in the socio-economic structures of the time and that most of the Jews in his home area would have lived their whole lives as poor tenants in debt to wealthy landowners. Thus the associations his hearers and the early Church would have made between debt and sin might be quite different to the associations made by a westerner today.

In the eighth and ninth centuries A.D. the Church's attitudes to usury became increasingly strict. During the reign of Charlemagne at the start of the ninth century usury was banned outright, with it even being declared a form of robbery and a sin against the seventh commandment: 'Thou shalt not steal.' In 850 A.D. moneylenders in Pavia Italy, were excommunicated (Homer and Sylla 1996, p.70) which was considered by the Church as the worst of all fates in denying the guilty a Christian burial and condemning them to an afterlife of eternal damnation.

Although usury was forbidden, other routes for borrowing did exist and were widely practiced. Lending in the form of a joint venture, with part of the profits used to repay the loan was acceptable. So, for example, funds might be provided to a merchant to purchase trade goods from overseas with the profits from the venture being proportioned between the merchant and the moneylender. However, if the ship carrying the merchant's goods was lost then the merchant would owe the money-lender nothing. Given that the lender could lose everything on what was potentially a very risky venture, high rates of return could be demanded. Interest-free lending was also acceptable and in its pure form was viewed by the Church as a charitable act – lending to one's brother in times of need. However, moneylenders often took advantage of this position, advancing funds without charge, but imposing penalties for late payment or a further fee to extend the loan beyond its agreed term.

While the Church publicly condemned usury, lending on interest no doubt took place in Catholic nations and was widely engaged in by bishops, princes and other senior figures in society, evolving as an activity openly condemned in public, but widely practiced in private. It is therefore probable that the true size of early medieval credit markets is under-represented in the historical record.

By the end of the twelfth century attitudes had softened somewhat and by the early thirteenth century the term 'interest' had come into common use. Usury was a charge made by a lender to secure a profit from a borrower – money made from money – but interest was compensation for loss of the use of funds during the period of a loan. If the moneylender had not lent the money, they could have reaped a profit from its productive or commercial use elsewhere, and should therefore receive recompense for their loss (Homer and Sylla 1996, pp.73–4). As lending on interest became more widespread in the eleventh and twelfth centuries, the increased availability of credit was no doubt one factor that helped support the resurgent medieval European economy. Small scale money lenders and pawnbrokers also operated in significant numbers throughout Europe, serving the lower orders of society, and many nations enacted legislation to limit the interest rates that could be charged – although how well these were enforced is open to debate. During the thirteenth century limits on interest rates in many European states were in the region of 10–20 percent per annum for personal loans, with anything above these rates considered usurious (Homer and Sylla 1996, pp.94–5). However, in some regions far higher rates were tolerated for certain types of lending. Pawnbrokers in particular appear to have had greater freedom to charge high rates. In England, for example, the legal maximum for pawn loans was set at 43.33 percent per annum in 1285 (but most cash loans on interest-bearing terms were technically outlawed until after the reformation). In Germany pawnshops were permitted to charge 173 percent and in Provence 300 percent (Homer and Sylla 1996, pp.94–5).

Lending on interest became increasingly common from the twelfth century onwards, but the Catholic Church remained suspicious of interest charges and firmly against usurious lending rates until relatively modern times.[3] Consequently, lenders had to be careful as to the rates they charged, lest they were accused of acting usuriously.

3.5 The Reformation

The Protestant Reformation of the sixteenth century saw religious strife across much of Europe which was accompanied by a polarization of positions on many issues depending on whether one fell into Catholic or Reformist camps. For the traditionalist there was little tolerance for the alternative views of the new churches and consequently the Catholic Church reasserted its position as to the evil and sinful nature of usury.

In theory the fundamental teachings of the new churches on usury were little different from the Catholic view. However, they had a more pragmatic approach to lending on interest. The Calvinists were the first Christian group to consider good economy, hard work and the capitalist ideal (achieved through hard work rather than idle accumulation) as a virtue in the eyes of God (Gelpi and Julien-Labruyere 2000, pp.50–1). To the Calvinist, lending in the right circumstances – in support of good and productive economy – was a wholesome and worthwhile activity. Calvin acknowledged the difference between the biblical prohibitions against 'biting usury' of the Old Testament, where money was lent without conscience, regardless of purpose or consequence and 'fenory' which is analogous to the gain reaped at the time of harvest over and above that which was sown (Kerridge 2002, pp.25–6). Fenory could be said to embody a conscious desire to increase the overall well-being of both borrower and lender and therefore not evil in its intent. In part, this could be taken to differentiate between consumptive and productive lending, a distinction recognized by the pre-Christian Romans. However, Calvinism was never more than a minor influence on wider Christian teaching and Calvin's general position on usury was not that different in practice from those of Martin Luther and other reformers; that is, that usury was only permissible under strict conditions, where the lender truly believed that in extending credit the borrower would also benefit from the transaction.

Newly Protestant England led the way in removing the barriers to interest-bearing credit. In 1545 Henry VIII repealed existing legislation against usury and interest on loans was permitted at a maximum rate of 10 percent. There was a temporary reinstatement of the bans against usury by Edward VI in 1552, but in 1571 usury was again permitted under the reign of Elizabeth I. After this time lending on interest was never again outlawed in England.

Although by the end of the sixteenth century the practice of lending on interest had become a legalized, regulated and well-practised activity in England and much of Europe, it remained much derided by the general populace. Both the Catholic and Protestant Churches continued to preach against the evils of usury and there are many examples in the record of the contempt and ridicule expressed against moneylenders and the usurious rates they often (illegally) charged. A measure of the force of this feeling is captured in the foreword to John Blaxton's 1634 text: 'The English Usurer' (Blaxton 1974):

> The covetous Wretch, to what may we compare,
> Better than Swine: Both of one nature are,
> One grumbles, the other grunts: Both grosse and dull,
> Hungry, still feeding, and yet never full...

> ...Nor differ they in death, The Brawne nought yields
> till cut in collers, into cheekes and shields,
> Like him the usurer, however fed,
> Profits none living, till himself be dead...

What this passage also displays is the direction in which the anger against lending took (and to some extent still takes today). While a borrower might be portrayed as acting foolishly, or as a spendthrift borrowing for immediate gain or pleasure, it was the moneylender who was always viewed as the transgressor, taking advantage of the poor, the stupid and the naïve – a view famously represented by the character of Shylock – the greedy and spiteful moneylender in Shakespeare's 'The Merchant of Venice'. However, despite continued opposition to money lending from a variety of sources, the use of various forms of credit continued to be exploited in England and parts of Europe in ever-increasing amounts by an ever-increasing proportion of the population.

3.6   A modern philosophy of credit

The eighteenth century saw huge social upheavals, with great strides made in the areas of economics, philosophy, science and industry, which drove the change from an agricultural society to an industrial one. As part of this revolution new ideas were being formed as to the appropriateness of usury and the laws that controlled it. In 1776 Adam Smith published his most famous work 'An Enquiry into the Nature and Causes of the Wealth of Nations' in which he argued that expensive credit led to the impoverishment of the agricultural worker (Jones and Skinner 1992, p.207), which today could be interpreted as applying to the general working man or woman. Smith also believed that excessive profits (such as the charging of high interest rates on loans) damaged the economy by taking away valuable resources that could otherwise be applied productively to improve the lot of individuals and wider society.

Smith's views did not in themselves bring anything new to the usury debate, but what is important about 'The Wealth of Nations' is that it provided the impetus for perhaps the most intelligent and perceptive discourse in favour of unrestricted lending practices to that time and arguably to date. In 1787 Jeremy Bentham published his 'Defence of Usury' (Stark 1952) in part as a reply to Smith's views on usury. Bentham presented a coherent and logical argument, without recourse to religious teaching, for treating lending on interest as a normal and not unnatural practice. As such, it was a practice that should not be constrained by interest rate ceilings or other terms which restricted the lender and borrower from striking a mutually acceptable bargain. At the core of Bentham's argument was that it was each person's responsibility to negotiate credit on the best terms they could. If the borrower felt they had borrowed at an uncompetitive rate, then all they had to do was borrow from a more competitive lender and repay the original debt. Bentham was also aware of the lessons of history and was of the opinion that whenever restrictive laws on usury were imposed, human ingenuity always found clever ways of circumventing those laws. Hence it was of little benefit to have them in the first place and a waste of resources which could be better applied elsewhere.

The impact of Bentham's work cannot be underestimated. While laws on usury and interest rates have remained, it represents a turning point from which lending laws in many countries would be grounded in secular argument rather than religious doctrine, and the basic arguments put forward by Bentham still form the basis of credit policies in many countries today.

3.7   From Victorian necessity to the First World War

There were a number of changes to English credit laws in the 234-year period between the reigns of Elizabeth I and Victoria, but most were minor, relating to the maximum legal interest rate and the regulation of pawn broking. The Bills of Sale Act 1854 abolished restrictions on interest rates and paved the way for consumer credit to become a standard feature of the Victorian era.[4] In contrast, legal limits on interest rates remained in many US states until 1981, and even today some states retain tight interest rate controls for some types of lending. However, after a court ruling allowing national lenders to charge common interest rates across all states, federal regulation now takes precedence over state law in most situations (U.S. Supreme Court 1978). Where state laws remain, many local lenders circumvent these by entering into agreements with federal banks whose registered offices are located outside the state (Peterson 2004, p.12). Therefore, for all practical purposes, state interest rate limits no longer apply. In many other countries however, including France, Germany and Holland, legal limits on interest rates remain. If one takes a wide historical perspective, then the uncapped rates that exist today in the UK (and effectively in the US) can be considered an aberration, rather than the norm.

The other major legal reforms of the Victorian era occurred in the 1860s. Prior to 1861 bankruptcy and escape from one's debts was only an option for merchants and traders owing considerable sums. People other than merchants and traders, who owed more than forty shillings,[5] were subject to insolvency law that empowered creditors to apply to the courts to either seize goods in lieu of the debt or seek the debtor's imprisonment until the debt had been repaid. For smaller amounts debtors were subject to the jurisdiction of local (county) courts. Courts were empowered to demand full payment of the debt, or to impose a repayment schedule for what was owed. Failure to meet the repayment schedule set by the court would result in asset seizure or imprisonment. It is estimated that by the 1790s roughly half of the entire prison population of England was accounted for by debtors (Finn 2003, pp.111–12). New legislation in 1861 and 1869 made bankruptcy available to all, subject to a fee of ten pounds,[6] and abolished the power of the courts to send those with large debts to prison. However, for those with small debts or without the funds to petition for bankruptcy, county courts retained the power to send them to prison right up until the passing of the Administration of Justice Act in 1970 (Finn 2003, pp.186–7).

Prior to the nineteenth century formal lending agreements had mainly been the domain of the well-to-do in the form of loans or mortgages secured against land or property. The working class did borrow extensively, but credit-debt relationships tended to operate on an informal basis with a network of debt and obligation existing within the local community, between merchants, friends, co-workers, employers and one's extended family. The early nineteenth century saw a shift towards more formal agreements being entered into by working and lower-middle class people who used credit in a number of different forms. Men were usually the wage earners, but it was women who were generally responsible for managing the household budget. It is therefore not surprising that the majority of working class credit was sought by women (Tebbutt 1983, p.47).

The tallymen (or peddlers) were travelling salesmen who worked door-to-door providing goods which were then paid for weekly, and were most common in London, Scotland and Northeast England (Johnson 1985, p.154). Retail credit worked through the relationship of local shops and their regular customers who would put items 'on the slate' or 'on tick' and settle their debts at week or month end. There was also a large trade in small scale, short term money lending, much of it remaining unlicenced after the Money Lending Act of 1900 which required moneylenders to be registered by law. However, the most widely used form of credit was pawning (or pledging) which remained popular in the UK until the Second World War. The laws governing the licencing and operation of pawnbrokers were revised in 1800 and again in 1872, and by the 1870s pawnbroking had become a huge industry.

The majority of the population lived week-to-week with little or no savings and employers offered no sick or holiday pay. Many people were employed in irregular or erratic occupations such as agriculture or dock work. Pawning provided a convenient way to cover short term drops in income or periods without pay. Consequently, most pawning consisted of low value, short term lending. It was not uncommon to take clothes or other items to pawn on a Monday, redeem them on Friday and then pawn them again the following Monday. The family's 'Sunday best' which were of no use during the week, were often used to provide this type of pledge and clothing was the most commonly pledged item. The pledging of jewellery and other valuables, which is perhaps most commonly associated with pawning today, was rare. The only jewellery of any worth owned by most people was their wedding ring with which they were loathe to part except in the most dire of circumstances.

The scale of the UK pawnbroking industry by the end of the nineteenth century was immense. Johnson (1985, p.168) quotes figures for 1870, when there were estimated to be around 150 million pawn loans issued in the UK, which had risen to 230 million by the industry's peak in 1914, equivalent to an average of between five and six loans for every man, women and child in the country. In the US pawning was also widespread, but to a lesser extent than in the UK.

The modern day residential mortgage had its roots in the Victorian era, arising from the building society movement. The idea of mortgaging one's assets to obtain credit was not new, but what the building societies did was to turn the mortgage principle on its head. Instead of using property as the security against which credit was obtained, the building societies offered the credit to buy/build the property in the first place. The first building societies appeared in the UK in the 1770s (Price 1959, p.14), and were originally set up as small temporary cooperatives whose members provided the money, time and labour needed to build each member a house in turn. When a house had been constructed for every society member the society was disbanded. In the 1840s a new breed of society appeared, with the aim of providing funds for members to buy property rather than building it for themselves. Many of the new societies allowed new members to join on an ongoing basis and also provided saving accounts to people who did not necessarily want to buy a property. These became 'permanent' societies that were never disbanded, and were sustained by a continual stream of new members.

The 1880s also saw the introduction of cheque trading in the UK. Independent companies would sell a customer cheques under credit terms, that could then be redeemed against goods at a range of associated stores. The stores would then be reimbursed for the value of the cheques by the chequing company (Johnson 1985, p.152). The chequing companies would make a return from the merchant in the form of a commission and from interest charged to the customer. In some ways these chequing facilities can be seen as a forerunner to the credit card accounts we know today.

While the British could be said to have driven much of the development of credit between the sixteenth and nineteenth centuries, new innovations in the US saw an increasing appetite for consumer credit at the end of the nineteenth century. The modern hire-purchase and installment loan agreements had their origins in the mid-nineteenth century and early forms of retail installment credit were being used on a small scale in the US soon after 1800 for the sale of clocks and furniture (Emmet and Jeuck 1950, p.265). As the nineteenth century drew to a close an increasing number of shops and particularly the new department stores, with their large floor area and wide range of diverse goods, had developed the concepts of hire-purchase and installment credit as standard mediums for the purchase of clothing and the many new consumer durables that appeared as a result of Victorian technological innovation.

Charge accounts were also popular. However, large department stores and retail chains comprising many different outlets, dealt with a far larger customer base than the small local stores that preceded them. Consequently, the customer was no longer someone who was known to the merchant. This led to some stores to issue charge plates to their customers – small metal plates containing the customer's details. The customer could then present the charge plate in any store and goods would be charged to the customer's account with some assurance that the customer was who they claimed to be. This was another development on the road towards the modern credit card.

The nineteenth century also saw the birth of the mail order catalogue companies. Improvements in rail and road transportation meant that goods could be dispatched to almost any location with ease and delivery could be guaranteed within a few days. Although some small scale operations had existed since the 1830s, the first full mail order catalogue in the US was launched by Montgomery Ward in 1872 and was aimed primarily at the large and isolated farming community where access to a diverse range of goods was limited by geography (Emmet and Jeuck 1950, pp.18–19). By the end of the nineteenth century the company was offering more than 10,000 different goods in its catalogue and was competing with the most famous of American merchants, Sears, Roebuck and Company. However, as Calder (1999, p.200) points out, Sears did not offer credit terms until 1911 and Montgomery Ward until 1921–2.

The original UK mail order catalogue company, Empire Stores, was founded in 1831, selling jewellery and fine goods. Initially it offered interest-free credit to 'customers of good standing' but soon began looking for ways to offer interest-free credit to working class people, and did so by organizing a system of 'watch clubs'. Each week club members paid a contribution towards the purchase of a pocket watch, which at the time was a much sought after item of new technology that the average working class person could not afford to purchase outright. The clubs were popular and quickly expanded to cover a wider range of goods. By the early-1870s, due to many clubs being distant from the physical stores, catalogues displaying goods were being produced and distributed to the clubs. Goods were then ordered, delivered and paid for by post. Full installment credit terms were being offered by the company some time prior to 1907 (Beaver 1981, pp.32–45). The second innovation that can be said to have originated with Empire Stores is the 'agency' model for mail order retailing. The agent (who presumably began as the named representative of the watch club) would act as the contact between the company and a number of 'customers' who were typically family, friends and neighbours. The agent would manage the relationship with the company, purchasing goods on behalf of themselves and their customers and collecting and making payments to the company. In return they received either a discount on their own purchases or a commission payment of around 10 percent. This model was adopted by all large mail order catalogue retailers in the UK and although in decline, the use of agents still accounted for a significant proportion of UK mail order catalogue sales in the late-2000s.

3.8   Between the wars

Retail installment credit and hire-purchase had been popular since the 1880s, but it was the interwar period of 1918–39 that saw these two types of credit rise to prominence. By 1935 it was estimated that in the UK 80 percent of cars, 90 percent of sewing machines and more than 75 percent of furniture were being purchased under hire-purchase agreements (Johnson 1985, p.157). In the US, with its geographically distributed population, the motor car was by far the biggest single factor in the growth of installment credit and in 1939 accounted for 34 percent of all new installment lending in that year (Klein 1971, pp.69 & 77). Hire-purchase, although similar in the method of payment to a personal loan, was attractive to lenders because it offered a secured medium, with goods legally remaining the property of the lender until the agreement was fully paid up. Therefore, with cars and other modern goods in great demand, there was always the option to recoup funds through repossession and resale should repayments fall behind schedule. Consequently, agreements could be entered into on a far more relaxed basis from the lenders' perspective. In support of the growth in the number of motor cars, the US also saw a number of oil companies offering charge accounts linked to their own-brand chain of gas stations as a means of encouraging loyalty in the fiercely competitive gasoline market.

At this time the possession of a car, washing machine, or any of the other consumer durables that had become widely available, was very much a middle class aspiration and consequently the use of installment loans and hire-purchase agreements were very much a middle class activity (Calder 1999, pp.202–3). As Calder notes in relation to the US experience, this represented a marked shift in the popular perception of installment credit from the end of the nineteenth century when it was viewed as an occupation of the lower classes and even described by some to be one of the lowest forms of credit available.

Pawning entered a period of decline after the First World War. Local shop credit and small scale money lending also went into decline after this time, albeit to a lesser extent.

3.9   The modern age

Arguably the biggest change in recent history in the way people borrow occurred in 1949 when three friends sat round a restaurant table in New York and thought up the idea of the universal credit card (Mandell 1990, p.1). The concept was revolutionary but simple, as so many important innovations prove to be. People would become members of a club. When club members went into a store or restaurant which recognized the club, they would not be required to pay for goods or services there and then, but would charge the goods to the club. The club would honour the debt and deal with the bothersome task of obtaining monies from the customer. In return for this guarantee of payment the merchant would pay a fee, of around 7 percent, to cover the club's costs. In addition, the club would charge members a fee for the privilege. To identify themselves, club members would carry a paper card, not dissimilar in principle to the charge plates some merchants had begun issuing to their credit customers some 50 years before. The name of this club was The Diners Club, and so the first credit card was born.

What differentiated The Diners Club from other forms of lending such as store or gas station credit was the fact that it was not confined to a single store or chain of stores, and once the initial agreement had been made, customers could (up to a point) continue to spend again and again without further authorization. The card could be accepted by any type of merchant for any type of good or service. The card company was effectively a middleman providing easy access to credit for the individual and security for the merchant. Therefore, a merchant could sell goods and services to a complete stranger safe in the knowledge that the credit card company would pay the bill.

For a number of years The Diners Club had the card market almost entirely to itself. However, as with all good commercial ideas competition eventually arrived, and it arrived in force. In 1958 both American Express and Carte Blanche entered the market, shortly followed by the two largest banks in America at that time, The Bank of America and Chase Manhattan. As the card market grew, The Bank of America offered its card services to other banks, allowing them to use its card processing infrastructure. This formed the basis of what became the VISA network in 1976 and all cards that use it carry the VISA logo. In response to Bank of America's growing domination of the card market, a number of other leading banks cooperatively set up their own card network which was re-branded as MasterCard in 1980.

While installment lending and mail order retained a significant market share in the unsecured lending market, by the end of the 1960s credit cards were becoming a common feature in the American consumer's wallet, with around 26 million cards in circulation by 1970 (Mandell 1990, p.35) – a phenomenal achievement in a period of just 12 years.

The rise of credit cards brought their own problems. Card companies would often mail customers out of the blue with a fully authorized credit card. If the card went missing or was misused, the card companies would pursue the individual for the debt, even if the card had never reached the customer in the first place. In the US the Fair Credit Reporting Act 1970 addressed many of these issues placing the burden of proof on the card companies to prove misuse, rather than the previous situation where the individual was forced to prove their innocence in what could be a costly and time consuming exercise. In the UK, the Consumer Credit Act 1974 replaced the hotchpotch of previous consumer credit legislation and provided similar protection for UK consumers.

With the arrival of the credit card – the most prominent of consumer credit tokens – individuals could buy what they wanted where they wanted without the need to have the money to pay for it. The credit card gave consumers a whole new dimension to their purchasing power.

The power to purchase whenever and whatever was only one of the impacts of credit cards. For the first time credit was visible, personal and said something about who and what an individual represented. For much of history debt had carried with it a stigma. To be identified as a borrower was something shameful and secret. Today the type of credit card you carry and the credit limit you command is a status symbol. As Morgan Stanley told us in their 2002/3 advertising campaign: 'Only 7 percent of communication is verbal' implying that your credit card says a lot about you, your attitudes and values. The trend for promoting prestige cards as status symbols came to prominence in 1981 when MasterCard launched its gold card to target what it saw as the most lucrative sections of the market, and for many people today the question is whether their plastic is silver, gold, platinum, green, black or blue. By the late-1980s affinity marketing had also become widespread, with card companies branding their cards with the logos of other companies, sports teams or famous people. There has even been a Star Trek card carrying a picture of the USS Enterprise, presumably with the goal of assisting the customer to boldly spend where they have never spent before!

The post-war years saw the UK fall some way behind the accelerating US credit industry. While credit cards were introduced to the UK in 1966 in the form of Barclaycard, the number of competing cards was small and the working classes were generally excluded from possession of a card either through choice or the conservative nature of the UK banking industry. Not surprisingly, the take-up of credit cards was slower in the UK than the US and it was the mail order catalogue retailers which expanded to service the retail credit needs of the UK population. Prior to the Second World War, mail order was popular mainly in the northern parts of the UK, in rural areas, and lower socio-economic groups. In the 1950s and 1960s mail order saw rapid expansion, accounting for approximately 8 percent of non-food retail sales by the late-1970s (Pederson 2002, p.168). In 1981 it was estimated that 20 million people purchased via mail order every year, with up to half a million orders being placed each day (Taylor 2002, p.116). It was not until the late-1980s and early-1990s that the UK credit card market really took off, and this can be attributed, at least in part, to American companies such as MBNA, Capital One and Morgan Stanley setting up UK operations in 1980s. These companies offered a range of new and competitive products often with lower interest rates than previously available and often without an annual fee.

As credit cards became more widely available in the UK, traditional mail order credit entered a period of decline and the industry looked to consolidate its position through various mergers and acquisitions. This was not a surprising development as a credit card generally offers the customer the ability to purchase more goods, at a wider range of stores, often at a lower price than that offered by a mail order catalogue. To some extent mail order catalogues have become the shopping medium for a much narrower range of customers. Principally, those with limited access to stores or the internet, those who struggle to obtain credit from other sources and older customers who have remained loyal to the catalogue ideal through long association, and who enjoy the familiarity of the catalogue experience.

The final push towards what could be considered as the modern lending environment came with the deregulation that occurred in the US and UK in the late-1970s and 1980s. In the US, with the implementation of the Depository Institutions Deregulation and Monetary Control Act 1980, most states either removed usury laws or raised the maximum interest rates that could be charged, leading to a more open lending environment in which competition could flourish. In the UK major changes to the regulation of the financial services market occurred between 1979 and 1987 resulting in a relaxation of market controls. Of particular note is the Building Society Act 1986. Prior to the Act banks and building societies focused on specific elements of the credit market. Building societies dominating the mortgage market while banks focused on bank accounts, overdrafts and personal loans. Following the new legislation, banks and building societies were able to offer more or less identical products and services, resulting in much increased competition within the consumer credit market.

3.10   The impact of technology

Technology has had a dramatic impact on the speed and sophistication of consumer credit markets in terms of the way credit is granted, managed and marketed. The industrial revolution provided the transport infrastructure to facilitate mail order catalogue retailing and the technological innovations which led to the development of so many of the consumer durables that customers ended up buying on installment credit or hire-purchase terms.

The IT revolution in credit started in the mid-1960s when the first banks and credit reference agencies computerized their customer databases and information processing systems, resulting in a huge increase in the amount of information lenders held about their customers and the speed with which such information could be processed. This allowed more subtle distinctions to be made between customers across all areas of the customer relationship, from marketing segmentation and product differentiation, via the application process, through to collections and debt recovery operations. The newly computerized systems facilitated more complex and efficient processing of this information, allowing financial organizations to apply mathematical and statistical models in real time to assess the creditworthiness of credit applications in seconds, where previously it could have taken days or weeks to process a credit application manually.

The other technological development of note was the rise of the internet in the mid-1990s. In one sense the internet did not offer anything new in terms of the types of credit available to the consumer. However, the lower costs associated with internet-only operation, without the requirement for a branch network or many other physical overheads, helped to stimulate competition with some lenders offering far more attractive credit terms than their traditionally branch-based rivals. The internet has also provided another channel for customer communication, and for many people it has proved to be the medium of choice, allowing credit applications and account management facilities to be accessed in the borrower's own home, at any time of day or night, at their own convenience.

3.11   Chapter summary

Credit-debt relationships have existed since prehistoric times, and the extent and sophistication of ancient credit markets should not be underestimated.

Throughout much of its history, credit has been defined largely by the prevailing moral climate and the resulting legislation to address the problems resulting from its use and misuse. However, what must be remembered is that although much of the historical record relates to the laws and restrictions on lending and the operation of legalized credit markets, the status of illegal and unregulated lending practices is less well understood. It is very likely that the role that this type of credit has played in society has been under represented, particularly during periods of history when lending on interest was highly regulated or banned altogether.

The technological advances made since the middle of the nineteenth century has significantly changed the way in which credit is marketed, granted and managed. Part of this change has been to facilitate new mediums of credit such as mail order and credit cards, but another aspect is the desire of the consumer to acquire a larger and larger number of the ever-increasing range of consumer durables on offer. A final observation is that limitations on interest rates have existed throughout most of history with relatively few exceptions. In a historical context, the relatively unrestricted nature of credit markets in the UK and US at the start of the twenty-first century – where interest rate limits apply in only a very limited set of circumstances – is arguably the exception rather than the rule. Given past history, it is not inconceivable that interest rate controls will again be applied at some point in the future in one or both of these countries, should the problems associated with credit once again reach a level deemed unacceptable by society at large.

3.12   Suggested sources of further information

Homer, S. and Sylla, R. (2005). *A History of Interest Rates*. Rutgers. After more than 40 years since its original publication, this remains a central text on the development of commercial and consumer credit markets around the world. The first ten chapters provide an abundance of information with regard to the history of consumer credit up to and including the Reformation.

Gelpi, R. and Julien-Labruyere, F. (2000). *The History of Consumer Credit: Doctrines and Practice*. St. Martin's Press. This book charts the development of consumer credit from earliest times to the present day with a strong focus on the development of consumer credit markets in Western Europe. At the time of writing, it is perhaps the only book devoted to the history of consumer credit in its entirety, as distinct from commercial credit or other areas of economics or financial services.

Calder, L. (1999). *Financing the American Dream*. Princeton University Press. Calder describes in great detail the development of credit in the US, focusing primarily on the period 1840–1940. An interesting, informative and well-researched read.

Lewis, M. (1990). *The Credit Card Industry: A History.* Twayne Publishers. Lewis provides a detailed account of the development of the credit card industry, primarily from a US perspective, but with some details regarding the introduction of credit cards in the UK and other countries.

4
Ethics in Lending

Ethics is the study of right and wrong. It is concerned with the decisions people make and whether or not these constitute 'good' or 'bad' behaviour. The chapter begins with a brief discussion as to why ethics is relevant to the operation of commercially-oriented financial institutions and briefly introduces ethics as a field of study. The discussion then turns to consider some of the ethical questions that have been raised about the nature of credit-debt relationships.

4.1   The role of ethics in financial services

Why consider ethics at all in a commercial setting? One view is that we live in a dog-eat-dog world where everyone must compete to achieve what they want in life, and one way to this is by working to maximize the profitability of the organizations that employ us. Making money is what commercial organizations are set up to do and what shareholders expect. Ethical considerations merely get in the way of this objective. It can also be argued that for an employee of a commercial organization to do anything other than trying to maximize the profitability of their employer, such as allowing its resources to be used for charitable purposes, is unethical because it acts against the interest of the shareholders to whom the employee has a responsibility in return for the wages they receive – a view espoused by the Nobel Prize-winning economist Milton Friedman (Chryssides and Kaler 1993, pp.249–54). Where controls are needed to protect employees, customers or others in the community against activities deemed to be unethical, then it is the role of government to legislate appropriately on behalf of these groups. Therefore, any action taken in a commercial setting can be said to be ethical as long as it complies with the law of the land. Legal compliance is normally a good thing because it is less costly than the legal fees, fines, imprisonment, loss of sales from bad publicity and so on, that arises from acting illegally.

One criticism of this argument is that secular laws are at best generalizations of ethical codes of conduct, representing a majority view of what does or does not constitute good behaviour. While there is often an overlap between legal and ethical activities, it does not necessarily follow that just because an action is legal it is also ethical. In the UK it is legal to give (but not sell) alcohol to a five-year-old child, yet few would agree with the ethical nature of this. Another criticism is that laws are often devised to deal with problems after they arise. It can take years to implement appropriate legislation due to the process of government and the limitation on resources that leads to some legislation taking preference over others. Even when ethical laws are passed quickly or preemptively, there are almost always loopholes allowing the unscrupulous to mistreat individuals within the law whilst ignoring the spirit of the law.

Another consideration is the nature of commercial organizations and their relationships with individuals. Commercial organizations are artificial constructs, with no concept of right and wrong in themselves. They have no inherent respect for persons or human rights. In most cases they exist with the sole objective of maximizing shareholder return – all other considerations are subservient to this goal. If a person behaved in this way, singularly focused on getting only what they wanted with no regard for others, the general consensus would be that at the very least they were selfish, immoral, and arguably, psychopathic.

If businesses only interacted with other businesses then it would be easier to accept the profit maximization principle. However, we all interact with commercial enterprise on a daily basis as workers, customers or individuals coexisting in a common environment, the control and management of which we have an understandable interest in. We should therefore, expect our relationships with business to mirror our relationships with other individuals, and we should expect commercial organizations to conform to the same standard of behaviour that we would expect when dealing with other people.

A more positive attitude towards corporate behaviour is achieved by remembering that organizations are controlled by shareholders, directors and managers, all of whom are human beings who, it would be hoped, have some personal ethical orientation. It is possible for shareholders to define non-monetary objectives within a company's article of particulars (the stated aims of a company created at its inception stating how it will operate) or for management to incorporate ethical ideals into the strategic objectives of an organization with the support of shareholders. The Cooperative Bank in the UK has operated an ethical commercial policy since 1992, formulated after a wide reaching consultation with its customers. The bank takes its social responsibilities very seriously and the implementation of its ethical policy is reviewed and reported upon annually by independent auditors (Cooperative Bank 2008). What is also encouraging is that rather than restricting its profitability, its ethical position has led to increased profits because of the positive image it presents. The bank has successfully incorporated its ethical stance into its corporate branding, making it stand out as offering something different from its competitors.

Further support for the value of having an ethical corporate policy was provided by a study of companies from the UK FTSE 350, undertaken by The Institute of Business Ethics. It concluded that those that had a stated code of ethical behaviour or who commented on ethical issues in their annual report, outperformed those who did not by a considerable margin (Webley and More 2003). The implication is that when companies act in accordance with some set of principles that take into account the impact of their actions on their customers, employees and the wider environment, then all groups benefit.

4.2 Ethics – a theoretical overview

In some circumstances ethics is used to refer to the set of rules by which individuals should abide. In others, it is viewed as the philosophy of action and consequence and the reasoning about how we, as human beings, should behave (Singer 1994, p.4).

Those who judge the rightness or wrongness of actions on the basis of the outcomes that result are termed consequentialists, while those whose actions are driven by rules or principles, with little regard for the consequences are termed non-consequentialists. To demonstrate the differences between these two perspectives consider the following question. Is it ethical to kill one person to save the lives of two or more others? If your answer to this is an unconditional yes, then this consequentialist view could be taken to imply a belief that it is ethical to carry out a medical experiment which kills the test subjects as long as it leads to the saving of a greater number of lives in the long run. On the other hand if your answer is a clear no, on the *principle* that it contravenes basic human rights, then this implies a non-consequentialist logic to your decision making. This is a very simplistic example and further arguments can be presented from both perspectives that give different answers to this question. If it is argued that killing test subjects in medical experiments causes significant harm to wider society, due to the fear and bad feeling induced by the chance of becoming a test subject and from the emotional harm incurred by the relatives and friends of the test subjects, then a consequentialist might decide the action is unethical under some wider measure of 'overall public good,' rather than just considering the consequences for the individuals directly involved. It might also be argued from a non-consequentialist viewpoint that the principle of saving many lives overrides that of protecting a single individual and therefore killing the test subjects is ethical in some circumstances.

4.2.1 Utilitarianism

Utilitarianism is the best known consequentialist model of ethical behaviour, encapsulating the idea of 'the greatest good for the greatest number.' Its formulation is attributed to the British philosophers Jeremy Bentham (1748–1832) and John Stuart Mill (1806–73) who developed the idea of an ethical action as one that maximizes the happiness and pleasure within the population as a whole. The only unethical action is the opposite – that which leads to pain or unhappiness. Why maximize happiness and not some other objective? Because in Bentham's view it is the only thing desirable as an end in itself. All other things are only of value insofar as they lead to that end of increased happiness (Chryssides and Kaler 1993, pp.91–2). However, as some people believe there are things other than happiness and pleasure that can be considered to be intrinsically good (such as gross domestic product or life expectancy) there can be consequentialists who are not utilitarianists (Singer 1994, p.243).

Utilitarianism tends to assume that the amounts of happiness and unhappiness can be measured so that alternative actions can be compared, making it possible to say objectively that the consequences of one action are better than another (Boatright 1999, pp.53–4). The main difficulty with formulating a utilitarian policy is how best to make this calculation. One approach favoured by economists is to represent levels of happiness and pleasure in terms of utility – allocating a numerical (often monetary) value to the desirability of each outcome. The outcome that yields the greatest overall utility is taken to be the most ethical. A more qualitative alternative to utility, which to some extent simplifies the problems associated with measuring outcomes directly, is to measure the popularity of actions in the belief that overall happiness and wellbeing can be represented in terms of popular approval; that is, when faced with two or more alternatives, to choose the one that the majority of the population believes will lead to the most desirable outcome. If more people agree that action X is preferable than action Y, then action X is taken to be the more ethical of the two. This is sometimes referred to as rule-based utilitarianism.

4.2.2   Kant's ethical theory

Immanuel Kant (1724–1804) is credited with advancing a non-consequentialist ethical framework based on duty and respect for others. Rather than asking what the impact of an action will be, Kant argued that an action is ethical if it is what a rational being would do and shows respect for other persons as rational beings (Boatright 1999, pp.56–7). In other words, one should be motivated to act in good faith, out of a sense of duty as to what is right and proper, which Kant termed the categorical imperative. Kant expressed the categorical imperative as: 'Act only according to that maxim by which you can at the same time will that it should become universal law.' The fundamental idea encapsulated in this statement is one of universalization. An ethical rule of behaviour is something that all rational people would universally agree with. The example given by Boatright (1999, p.57) is the problem of how to choose the best way of dividing a chocolate cake between a number of people. While everyone might want the whole cake for themselves, the only consensus (and hence ethical) decision that can be arrived at is to divide the cake equally amongst everyone.

Kant also presented a second formulation of the categorical imperative, as a respect for individuals, which can be taken as complementary to the universalist principle; that is, people should not be treated as objects, but as other sentient beings with the right to their own life and opinions and should never be used merely as a means to one's own ends. This idea is often expressed by what has become known as the Golden Rule: 'Do unto others as you would have done unto you.' However, as Olen and Barry (1989, p.8) point out, this implies that we should carry out actions such as giving all our money to complete strangers because this is what we would want them to do for us. Consequently, it is the negative version of the Golden Rule that is often the most insightful: '*Do not* do unto others as we would *not* have done unto us.' This places the emphasis on what we should do to avoid inflicting harm, rather than maximizing the wellbeing of others.

4.2.3   Higher moral authority

Religious teaching forms the basis of many people's lives, with God-given law forming the basis of the ethical framework within which they operate. The fundamental principle is that God is a better judge of right and wrong than we are. Perhaps the best known example of this type of law are the ten commandments, given by God to Moses: 'Thou shalt not kill,' 'Thou shalt not steal,' and so on, which have the general support of many religions as well as agnostics and non-believers. However, no system of religious laws deals with all possible situations that people encounter in their daily lives and the application of reason is always required to interpolate and apply what is believed to be God's will to specific situations. So while there are no holy scriptures relating to the application of stem cell research or the use of nuclear weapons, it is still possible to formulate a theologically derived moral stance on these issues.

4.2.4   Natural law, virtue and human rights

Aristotle (382–22 B.C.) believed that for everything in nature there was a right and proper purpose – a natural law to which it should conform (Crisp 2000, pp.15 & 23). This principle also applied to human beings and human activities, with the ultimate purpose being to be fulfilled in one's life. This was achieved partly through fulfilling social responsibilities such as being a good parent or a conscientious worker, but also as a rational being to be guided by reason so that we control our emotions, live disciplined lives and do not give into sudden temptation to do foolish or extravagant things. Aristotle called these principles 'virtues' and concluded that there were inherently virtuous modes of behaviour beyond any man-made rule or law. Over the next two millennium this concept evolved into the concept of natural rights or human rights as we know them today. There are certain things that an individual has a given right to do, and certain things an individual cannot be denied, that should be beyond the power of any individual, government or other power to grant or deny. The role of government is simply to accept and protect the rights of its citizens. One of the key figures in formulating these ideas into a modern setting was John Locke (1632–1714) who espoused the philosophy of the right to life, liberty and property for all. These ideas were later incorporated into the American Declaration of Independence in 1776 and the French Declaration of the Rights of Man in 1789 (Chryssides and Kaler 1993, pp.101–2). Today the list of generally accepted human rights has grown to include concepts such as the right to free speech, free association, religious freedom and choice of sexual orientation.

One question that naturally arises is, where do these rights come from? The traditional view was that they were 'God given.' Some modern philosophers find this a difficult position to adopt, and an alternative view, formulated by the philosopher John Rawls (1921–2002) is that we should move beyond the idea that society merely protects the rights of individuals, to one where we define rights as those that should be granted by a just society (Olen and Barry 1989, p.15).

In many ways the concept of human rights can be considered a natural complement to Kantian ideas of duty and respect for individuals. So for example, it could be argued that workers have a basic <u>right</u> to receive a minimum wage for their labour, while employers have a <u>duty</u> to provide fair wages.

4.2.5 Ethics in practice

Putting ethical theories into practice in the real world can be difficult. Arguably, all of the ethical frameworks discussed previously can be found lacking when applied to some real world situations. Pol Pot in Cambodia and Stalin in Soviet Russia both applied what can arguably be described as extreme utilitarianist ideals to government policy during the twentieth century, putting the welfare of the state before that of the individual citizens that comprised the state. In both cases millions of people were deliberately killed as a direct result of their policies. The (mis)interpretation of religious teachings has been used as the excuse for many wars and acts of terrorism throughout history, and as the justification for applying unjust policies to some minority groups. It can also be argued that to follow a Kantian or human rights philosophy entirely can lead to equally poor decisions, and in the extreme can conceivably lead to catastrophes that could otherwise be avoided. This is because someone does what they believe should be done, not what avoids some ultimate disaster – a justification used in the 2000s by the UK and US governments to deny basic human rights to 'suspected terrorists' at Guantanamo Bay in the US and Belmarsh Prison in the UK.

Another difficulty is that many issues are extremely complex and the full facts may not be known or are disputed. Also, people may have different value systems, particularly if they are coming from different cultural or religious perspectives. Individuals with a North American or Western Europe heritage may consider it unethical to offer a payment to a government official to speed up a particular government process.

In countries such as Nigeria and Bangladesh, what westerners would consider a bribe is a widely accepted practice engaged in at all levels of society, and in some cases things won't get done at all unless a suitable payment is offered. When people hold opposing views it can be impossible to form a consensus as to whether a particular action is right or wrong, moral or immoral. Well-known issues such as, abortion, euthanasia, animal rights and capital punishment all fall into this category, with it being possible to argue a different but convincing case from many different perspectives.

In life, people naturally adopt ethical frameworks that encompass both consequentialist and non-consequentialist perspectives to generate their own individual views of what constitutes good behaviour, and no two individuals will have exactly the same viewpoint on every subject and every situation. However, the one assertion that can be said to apply across all ethical frameworks is the notion that ethics carries with it the idea of something more important than the individual. An ethical action is one which the perpetrator can defend in terms of more than self interest (Finlay 2000, p.75). To act ethically, one must at the very least consider the impact of one's actions in respect of other individuals and society at large.

4.3   The charging of interest

The oldest moral arguments about credit have centred around the use of interest as an appropriate mechanism by which an income is earned. From a western perspective, where interest is considered a standard element of most commercial credit agreements, it is important to remember that there are alternative methods for earning an income, and it is certainly feasible to run a profitable credit business without recourse to interest. Perhaps the best known example is the American Express charge card, where income is generated almost entirely from annual fees and merchant fees.

Aristotle opposed interest because it contravened natural laws of reproduction – an argument few would support today. The Bible, Qu'ran and Torah all share prohibitions against lending on interest and historically it is from religious groups that the strongest opposition to interest has been voiced. For Christians and Jews the blanket bans against charging interest were originally circumvented by interpreting the ban as only applying to those of the same faith group. Thus the historical association of Jews as moneylenders arose because they were permitted to lend to non-Jews, while Christians were allowed to borrow from them. In later times it became acceptable to charge a reasonable rate of interest to cover the return that would have been made if the lender's money had been invested elsewhere. For Christians and Jews the debate has moved on to consider where the boundary lies between reasonable and extortionate (usurious) rates of interest.

In Islam the ban on interest remains. However, the ethical arguments currently used by Islamic scholars in support of the ban are similar to those put forward by Judaeo-Christian philosophers in the past. They also have merit from humanist and economic perspectives and should therefore not be considered as exclusively theological arguments as to why charging interest is wrong. As described by Mills and Presley (1999, pp.10–11) different arguments are usually put forward against charging interest on investment (productive) loans and consumptive loans respectively.

The main argument against charging interest on investment loans is that it creates an unfair allocation of risk between borrower and lender should the venture fail. In a competitive market all business ventures carry with them an inherent risk of failure and it is the borrower who shoulders the greatest risk. If the venture fails the lender still has claim on the funds advanced, but the borrower has lost capital and interest, as well their own time and money. The lender has no concern about the success of the venture, only in the return of the original loan plus interest. The converse is also true. If the venture is very successful, then the borrower will receive a far larger share of the profits than the lender.

Ethical lending arrangements in compliance with Islamic (*Shari'ah*) law are those where risk and return are shared between lender and borrower, creating a joint concern for the venture's success. The credit-debt relationship is based on a partnership; one party provides the finance, the other the expertise to undertake the venture.

Consumptive lending, either to provide immediate necessities or for personal gratification, generates no returns in which the lender may share, and can also be argued to break Islamic principles regarding wealth and property ownership. While increasing one's personal wealth is considered a good and wholesome activity, it is something that brings with it certain responsibilities. One of these is the payment of the *Zakat*, an annual tax of 2.5 percent of an individual's assets. While its primary purpose is to provide for the poor and needy, the *Zakat* also acts as a redistribution mechanism, discouraging the concentration of wealth into fewer and fewer hands over time. Another tenet held by Islam is that wealth, particularly monetary wealth, is not something to be hoarded. Spare capital should be employed productively for the benefit of oneself, one's family and the community. The fact that someone has money to lend implies an excess (a hoard) and consumptive lending does not create wealth through productive investment or trade, but merely results in a transfer of wealth from one part of the community to another. Where interest-bearing credit is advanced to the poor to meet immediate personal need such as food, clothing or shelter, it acts against the redistribution of wealth, taking a proportion of what little they already have for the benefit of those who already have more than enough. In effect the interest charge can be considered as a tax paid by the poor for the goods and services they need to survive. If someone is in need then this should be met through charitable means, which may be a gift or a loan made on interest-free terms.

4.4   Interest or usury?

For those who accept interest as a legitimate charging mechanism, it is a matter of debate as to what constitutes an acceptable rate of interest, and at what point the charge made for credit can be considered usurious. The first question is whether usury even exists; that is, is there a rate of interest at which it can be considered unethical to lend? If usury is a valid concept, then a second question is, where does the boundary between fair and usurious interest rates lie?

4.4.1   Jeremy Bentham's 'Defense of Usury'

One view is that in a free market conforming to established principles of supply and demand usury is a flawed concept. The charges made for credit should be determined by market forces, with there being no need for legislation to limit the interest or other fees that a lender may charge. The main points in this argument were formulated by Jeremy Bentham (of utilitarianist fame) and presented in his treatise 'Defense of Usury' (Stark 1952). Bentham argued that a rational individual should always be able to obtain the best market rate on offer where competitive pressures keep market rates as low as possible. The price a lender obtains for the use of their money is no different in principle to a farmer obtaining the best possible price for their crop – if a buyer is willing to pay more than someone else then so be it. In Bentham's eyes there was no such thing as usury in normal economic circumstances. If an individual did happen to take a loan at an uncompetitive rate, then all they had to do was find a better deal, borrow again and repay the original loan (Stark 1952, pp.141–2). This principle works well for many modern day consumers and one can see it being applied through the large number of re-mortgages and consolidation loans taken out each year, and the widespread practice of card surfing to transfer credit card debt from a high rate card to a lower rate one. The only case where Bentham believed usury could be said to exist is where the rate charged was 'more than usually charged by men' implying situations where the lender misrepresented or misled the borrower in some way, or where the terms of the agreement resulted from some external factor not directly related to the credit agreement in question.

Bentham's arguments are appealing, particularly in relation to business lending where the borrower has access to professional advice and expertise, enabling them to negotiate with a lender on an equal footing. However, it could be argued these arguments are deficient when applied to modern consumer credit markets. Just as someone can be ripped-off and end up paying over the odds for consumer goods or services, so they can pay more than they should for a loan, and in today's markets it's often not simply a case of finding a cheaper loan elsewhere. Many credit agreements come with penalty clauses which costs the borrower dearly if they repay the loan before the agreed repayment date.

Bentham's assertions were also based on the concept of the rational borrower, acting in full knowledge of the agreement they were entering into. Yet, despite legislation such as the UK Consumer Credit Acts 1974 and 2006, and the US Truth in Lending Act 1968 that give detailed and specific instructions about the information that lenders must provide about their products and repayment terms, there is considerable evidence that a significant proportion of the population does not understand the terms under which credit is provided to them. In a survey carried out in the US, it was reported that at least 40 percent of people do not understand the relationship between the interest rate and the APR quoted by lenders (Lee and Hogarth 1999). A UK survey in 2002 reported that 75 percent of those with hire-purchase agreements and 63 percent with loans did not know the interest rate they were being charged on their debts (Kempson 2002, p.50). Why do so many people know so little about the credit agreements they enter into? One reason is that credit agreements are relatively complex, requiring a high level of literacy and numeracy to understand them. Very few people are completely illiterate, but in the US studies have reported that 34 percent of adults have only a basic or below basic level of literacy (Kutner *et al.* 2005, p.4).[1] In England 16 percent of adults are described as having a level of literacy at or below that expected of an 11-year-old (Williams *et al.* 2003, p.18). Similar figures exist for numeracy.

Another assumption made by Bentham was that individuals enter into a credit agreement freely and then have the ability to borrow again, should the rate of interest be overtly high. This is not necessarily the case. Returning to the example of the farmer and his crop, it seems quite reasonable that under normal circumstances they should be able to sell it for whatever price they can get, but what about in times of famine when people are starving, and the farmer is the only supplier? Is it right for the farmer to maximize their profit from a starving individual, who is in no position to bargain for a good deal? A more ethical decision might be to give away some of the produce for free as an act of charity, or to charge only a 'reasonable rate' representing the farmer's costs and some acceptable level of mark up. Sometimes only a single lender may be willing to lend to an individual. In other situations someone may be forced to borrow to meet the immediate needs of themselves or their family. These two factors often come together with people being forced to borrow from a single source of credit that can effectively charge whatever rate they wish. The borrower, with an overwhelming concern for today's immediate needs, will willingly enter into a credit agreement without consideration of the long term consequences of their actions.

While Bentham may have been aware of such problems, this did not detract him from the belief that interest rates should not be regulated. In particular, he believed that where attempts had been made to impose interest rate ceilings, lenders always found ways around them. For example, prior to the relaxation of American interest rates in 1980, credit card issuers increased their revenue by imposing annual fees to make up for the low interest rates they were allowed to charge. Bentham's other argument against setting maximum permissible interest rates through law was that if a lender was unwilling to lend to an individual at a legal rate of interest, then the borrower would be forced to seek a loan from an illegal source that would charge an even higher rate than they would have charged in an unrestricted market, to cover the added risk imposed from operating illegally. The illegal status of these types of agreement would also mean that the number of lenders offering these higher rates would also be much reduced. Hence, there would be less competition, pushing rates up still further. In summary, Bentham believed that the net result of any legislation to limit interest rates would be for those denied credit by mainstream lenders to end up paying more for the credit advanced to them than they would otherwise have paid in a market in which no restrictions existed. Was Bentham right in his belief? A report by the UK government (Department of Trade and Industry 2004) came to the following conclusions:

- In those countries where interest rate ceilings existed, the use of legalized sources of credit by low income households was less than in those countries where no ceilings existed.
- In France and Germany, where interest rate ceilings existed, those on low incomes were more likely to admit to using illegal moneylenders than in the UK where no legal limits on interest rates existed.
- There was less product diversity in markets where interest rate ceilings existed, and when ceilings were imposed some lenders subsequently withdrew from the market (resulting in reduced competition).
- The introduction of interest rate ceilings resulted in credit charges being applied in other ways. In particular, through penalty fees, and it was low income/high risk individuals who tended to incur these fees, not those who were better off or who had a lower risk of defaulting.

Similar conclusions were drawn by a report into the effect of interest rate limits across different US states (Staten and Johnson 1995, pp.48–50), and these findings would tend to support Bentham's views. This does not mean that charging high rates of interest is ethical: it merely means that simple legislation to define a maximum legal rate of interest does not address the problem of high cost credit encountered by those members of the community who are unable to secure credit from mainstream sources.

A final comment on Bentham's arguments is that they were made primarily on economic grounds. The borrower and lender agree the charges levied because they both believe that the benefit they will receive will be worth the expense. What Bentham does not discuss in any detail is the hardship that can result when a borrower faces unforeseen repayment difficulties. A rational borrower will normally make two key assumptions when they enter into a credit agreement. First, that their circumstances will not deteriorate over the term of the agreement. Second, that given their current circumstances, they will be able to afford the credit they have agreed to borrow based on their expectation of the cost of credit at the time the agreement was entered into. From the borrower's perspective, interest as a charging mechanism works well if these two assumptions are borne out. However, if the borrower finds themselves in financial difficulty and in arrears, then the amount owed can increase rapidly, soon overwhelming the ability of the individual to repay, even if their circumstances subsequently improve. The greater the rate of interest the more pronounced this effect will be. Ward (2004) reports the case of a couple who borrowed a sum of $11,500 in 1989 at an interest rate of 34.9 percent – similar to that being charged by some UK store card issuers at the time. By 2004 the debt had risen to $768,000 due to the couple falling into arrears a few months into the agreement, with interest continuing to be charged on the original sum, the penalty charges that were levied and interest that had already accrued. This is despite the couple resuming repayments a few months after their initial difficulties arose.

This case also demonstrates a fundamental difference between a simple trade agreement and a credit one. With a trade agreement, the exchange of goods and money occurs instantaneously. The costs and benefits to both parties are evaluated at a single point in time when the transaction occurs. With a credit agreement the actual costs and benefits are not known for certain. There is an inherent uncertainty due to the time/ risk dimension of the transaction. If a borrower experiences repayment difficulties then their benefit will decrease to the lender's advantage because extra interest charges and penalty fees apply. A lender might lose out if a borrower experiences repayment difficulties resulting in a loss of funds, but a borrower always will.

One conclusion that might be drawn from the discussion so far is that usury is a valid concept, but only in certain situations. Where individuals are well informed, fully understand the terms of the agreement, behave in a rational manner and have the ability to shop around for their debt, then it is difficult to argue a case for usury. However, there are cases where a lender takes advantage of an individual's ignorance or personal situation to make an unacceptable level of profit by charging an extortionate level of interest or other fees on a loan, and in these cases it is valid to consider these arrangements to be usurious. This is broadly in line with the definition of usury incorporated within the UK Consumer Credit Acts 1974 and 2006. The Acts, while not defining a statutory limit on the interest rate that may be charged, permits a court to modify the terms of an agreement if the interest charged is deemed to be 'unfair' or which 'otherwise grossly contravenes ordinary principles of fair dealing' (Skipworth and Dyson 1997, p.150). It was this legislation that led to a court decision writing off the $768,000 debt because it was deemed to form an extortionate (usurious) credit agreement (Ward 2004). The key question of course, is how to determine when the charges relating to a credit agreement are 'unfair.' This question is discussed in the following section.

4.4.2   The principle of reasonable return

If someone borrowed $1,000 one day and repaid $1,010 the next, would this be excessive? What if they borrowed $1,000 on the first of January and repaid $2000 on the tenth of April (100 days later)? In both cases the annual equivalent rate of interest is 365 percent, but it can be argued that the second is a much more extortionate agreement than the first. This is because the lender's administrative costs are the same, regardless of the size or term of the loan. If it costs $9 to arrange the necessary paperwork and so on, then in the first case the lender only makes a return of $1. If exactly the same loan was repeated every day for 100 days then they would make a total profit of $100. In the second case, where the loan was only arranged once, the lender would make a return of $991. Yet, in both cases the borrower would pay the same amount over a period of 100 days.

Consider another question. Is an interest rate of 20 percent per annum extortionate? For a US mortgage in the late-2000s almost certainly, for a personal loan maybe, for a store card – probably not. The key difference is the cost (and risk) of providing each product in relation to the income received. This is one reason why mortgages, which are usually for large sums over long terms have much lower interest rates than personal loans, which in turn tend to have lower rates than credit and store cards (their secured status is the other reason mortgage interest rates are low).

One view is that a lender has the right to make a return on their investment that reflects their costs plus a reasonable mark-up. What constitutes a reasonable rate of return for a credit agreement to be considered ethical? There is no single answer to this question, but one approach is to follow the arguments first put forward by the medieval Christian philosophers. A reasonable return is defined as the equivalent return that could have been made through investing in some alternative venture. One measure commonly used to assess the relative profitability of limited companies is the Return on Capital Employed (ROCE). The ROCE is a measure of the net annual profit as a proportion of the total funds invested in the company in terms of buildings, machinery, investments and so on. If a company has employed capital of $20 million and makes a net annual profit of $2 million, the ROCE would be 10 percent (100 * $2m/$20m).

The average ROCE for non-financial UK companies is about 5 percent. The average ROCE for specific industry sectors ranges from close to zero for engineering companies, to over 20 percent for pharmaceutical companies (Experian 2004). The average return made by the major UK banks is around 14 percent (Bank of England 2008, p.62). If, for example, 14 percent per annum is taken to represent a reasonable return for a credit agreement, then a reasonable charge for credit could be defined as a lender's costs plus 14 percent.

Take a credit card as an example. By using some of the figures quoted in Chapter 6, it is possible to (very roughly) estimate that the average cost of providing credit for a typical credit card is equal to about 12 percent of the money lent per annum. So for every $1,000 lent, it costs about $120 in bad debt, cost of funds, staff wages and so on. Therefore, if income is generated from interest alone, the rate that would need to be charged to generate a 14 percent return would be 26 percent (12 + 14). As discussed in Chapter 6, not all revenue comes from interest. If merchant fees, charges, insurance revenue and so on were expressed as an interest rate they would probably be equal to an interest charge of about 7 percent. Taking this additional revenue into account, the rate of interest a lender would need to charge to achieve a 14 percent return on investment is approximately 19 percent (26 − 7). If a different return is deemed acceptable, then the figures can be reworked. So if a return of 5 percent was the maximum ethically acceptable, then an interest rate of 10 percent could be justified ((12 + 5) − 7).

In practice of course, the situation is more complex. Most credit card providers apply pricing-for-risk strategies, offering credit at different interest rates to different customers, based on the estimated revenue and bad debt they are likely to generate. For example, the typical interest rate being quoted by Barclaycard (the UK's largest credit card provider in 2008) for purchases made using most of its credit cards was 14.9 percent. However, the range of different interest rates being advertised on the Barclaycard website varied from 6.8 to 27.9 percent (Barclaycard 2008).

If the argument for setting interest rates on the basis of reasonable return is taken to its logical extreme, then for some credit agreements interest rates of hundreds of percent are justifiable on the basis of the costs of provision and the chance of the money not being repaid, or as Lord Bramwell argued in more poignant terms: 'Suppose you were asked to lend a mutton chop to a ravenous dog, upon which terms would you lend it?' (Kerridge 2002, p.11). The principle of reasonable return has been used successfully in the UK courts to justify annualized rates of interest far in excess of 100 percent on pawn loans and low value cash loans by door-to-door lenders.

The major criticism for justifying credit charges as morally acceptable on the basis of reasonable return is that it is a one-sided argument.

It gives no consideration to the costs or benefits incurred by the borrower. At best, most lenders would argue that if the borrower agrees to the terms of the agreement, then they must believe that they will benefit from it. Yet, as the cost of credit rises, so the overall net benefit to the borrower will diminish. If the lender makes only a reasonable return, but the borrower is paying a very high price (including costs in terms of penalty charges, mental stress, the risk of bankruptcy and so on) then the overall net benefit of the transaction is likely to be negative. If one adopts a utility perspective and considers the overall net benefit as the measure by which credit agreements are judged, then it is hard to justify a credit agreement as ethical solely on the grounds of reasonable return. There may also be some cases where it is impossible to ethically justify a commercial lending agreement because the costs that a lender needs to impose on the borrower in order to make a return on their investment cannot be justified in terms of any benefit that the borrower may receive.

4.5   A right to credit?

The list of rights individuals possess seems to grow every year. Whereas an individual's rights might once have been expressed simply as the right to life, liberty and property, today there is a much longer list of rights that citizens of Western Europe (and to a lesser extent the US) take for granted – the right to education, health care, a minimum wage and so on. However, there is no country in the world where there is an indelible 'right to credit.' If a lender does not wish to lend to an individual then there is no compulsion for them to do so.

Should there be a right to credit? Credit is only a means to an end. It is only useful if it is used to fund some tangible product or service that the borrower needs or desires. Therefore, one approach is to ask if access to credit is something that is essential for access to goods or services that society deems necessary for an individual's rights to be fully exercised. If denying credit can be said to limit or exclude someone from exercising their basic rights, then there is a case that access to credit should also be right that an individual possesses. So if things such as health care can only be obtained by presenting a credit card or employment can only be secured on the basis of having a satisfactory credit history, and access to these things are taken to be basic rights, then access to credit should also be a right.

Whether or not credit can be viewed as a fundamental right, there is a widely held view that it is in everyone's interest for greater access to credit to be made available – particularly for groups such as the poor, those who are less creditworthy and those who cannot obtain credit because of the low value of credit that they require. Is this a worthy ideal? Merely arguing for greater access to credit is not a justifiable goal in itself. Nor is it justifiable purely on economic grounds, on the basis that more credit contributes towards economic growth, which in turn improves the wellbeing and happiness of the populace. As observers such as Hamilton (2004) and Layard (2006) have noted, there is plenty of evidence to support the view that in developed countries high economic growth does not necessarily lead to a happier or more contented populace. If anything the converse is likely to be true, if the increase in wealth ends up in the hands of a few, widening the gap between rich and poor – a situation that occurred in both the US and UK between the 1980s and late-2000s.

If one accepts the argument presented at the end of section 4.4.2, then there will be some groups of people where the case for providing credit within a commercial framework cannot be justified on ethical grounds. In these situations, one answer is to make low cost credit available through charitable or government schemes where a low level of profit (or even some level of loss) is an acceptable price to pay for making credit more widely available. If a lending institution wishes to demonstrate its ethical credentials then one option that could be taken is to allocate some proportion of its funds to charitable lending schemes targeted at those who cannot obtain commercial credit at a reasonable cost.

Another approach is to set up a non-monetary scheme operated on a charitable or cooperative basis, where goods and services are provided and paid for in kind at a later date – a form of barter. For example, if one member of the scheme – who happens to be an experienced gardener – requires a new bed, and another member has a spare bed and needs some work doing in their garden, then the bed could be exchanged in return for a number of hours spent working in the original owner's garden.

4.6 The use of personal information in credit granting decisions

Consider the following list of personal characteristics:

- Race
- Religion
- Age
- Address details
- Time lived at current address
- Education

- Gender
- Sexual orientation
- Marital status
- Number of dependents
- Residential status

- Occupation
- Time in current employment
- Income
- Partner's income
- Previous credit history

Which of the above is it ethical to use when making a decision about whom to lend money to? In some countries it would be acceptable to use any of these characteristics. In many others race, religion, gender and sexual orientation are all frowned upon and/or illegal. In some, such as the US, the use of marital status and age are also considered dubious and subject to regulation.

One argument deriving from a human rights perspective, is that a person has a right not to have decisions made about them using information over which they have no control such as their race or gender. It is only ethical to make decisions using factors that reflect the choices they have made throughout their lives, such as their occupation, education or residential status.

For some characteristics such as religion, sexual orientation and so on, there are questions over whether these are chosen or inherent and therefore whether or not they should be used in decision making. While people do have some choice in these matters there is undoubtedly an inherited component. People are usually of the same religion as their parents, even though in theory there is nothing to stop them from choosing to follow another religion or declaring themselves atheist. Therefore, it is perhaps prudent to also consider whether the use of these types of personal information are ethical. One could also question the use of fairly innocuous items such as income or education, if there is some evidence of prior prejudice that has led to that situation. If women and men are paid different rates for the same work, then the indiscriminate use of income is questionable. A better approach might be to consider male and female income as separate characteristics.

A similar argument is that information about one aspect of someone's life should not be used to make decisions about another. Why should someone be considered a worse credit risk just because they decide to work for a bank rather than being a teacher, or because they live in the country instead of the inner city? Taking this argument to its logical conclusion, it could be argued that the most ethically acceptable information to use when making decisions about an individual's creditworthiness is their credit history; that is, their previous behaviour when using credit in the past. In the US and UK where previous credit history is widely available via credit reference agencies, the major component of most credit granting decisions is the individual's credit history. However, in countries such as Australia and France access to credit history is more limited and there is naturally a greater emphasis on personal characteristics such as age, employment status, residential status and so on. There is also the issue of first time credit users, for whom no credit history will exist. In these circumstances there is little choice but to use other information that is available.

An alternative argument is that it is not the type of information that is used to make decisions that is important, but the process by which decisions are arrived at. As long as an impartial process is used that produces some objective measure of how a customer will behave (such as credit scoring which is discussed in Chapter 7) then it is acceptable to use any available information to make a credit granting decision. So if there is some quantitative evidence that say, men are better credit risks than women or vice versa – then so be it.

4.7 Over-indebtedness and responsible lending

Over-indebtedness occurs when someone borrows beyond their means, or finds themselves in a position where they do not have sufficient funds to cover their debt repayments. Whose responsibility is over-indebtedness? If it arises from a change of circumstances, such as illness or being made redundant, then arguably no one's – it's just one of those unforeseen events that are outside of anyone's control, and it is estimated that in the US about 90 percent of bankruptcy can be attributed to such events (The American Bar Association 2006, p.201). If it occurs because someone has run up more debt than they can afford, then one view is that the responsibility is entirely the borrower's. They should know what their income and outgoings are, and how to manage their budget. It is their responsibility to know how much debt they can afford and not to borrow beyond this level. The other side of the argument is that it's all the lender's fault. Credit is supplied indiscriminately by companies who have no concern for people's financial circumstances. They will lend to people who do not know or fully understand the terms under which they borrow, and they don't care if they are borrowing beyond their means, just so long as they can make a profit from them. If they end up with financial difficulties then so much the better because of the extra fees that can be charged.

The big lenders are household names with established reputations, and there is an element of trust that many people, rightly or wrongly, place in them. People expect to be treated reasonably and not to be taken advantage of. Much marketing activity is focused in this direction, encouraging people to believe that the lender has their best interests at heart and that they should trust them, when in reality this may not be the case. Some might argue that a rational individual should know that commercial organizations are in it for the money, and should take this into account when making an informed choice. Yet it's hardly a fair fight, pitting the knowledge and experience of the average person in the street against the thousands of hours of effort that have been expended by marketing professionals to persuade them that the product is the right one for them. The result is that an unrealistic and over optimistic picture of the product is presented to the customer – the good things are made to seem better than they really are, the bad things not so bad. Great efforts are made to hide or disguise the true costs of credit as much as possible within the bounds of the law. So while the typical APR may be shown prominently, fees for late payment, going over limit, early repayment and so on are buried in the small print. Some lenders will position optional charges as mandatory. For example, when asked for a quote for a loan, to automatically include a charge for payment protection insurance. A quote without insurance will only be arrived at if the borrower explicitly asks for it. Another problem is unsolicited credit. If a lender automatically mails an individual saying that they have been deemed suitable and/or pre-approved for a loan, or they increase the credit line on a credit card, overdraft or some other facility, the borrower may take this to imply that the institution has assessed their situation and believes they can afford to service the new debt being offered to them. All of these factors make it very difficult for someone to make an objective assessment of the credit on offer.

Both sides of this argument have some merit. Perhaps a pragmatic approach is to accept that both the lender and borrower have some shared level of responsibility to ensure that any credit-debt relationship entered into is affordable. A borrower should think about what they can afford and be honest in their dealings with the lender. A lender should not advance credit if they have good reason to believe a customer is likely to find it difficult meeting the repayment schedule.

To what lengths should a lender go to help prevent someone becoming over-indebted? The main problem lenders face is that while indebtedness is a simple concept in principle, in practice there is no widely accepted definition that lenders, governments or other interested parties have agreed upon (Consumer Affairs Directorate 2001, 2003). One reason why this situation exists is because it is difficult to come to a consensus as to what constitutes disposable income. Is it income remaining after the bare essentials of food/clothing/shelter have been met, or should it include expenditure on pensions, holidays, eating out and so on? Is a car an essential item of expenditure? If so, then what type of car? A second reason is the relationships between individual and household finances. If an individual applies for credit, should the income and outgoings of other household members be included or excluded in any assessment of their ability to pay?

Even if a precise definition of indebtedness can be arrived at, establishing the affordability of debt is not straightforward in a practical lending environment. First, many lenders do ask some simple questions about income and expenditure in order to try to establish the affordability of new debt, but individuals may simply lie about their true income/expenditure in order to obtain credit, particularly if they are desperate to obtain new funds. Second, asking individuals detailed questions about income and expenditure can act as a barrier towards selling products and services, leading people to apply for credit elsewhere. Therefore, there is little incentive to seek a lot of information about expenditure unless it can be assured that the competition are taking a similar line. Third, credit granting is a business in which many customers shop around for credit and make extensive use of balance transfer and debt consolidation services. In some circumstances this will actually help to reduce indebtedness if the new debt is at a better price than the old one. If someone with a high level of debt on a credit card applies for a new card with a lower interest rate, and has the intention of using the new credit to pay off the existing debt, it is not necessarily the best policy to decline them. However, there is no way of ensuring that they won't transfer the debt and then continue to run up new debt on their old card.

To tackle these issues, a pragmatic approach taken by the UK Government Taskforce on Over-indebtedness (which included industry as well as government representation) was to define the conditions for which individuals have a high likelihood of being over-indebted, and by implication, should not be advanced further credit without good reason. A household was defined as having a high risk of being over-indebted if any one of the following conditions were met:

- Having four or more credit commitments (this excludes mortgage and utility payments, and debt on credit and store cards that is paid in full each month).

- Spending more than 25 percent of gross income on credit, excluding mortgages.
- Spending more than 50 percent of gross income on credit, including mortgages.

This is a very simple set of conditions that will not identify everyone that is over-indebted. Conversely, some people will match these conditions and not be over-indebted. However, it is simple, easy for the general public to understand, and is something that most lenders could implement easily within their systems. It is also the case that in many countries the information required to establish if these conditions are satisfied can be obtained from a credit reference agency. Very little information needs to be obtained directly from the individual. The taskforce reported that 7 percent of UK households satisfied one or more of these conditions and would be classified as over-indebted (Consumer Affairs Directorate 2003, p.12).

4.8   Chapter summary

Ethics is the study of whether the decisions people make constitute good or bad behaviour. Ethics can be a very personal thing and in many situations different people will have a different view as to what is ethical or not. The role of this book has not been to make any definitive statements about the precise factors that determine whether or not the terms of a credit agreement can be described as ethical or unethical, but to raise the reader's awareness of some of the ethical issues that can be raised about commercial credit-debt relationships. Some key questions to consider are:

- Does the advertising used to promote the product reflect the true benefits and costs that a borrower is likely to incur from using the product; that is, are the full terms and conditions of the product presented in such a way that a typical customer can easily evaluate the true costs and benefits for themselves?
- What rate of return is being made by a lender on the product they are providing?
- What benefits do borrowers receive from the credit they receive?
- What costs do borrowers incur for the credit they receive? This includes costs that arise during the course of a credit agreement that were not envisaged at the outset. These costs may be in terms of stress or other psychological factors, not just in monetary terms.

- Taking both the borrower's and lender's interests into consideration, is there some overall net benefit to the relationship for each party? If only one party benefits then it is questionable whether the credit agreement is ethical.
- At the time when a customer signs an agreement, have reasonable attempts been made to ensure that they understand the terms of the agreement and the consequences of non-payment or default?
- What information is used to make credit granting decisions, and how is it used?
- Is credit being advanced when it is known (or could easily be determined) that a borrower is already over-indebted or is otherwise likely to experience difficulty repaying the debt?

It should also be remembered that we live in the real world – things need to work, money needs to be made and spent. To achieve a perfectly ethical lending environment is probably impossible. However, an admirable goal is to always be working towards the ideal, not away from it. Whenever a decision is made about how credit is marketed, sold and managed it is worthwhile considering how this impacts on the parties involved and whether or not the overall benefit to the lender, borrower and society justifies the decision made.

4.9   Suggested sources of further information

Chryssides, G. D. and Kaler, J. H. (1993). *An Introduction to Business Ethics*. Chapman and Hall. This is an excellent introduction to business ethics. It is very readable and provides a comprehensive overview of ethics and its application to business. It includes contributions from some of the world's leading economists, philosophers and business leaders.

Singer, P. (ed.)(1994). *Ethics*. Oxford University Press. Provides a broad introduction to the study of ethics, bringing together and providing commentary on some of the most influential texts throughout history.

Mills, P. S. and Presley J. R. (1999). *Islamic Finance: Theory and Practice*, Macmillan Press Ltd. Provides a detailed analysis of Islamic perspectives on finance and credit and contrasts these with the position taken historically by Judaeo-Christian philosophers.

Bentham, J. (1787). *Defence of Usury*. Kessinger Publishing. This is an e-book version of Bentham's work, for those interested in the source material behind his arguments against unrestricted interest rate charges.

5
Legislation and Consumer Rights

As discussed in Chapters 3 and 4, debt has caused many problems over the ages, and there have been many ethical concerns raised over the terms and conditions under which credit agreements operate. It is therefore, not surprising that consumer credit is subject to extensive legislation in many regions throughout the world. In this chapter the main UK and US legislation relating to consumer credit is described. Other jurisdictions have their own laws relating to consumer credit, but laws in many regions have been drafted to address similar issues to those addressed by US/UK law.

The first half of the chapter discusses relevant UK legislation. In particular, The Consumer Credit Acts 1974 & 2006, The Data Protection Act 1998 and parts of The Enterprise Act 2002. The second part of the chapter looks at US legislation. This includes the Consumer Credit Protection Act 1968 and its various sub-chapters, as well as The Federal Bankruptcy Code 1978.

Even a single piece of legislation can require a weighty volume to fully explore all its nuances, and the form of words used by the legal profession is notoriously difficult to understand for those who have not received appropriate training (I include myself within this category!) Therefore, the objective is to introduce the reader to the general principles and highlight the most important issues in simple language. It is not my intention to cover every aspect of the law or every situation that may conceivably be encountered.

5.1   The Consumer Credit Acts 1974 and 2006 (UK)

The major UK legislation covering consumer credit in the UK are The Consumer Credit Act 1974 and The Consumer Credit Act 2006. The 2006 Act updated the 1974 in a number of areas and we will simply refer to them as 'The Acts'. Credit agreements that are fully covered by The Acts are described as regulated agreements. Some types of agreement are classified as unregulated agreements and are exempt from many of the provisions within The Acts. These include:

- Credit agreements secured on land, where credit is provided by a recognized institution. This mainly covers mortgage lending by banks and building societies.
- Credit agreements where the number of repayments is four or less and the term of the loan is less than a year, except where the credit is a hire-purchase agreement, conditional sale agreement, secured on land or secured against a pledge (a pawn agreement).
- Credit agreements where the charge for credit (the APR) is no more than 1 percent above the Bank of England base rate. The intention of this exemption is to exclude low cost loans made by charities, cheap loans by employers to their employees and so on.

What can be confusing is that while The Acts primarily apply to regulated agreements, some sections apply to both regulated and unregulated agreements. In particular, unregulated agreements are subject to the regulations covering the advertising of credit and unfair (extortionate) credit agreements.

5.1.1   Credit licence

A credit licence is required by any individual or organization engaging in any of the following activities:

- Operating a consumer credit business.
- Operating a consumer hire business.
- Running a credit brokerage.
- Providing debt adjusting and debt counselling services.
- Undertaking debt collecting activities.
- Operating a credit reference agency.

Credit licences are obtained by making a successful application to the Office of Fair Trading. It is a criminal offence to operate a credit business without a credit licence. A credit agreement entered into with an unlicenced credit provider is legally unenforceable.

5.1.2   Requirements for a legally binding credit agreement

For a regulated credit agreement to be legally enforceable three conditions must be met:

1. A copy of the agreement's terms and conditions must be provided to the applicant before the agreement is signed.

2. The form and contents of the agreement must comply with the provisions specified within The Acts.
3. The agreement must be signed by the borrower. This includes electronic signatures so that agreements can be made over the internet.

If a credit agreement does not meet any of these conditions then the agreement is not enforceable and the lender can take no action to force the borrower to pay. In this scenario, the only way for the agreement to become enforceable is for the lender to apply for an enforcement order via the courts. The Acts give the courts considerable discretion as to whether or not to grant an enforcement order, and they are only likely to issue an order if the original agreement contains all of the correct content, but it is not laid out in the format specified in The Acts; that is, the agreement contains the correct information, but in the wrong order or using the wrong form of words. In other situations it is doubtful that an enforcement order would be granted.

Once a borrower has signed the agreement, a copy must be dispatched to them within seven days. At any time during the course of the agreement the borrower has the right to request that further copies are made available to them.

After an agreement has been created, for regulated fixed sum agreements, lenders must issue a statement of account at least once every 12 months. For running account credit, lenders must provide debtors with information about the account, such as the interest rate(s) charged, and the consequences of making only minimum repayments or failing to make repayments.

5.1.3   The right to cancel (right of rescission)

A cancellable agreement is one where the following conditions are met:

- Face-to-face negotiations have taken place between the borrower and the lender (or their representative) about the terms of the agreement. Negotiation is understood to mean that a statement had been made that is capable of persuading the borrower to enter into an agreement (Skipworth and Dyson 1997, p.71). Satisfying a simple request for information would not be considered to constitute negotiation.
- The credit agreement was not signed on the lender's premises. This includes premises where there is a linked transaction. For example, if a car dealer used a finance house to supply credit agreements to its

customers, then the dealer's forecourt would be considered as if it were the lender's premises.

The key issue is where the agreement is signed, not where any negotiation occurred. So if a salesperson leaves you with a credit agreement after visiting your home and suggests that you 'come on down' to the store to sign it, it is probably prudent to sign it beforehand. If it's signed on the lender's premises then there is no right to change your mind.

Where a borrower wishes to cancel a cancellable agreement, they must inform the lender within five days of receiving their copy of the signed agreement. Once an agreement has been cancelled, all money or goods advanced to the borrower under the terms of the agreement become owing.

The *Financial Services (Distance Marketing) Regulations 2004* (2004c) apply to all credit agreements made at a distance, where there has been no face-to-face contact with the lender or their representative. The regulations apply to credit agreements made by post, over the phone or via the internet, and take preference over the cancellation rights granted within the Consumer Credit Acts. The regulations give the borrower the right to cancel the agreement within 14 days. It should be noted that the 14 day cancellation period begins on the date that the agreement is signed, not from the date that a signed copy of the agreement is received by the borrower.

5.1.4 Advertising

Promotional material for both regulated and unregulated credit agreements must comply with the *Consumer Credit (Advertisements) Regulations 2004* (2004a). In particular, these require all promotional materials to:

- Use plain and intelligible language.
- Be easily legible (or, in the case of information given orally, be clearly audible).
- Specify the name of the advertiser and (except for radio and TV advertising) provide a contact address.

If the material only contains general information along the lines of 'we provide unsecured loans for any amount between $10,000 and $60,000' then this is all that has to be complied with. However, once any claims are made that could be considered an incitement to apply for credit such as 'come to us for one of the best deals in town' or the lender wishes to advertise the repayment terms of their agreements, then the regulations define the information that must be provided about the terms. This includes the amount of credit available, what the regular repayments will be and how often they have to be made, the total amount payable and so on. The most important item of information that must be displayed is the 'typical APR'. This is the APR that at least 66 percent of agreements will be charged at that rate or lower. The typical APR must be displayed more prominently than any other interest rate or charge. For revolving credit agreements the APR quoted must be that for purchases (rather than for cash withdrawals or credit card cheques) and the APR calculation must be based on a nominal credit limit of $3,000, repaid in 12 equal installments over a 12 month period, beginning at the end of the first month. The only exception to this is if the credit limit is known to be lower than $3,000, in which case the actual limit can be used in the APR calculation.

Where the borrower's home is required as security, a statement warning the borrower that their home is at risk if they do not keep up repayments on their loan must also be made. The form of words that must be used to do this is specified by The Acts.

5.1.5   Credit tokens

A credit token is any card, document, voucher or thing that allows someone to obtain credit. The most well-known credit tokens are credit cards, store cards and charge cards. A token such as a debit card or cheque book is only defined as a credit token if it permits someone to become indebted. For example, by becoming overdrawn on a bank account. It is a criminal offence to supply a credit token to someone who has not applied for it.

An individual is only liable for debt incurred using a credit token once they have taken possession of it. If a credit token is stolen in transit, the individual it is intended for has no liability for it. If a token is lost or stolen after someone has taken possession of it, then the borrower is only liable for a maximum of $100 if they report the loss as soon as they become aware of it. However, if they give consent for someone else to use their credit token then they are fully liable, should the other person misuse it. This is important for cases where a second credit token is requested by an individual to be used by their partner. Unless the application is made in joint names, the responsibility for the debt created through the use of the token remains with the original recipient.

If there is some dispute over whether or not a transaction made using a credit token was permitted by the authorized user, then the burden of proof is on the credit provider to prove who made use of it. If it cannot be established that the authorized user was responsible for a transaction, then they are not liable for it.

5.1.6 Early settlement

For regulated fixed sum agreements, a borrower has the right to settle the agreement early; that is, to repay the remainder of what they owe at any time. For most types of fixed sum credit, interest and other charges are calculated and added to the sum borrowed at the beginning of the agreement and this total amount is used to calculate the fixed monthly repayment. Therefore, when an agreement is settled early, the amount still owing needs to be recalculated to take into account the period for which interest will no longer be charged. For credit agreements entered into before 31 May 2005, the calculation of the amount owing is based on the rule of 78 method, as specified in the *Consumer Credit (Rebate on Early Settlement) Regulations 1983* (1983). The rule of 78 method can still be applied to these loans until 2007 for loans lasting ten years or less and until 2010 for loans lasting more than ten years. For loans taken out since 31 May 2005, the method for calculating the amount owing is defined within the *Consumer Credit (Early Settlement) Regulations 2004* (2004b). The main difference between these two schemes is that the new regulations result in the lender paying a maximum of (approximately) one month's additional APR charge for settling early, while under the UK implementation of Rule of 78, the lender could charge the equivalent of about two months of extra payments. Therefore, the 2004 regulations result in a better deal for the borrower.

In order to settle a loan agreement early, a borrower must make a formal request (usually in writing). The lender then has 12 working days to respond by sending the borrower a settlement quotation, detailing the amount of the loan owing under the terms of the agreement, the amount of any rebate (the reduced amount of interest resulting from repaying early) and the total amount that the borrower must pay to settle the debt. The lender will also specify a settlement date by which time the borrower must repay the debt. If the debt is not settled by the settlement date, then a new early settlement request will be required. The settlement date must be at least 28 days after the request for settlement was made, but a lender has the option to extend the settlement date by up to one month. The settlement figure is based on the assumption that the standard repayments continue to be made and interest continues to be charged until the settlement date. Therefore, in most cases lenders will make full use of their option and set the settlement date to be one month and 28 days after the request for early settlement is made. If any payments are due between the request for early settlement and the settlement date, then the borrower must continue to make these payments.

5.1.7 Charges for delinquency

If a borrower is behind in their repayments a lender is allowed to charge simple interest on the arrears, but not compound interest (See Appendix A for details of simple and compound interest). The rate of interest can be no more than the contractual rate stated within the credit agreement. However, some lenders have been known to state two rates of interest within credit agreements, with the second rate only being applied when accounts are in arrears (Skipworth and Dyson 1997, p.96). This has been reported to be a common practice in relation to overdraft agreements, where banks charge a much higher rate of interest on the entire overdraft, even if the amount by which the borrower exceeds the agreed limit is negligible. The example given by Corby (2004) was of a typical overdraft facility where an interest rate of 7 percent was charged for any amount up to the agreed limit of $500. If the overdraft became $501, then a new rate of 29.9 percent would be charged on the entire $501, not just on the additional $1. This is in addition to an over-limit fee of about $50. While commonly applied, the legality of these types of charges is questionable. What also has questionable legal status is the charging of penalty fees for late or missed payment. Under UK law a lender can only charge for any loss they have suffered. If interest is being charged on the amount in arrears, then arguably this already covers the lender's costs and the borrower cannot be held liable for any other fees. If some action is taken to recover the arrears, such as writing a letter or making a phone call, then there is perhaps a case for charging a fee. However, as discussed in Chapter 6, the actual cost of chasing up late payers is usually only a fraction of the amount charged and in the UK the OFT has taken action to limit the penalty fees that lenders can charge. As Corby (2004) notes, if a borrower challenges a lender about a penalty charge, they will often back down and remove the charge from the account. If not, then the enforceability of such charges in a court of law is questionable.

5.1.8 Court action to recover debt

If a borrower defaults on the credit advanced to them, the lender may seek to take legal action through the courts to recover the debt. Before court action can be taken, the borrower must be issued with a default notice stating what breach has occurred and what action is needed to bring the debt back within the terms of the agreement. The form and content of the default notice must comply with the conditions laid down by The Acts. The borrower then has 14 days to rectify the problem before any further action can be taken. If the lender and borrower subsequently fail to reach an agreement, the lender may then apply for a court to make a judgement against the borrower; that is, for a county court judgement (CCJ) to be made. A borrower may contest the judgement, if they feel that the terms under which it is being applied for are incorrect. This is only likely to be successful if they can show that they have in fact paid the debt, or that they had come to some prior arrangement with the lender that had subsequently not been honoured – so if a lender had agreed in writing to write-off a debt, they could not then change their mind and take court action against the borrower. The borrower should also consider very carefully before making a challenge, because if it fails they may be liable for any additional costs incurred by the lender.

As part of the court proceedings, the borrower's income and outgoings will be assessed. The court will then make one of the following judgements:

- If the borrower has sufficient disposable income, then they should continue to pay the installments demanded by the lender.
- If the borrower only has enough income to meet a portion of the repayments demanded, then a new repayment schedule may be defined based on the borrower's disposable income. If the amount of disposable income is very small, this may mean a repayment schedule lasting many years, with only a token payment being made each month.
- If the borrower has no assets or income, or is facing some critical situation (such as being terminally ill) the court may agree to suspend any payments for a period of time.

The court may freeze the debt at the point a judgement is made, stopping new interest or other charges being applied, but in some situations they may allow the contractual rate of interest to continue to be charged. If either party disagrees with the court's ruling, then both have the right to ask for the decision to be reviewed by a district judge within 14 days. If someone does not keep to the terms of a judgement and if the lender wishes to pursue the debt, several courses of action are available. If the debt is large then a petition for bankruptcy can be made (discussed later in the chapter) or an enforcement order can be applied for. An enforcement order allows money to be taken directly from a debtor's bank account, or for bailiffs to be appointed to recover goods in lieu of the debt. Bailiffs have significant albeit limited powers. They cannot force entry to a person's premises and there is no legal requirement to let them in, but if they find an unlocked door or window, or gain access to a property by climbing walls or fences, then this is permissible. Once inside a property they can force entry to other parts of the building. Bailiffs are not allowed to take essential items such as clothing, bedding or furniture, or items such as tools that are required for someone's employment. Another option is for the court to grant a charging order. This secures the debt against the debtor's property, usually their home. The debtor is not forced to sell the property, but if they do sell it at some time in the future, then the proceeds from the sale must be used to pay the debt.

5.1.9   Repossession of goods under hire-purchase and conditional sale agreements

With a hire-purchase agreement the title (ownership) of the goods does not pass to the hirer until they have exercised their right to purchase. Therefore, if the terms of a hire-purchase agreement are breached, action can be taken to recover the goods. As with other types of regulated agreement, a lender must issue the borrower with a default notice and allow the borrower 14 days to rectify the situation before any further action can be taken. If the borrower has not complied with the default notice, the lender can then repossess the goods. However, they are not allowed to enter the borrower's property unless they have obtained an enforcement order from the courts permitting them to do so. A court order is also required before repossession can occur, if the borrower has paid more than one third of the total price of the goods. If the borrower has subsequently sold the goods to a third party the lender is still entitled to repossess the goods. Therefore in these cases, it is the third party that generally suffers the greatest loss. These principles also apply to conditional sale agreements.

5.2   The Enterprise Act 2002 and bankruptcy (UK)

Bankruptcy (personal insolvency) occurs when a court issues a bankruptcy order, confirming that an individual is unable to pay their debts. Once a bankruptcy order has been made against an individual their assets can be seized, including their home and the contents of any savings and deposit accounts. The proceeds from the sale of assets are shared amongst those to whom the individual is indebted. Bankruptcy is generally seen as an action of last resort, when all other means of coming to an agreement with creditors has been exhausted. The law covering personal insolvency is covered by the Enterprise Act 2002.

5.2.1 The road to bankruptcy

There are two ways that someone can be declared bankrupt. The first is for them to make a voluntary petition for bankruptcy when they know that their debt situation is untenable. The rationale for making a voluntary petition is to get debts cleared as quickly as possible, rather than waiting to go through what could be a costly and drawn out process with creditors and the Official Receiver. This may be a good route for someone to follow if they have few assets and considerable debts, even if they are not currently experiencing repayment difficulties. Voluntary bankruptcy is a relatively straightforward process, requiring the individual to complete a petition for bankruptcy and a statement of affairs document, and for these to be submitted to the county court together with the required fee.[1] Once the petition has been submitted bankruptcy proceedings can be very quick, possibly being completed on the same day that the petition was made.

The second way to become bankrupt is for one or more creditors to make a bankruptcy petition against the individual if the amount owed is more than $1,500. Given the cost of making a petition,[2] lending institutions are only likely to make one if they believe there is a reasonable chance that they will recover a considerable sum from the borrower. If they know that someone has no assets or income, then there is little incentive to incur the costs associated with a bankruptcy petition.

If the debt is for less than $1,500 then a petition for bankruptcy cannot be made. However, if two or more creditors are each owed sums of less than $1,500, but the total owed between them is more than $1,500, then a joint petition can be submitted.

Before a petition can be submitted to the courts, the lender must present the borrower with a statutory demand giving them 21 days to pay the debt. All reasonable steps must be taken to present the statutory demand in person. It can only be sent by post after a court has determined that reasonable efforts to deliver it in person have been made, but that these have proved to be ineffective. A petition for bankruptcy can be made 21 days after presenting the statutory demand. However, the date for the court to rule on the petition must be at least 14 days after the petition. During this time an individual can apply for an adjournment to the court hearing of up to several weeks if they can persuade the creditor or the judge that they will acquire the means to settle their debt in the meantime. As Brumby *et al.* (2004) point out, a petition for bankruptcy can only be made for sums in excess of $1,500. If the statutory demand is for say $2,000, and the debtor pays $600, the amount owing falls below $1,500 and therefore a petition can no longer be made.

It is important to note that the courts have considerable discretionary powers when considering a petition for bankruptcy. The court can grant an adjournment of bankruptcy proceedings to give the debtor time to pay, or allow a charging order to be made against the debtor's property (their home) if the value of the property is greater than the outstanding debt.

5.2.2 After a bankruptcy order has been granted

If the petition for bankruptcy is successful, the Official Receiver will become involved. The Official Receiver is the government department responsible for managing bankruptcy proceedings. Its main responsibilities are to assess the bankrupt's assets and to take responsibility for selling these assets to meet the demands of creditors. Individual creditors can take no action themselves to recover property, cash or anything else from the debtor.

The Official Receiver will not look to seize everything a bankrupt owns. Things that are required for a person to continue living a normal life and to enable them to continue in their employment, such as their clothes, furniture and car, will not be seized. With regard to the bankrupt's income, the Official Receiver will assess their normal living costs and will take any spare income that they have.

After being declared bankrupt a person usually remains in a state of bankruptcy for a year. During this time a number of restrictions are placed upon their activities which include not being permitted to:

- Obtain credit for more than $1,000, without first disclosing to the person they intend to borrow from that they are in fact bankrupt.
- Dispose of assets bought on credit terms within the 12 months prior to bankruptcy.
- Leave the country with property worth more than $2,000.
- Act as a company director, or to be involved in any way in the running of a company as if they were a director.

After a year, a bankrupt is discharged. At this point the slate is wiped clean with all outstanding debts being written-off and there can be no further claims on the individual's assets. The restrictions imposed during the course of the bankruptcy are also lifted. However, credit reference agencies will maintain records of the bankruptcy for six years. Therefore, the ability of an individual to obtain credit, including a mortgage, may be restricted for a considerable period of time because most lenders view a previous bankruptcy as a strong indicator of poor creditworthiness.

5.2.3 Individual Voluntary Agreements (IVA)

For debtors owing sums greater than $10,000, who have some disposable income, a possible alternative to bankruptcy is an Individual Voluntary Agreement (IVA). An IVA is a legally binding agreement between an individual and all of their unsecured creditors (so secured debts such as a mortgage can not be covered by an IVA). The main benefit of an IVA is that it allows a debtor to remain in control of their assets and avoid the stigma and legal implications of bankruptcy.

A standard IVA will be an agreement to pay a proportion of an individual's outstanding debt, via regular installments, over a period of up to five years. In most cases this will cover only a proportion of someone's outstanding debts, with creditors writing off the rest. By law, the process of creating and managing an IVA must be undertaken by a Licensed Insolvency Practitioner (LIP). The LIP will manage the creation of the IVA, negotiate with creditors and manage the collection and distribution of payments once the agreement is in force. For their services the LIP will usually charge fees of anything between $1,500 and $6,000, and it is the creditors who pay for this service (Brumby *et al.* 2004, p.67). For an IVA to proceed 75 percent of creditors (by value) must agree to the IVA proposal put forward by the LIP on behalf of the debtor. Therefore, amounts put forward in the proposal represent something of a balancing act. They must be within the debtor's ability to pay, while offering enough for the majority of creditors to accept it.

5.3   The Data Protection Act 1998 (UK)

In 1995 the EU directive 95/46/EC laid a responsibility on governments of EU member states to implement legislation giving people certain rights over how public and private organizations obtained, held and managed information about them. In the UK the directive was implemented within the Data Protection Act 1998.

The Data Protection Act is a general piece of legislation that applies to all personal data held by organizations operating in the UK. Any organization that holds or processes personal data must register with the Information Commissioner or be liable for criminal prosecution. The Act applies only to information about living individuals and ceases to apply once someone has died. A few government institutions, such as the security services MI5 and MI6, are exempted from the legislation on the grounds of national security.

The Act is centred around the eight data protection principles which can be summarized as:

- An individual has the right to decide who has access to any data about them and the uses to which that data is put.
- Any organization holding or using personal data must obtain permission from the individual to hold and use their data, and to only use it for the agreed purposes. The data held should not be excessive and should not be kept for longer than necessary for the agreed purposes to be carried out.
- Data should be accurate and up-to-date. This does not mean that data cannot contain errors, but that reasonable care must be taken to ensure accuracy and a suitable process must be in place to correct errors when they come to light.
- Security measures should be in place to prevent accidental loss or damage, unauthorized access or misuse of personal data. In practice, this means that reasonable disaster recovery and backup procedures should be in place, and only those who have received authorization from the institution holding the data should have access to it.

For financial services organizations it is usual to include a statement about data protection within the terms and conditions section of the application form that someone signs when applying for credit. This gives permission for their data to be used for the required purposes. There are no prescribed form of words for this, but a typical data protection statement is along the lines of that shown in Figure 5.1.

The main purpose of a data protection statement is to allow the company to manage the credit agreement. The phrases in bold italics in Figure 5.1 (which would not be in a different font in a real data protection statement) give the organization permission to use the information someone provides for other purposes. This is particularly relevant for large organizations offering a wide range of products and services, or who enter into joint ventures with third parties. This is because it gives permission for information obtained in relation to one product or service to be used to assess and/or manage other products and services that they or an associated organization currently offer, or may offer, at any time in the future.

USE OF PERSONAL INFORMATION

We will store and process personal information about you within the information systems of the company. This includes information we may obtain from third parties such as a credit reference agency, or from other organizations to whom you have previously given permission to share your personal information with us.

We will use this information to manage your account and to provide you with regular information about the status of your account. This includes using your personal information to assess the status of your account or for research purposes, *and to continue to provide you with improved products and services*. We may, from time to time, inform you of new products and services that may be of interest to you.

We will obtain and provide information about you to credit reference agencies and fraud prevention agencies to:

-Assess enquiries when you apply for any of the company's products
-Assist in managing your account(s) on an ongoing basis, by finding out about the status of your accounts with other lenders.

Credit reference agencies maintain a record of our enquiries and may give out information we provide them to other lenders, insurers and other organizations. This also applies to fraud prevention agencies if you give us false or inaccurate information or we suspect fraud.

The information you provide may also be used to make future assessments for credit and to help make decisions on you and members of your household, about any credit or other products or services that we provide, and for debt tracing and to prevent fraud and money laundering.

We may give information about you and how you manage your account to people who provide a service to us or are acting as our agents, on the understanding that they will keep the information confidential.

Figure 5.1   A UK data protection statement

5.3.1   The right of subject access

The Data Protection Act grants everyone the right of subject access; that is, the right to be provided with a copy of any data an organization holds about them within 40 days of a written request being made and payment of a small fee towards the organization's administrative costs.[3]

Dealing with a subject access request can be a lengthy and time consuming process, requiring detailed searches across all of an organization's computer and manual filing systems. While an individual has the right to request copies of all of the information an organization holds about them, in nearly all cases they are actually looking for some specific information in order to understand why certain decisions were made about them. It therefore makes sense to design the process for dealing with subject access requests so that it encourages people to say what they are looking for; for example, by providing a questionnaire that enables them to highlight certain areas of interest. The response to a subject access request must not only include the data requested, but also an explanation of what the data means, particularly if it includes codes or abbreviations which cannot be interpreted easily.

In relation to credit, probably the most common reason for a subject access request is to find out why a credit application was declined. All competent lending organizations maintain copies of the information used to assess credit applications for at least 12 months. Therefore, if an individual has been declined and subsequently makes a subject access request, a lender should be able to provide detailed information about the application. This should include the information used in the credit granting process, the decision codes assigned to the application and details of any credit scores used.

Sometimes someone may be referred to a credit reference agency if data was obtained from one. While it can be worthwhile to query the data held by a credit reference agency, it remains the lender's obligation to provide details of any personal data they hold and what it means, whatever the original source. If the data they hold is in error then they are obliged to correct it. However, if data originally obtained from a credit reference agency contains errors then it is a good idea to also make enquires with the credit reference agency because if the errors are not corrected then they will be passed on to other organizations when another credit search is made.

Another common reason for making a subject access request is to obtain copies of account statements at a much lower cost than organizations officially charge. If someone wants copies of 12 months of credit card statements at a cost of say $10 each, then this would cost $120. This compares to the maximum cost of $20 for a subject access request to obtain the same data.

5.3.2 Data controllers and data processors

An organization with permission to hold or process someone's data is termed a data controller, and it is the data controller that has responsibility for ensuring that the data is managed within the law. If data is passed to another organization that holds or processes data on behalf of the data controller (termed a data processor), then the responsibility for the integrity of the data remains with the data controller – it does not pass to the data processor. The data controller is also responsible for providing details of any data held by a data processor as part of a subject access request.

5.3.3 The right to prevent direct marketing

An individual has the right to request, at any time, that data held by an organization is not used to mail them with any information about the organization's products and services. This overrides any previous permissions given for this purpose. Organizations therefore need to maintain lists of individuals who have expressed this right so that they can be removed from mailing lists.

5.3.4 Automated decision making

An individual has the right to have any decision that was made by a computer or other automated system reviewed manually. For credit providers this means that if an individual is declined for credit due to a computer generated credit score, the applicant can request that the application is reviewed by a person. There is however, no requirement to come to a decision that is any different from that generated by the credit scoring system, or to provide any further justification for the decision that was made.

5.4 The Consumer Credit Protection Act 1968 (US)

The legal situation in the US regarding consumer lending is complex, with a mixture of state and federal law, and most states have their own laws regarding lending practices. In particular, state legislation covers the legal rate of interest that can be charged and the practices that can legally be employed to collect delinquent debts. However, where Federal legislation exists, it takes priority (preempts) state legislation. Federal law covering consumer credit agreements is contained within The Consumer Credit Protection Act 1968. The Act comprises six subsidiary acts (sub-chapters), each of which is discussed in the following sections.

5.4.1 The Truth in Lending Act 1968

The Truth in Lending Act is designed to provide consumers with clear information about the terms and conditions of the credit they are offered. It places an obligation on lenders to clearly state the terms of a credit agreement in the text of the credit agreements that customers sign, as well as in promotional literature. In particular, the total charge for credit and the APR must be clearly displayed. Once a credit agreement has been signed, the Act requires more detailed information about the interest rate, repayments and the outstanding debt to be included within customers' regular statements.

A further feature of the Act is that it limits consumer liability with respect of credit tokens (credit cards in particular) in two ways. First, individuals have no liability for unsolicited credit cards, sent to them without their consent. Second, if someone has consented to receiving a credit card, then they are only liable for transactions that they themselves have authorized. If a credit card is used without the card holder's consent, then the card holder is not liable. The only exception to this is if the unauthorized transaction occurred before the card holder informed the card issuer that unauthorized use might occur, for example due to loss or theft of the card (Jasper 2006, p.34). In this case the maximum liability is $50.

The Fair Credit Billing Act 1986 is an amendment to the Truth in Lending Act, allowing a customer to challenge the accuracy of the information provided on their credit card statements. If a customer believes the information on their statement is incorrect, for example the interest calculation is erroneous or the statement contains transactions that the customer did not make, then the customer can request that the card issuer investigates the error within 90 days.

5.4.2   Garnishment restrictions

Under certain circumstances US courts may allow deductions from someone's wages at source, to meet debt repayments. Under Federal Garnishment Restrictions the total amount that may be taken from someone's wages to meet credit commitments is limited to 25 percent of net earnings, after tax and other mandatory deductions.

5.4.3   The Fair Credit Reporting Act 1970

The US has no equivalent to EU data protection laws. Instead, personal data is viewed as a commodity that any person or organization can obtain and use however they wish. Where legislation exists, it is to protect individuals from having their data misused within the context of specific situations. The Fair Credit Reporting Act (amended with the Fair and Accurate Credit Transaction Act 2003) puts in place controls over how credit reference agencies manage the data they hold and the purposes to which such data can be put. The most important aspects of the Act are:

- Individuals have the right to obtain a free copy of their credit reports, and any other information held in their credit file,[4] every 12 months, from each of the three main credit reference agencies; that is, the information the Equifax, Experian and TransUnion credit reference agencies hold about them.
- The data held by credit reference agencies must be accurate. An individual has the right to challenge the accuracy of information held by credit reference agencies and any inaccuracies that are found must be corrected.

- Credit reports may only be supplied by credit reference agencies for certain limited purposes. Primarily this includes credit referencing and employment vetting (Jasper 2006, p.37).

5.4.4   The Equal Credit Opportunity Act 1974

The Equal Credit Opportunity Act is intended to prevent unfair discrimination against people within certain social groups when applying for credit. The Act prohibits credit decisions being made wholly or partly on the grounds of Race, Religion, Gender, Nation of Origin or Marital Status. Age can be used in decision making, but the Act prohibits negative discrimination on the grounds of age. The Equal Credit Opportunity Act also prevents lenders from discriminating against individuals because they have exercised their rights under any chapter of the Consumer Credit Protection Act. For example, it would be unlawful for a lender to decline an existing credit card customer for a personal loan, because the individual has a history of querying the information on their credit card statements, as is their right under the Fair Credit Billing Act 1986.

The Act also places an obligation on lenders to tell consumers within 30 days of a credit application being completed, whether or not their application has been accepted. This must be in writing, and if a credit application is declined, then the applicant has a legal right to be told why. Similarly, a reason must be given if a lender decides to close someone's account (Jasper 2006, p.40). This has important implications for lenders who make extensive use of credit scoring, because it means that they must be able to deduce from the credit scoring system the reasons why a specific individual was given a certain score.

5.4.5   The Fair Debt Collection Practices Act 1977

The Fair Debt Collections Practices Act 1977 is intended to protect individuals from unfair, threatening or intimidating practices employed by debt collectors. In particular the Act requires that debt collectors:

- Must not communicate with a debtor at an unsocial or inconvenient time. For example, calling a debtor in the middle of the night.
- Engage in threatening or abusive behaviour.
- Contact a debtor at their place of employment without their permission.
- Make unfair claims or representations. For example threatening that someone's property will be possessed in lieu of a debt, if in fact this is not the case.

- Must not deal with an individual directly if they have appointed an attorney; that is, they must deal with the attorney not the debtor.

The Act requires that when an individual is in default and a lender has decided to initiate debt collection action, the debtor must be provided with details of the debt in writing. If the debt collector is a third party, acting on behalf of the lender, then they must also state who they are collecting debt on behalf of. A debtor then has 30 days to contest the debt in writing if they believe that they do not owe the debt. The debt collector is then obliged to provide proof of the debt before collections action can continue.

5.4.6   The Electronic Funds Transfer Act

This Act covers electronic transfer of funds, using a debt or credit card to draw funds from bank accounts and card accounts. The primary provision of the Act in relation to consumer credit is to limit liability of card holders for unauthorized transactions that occur electronically.

5.5   The Federal Bankruptcy Code 1978 (US)

In the US the law governing bankruptcy is covered by The Federal Bankruptcy Code 1978, which was updated with the implementation of the Bankruptcy Abuse Prevention Act 2005. There are some similarities between bankruptcy in the US, UK and other regions, but one of the main features of US bankruptcy proceedings is that the decision to petition for bankruptcy is entirely the responsibility of the debtor. Bankruptcy is primarily seen as a way for a debtor to be released from their debt obligations, rather than as a mechanism by which creditors can recoup their funds. Unlike the UK, a creditor can not file a petition seeking to make someone bankrupt. Instead, the standard course of action for a creditor faced with a defaulting customer is to sue the customer in the courts in order to obtain a financial settlement covering the unpaid debt. The main incentive for a debtor to file for bankruptcy is that once the petition for bankruptcy has been filed, all collections/ legal action against the debtor must cease and any foreclosure proceedings against the debtors property must be halted, pending the outcome of bankruptcy proceedings.

Under The Federal Bankruptcy Code several different types of bankruptcy are defined, covering different commercial and personal insolvency situations. Those relevant to individual consumers are covered by Chapter 7 and Chapter 13 of the Code. These are referred to as Chapter 7 and Chapter 13 bankruptcy respectively.

Bankruptcy proceedings differ somewhat by state, but in general the process for filing is as follows. Before filing for bankruptcy, the debtor must obtain credit counseling up to 180 days before they file. This may be individual or group counseling, with the objective of ensuring that the debtor fully understands the nature of bankruptcy, and is entering into it with full knowledge of the consequences of doing so. The counseling must be from an approved credit counseling agency, and a certificate confirming that counseling has taken place is required by the courts before bankruptcy proceedings can proceed (The American Bar Association 2006, pp.221–2 & pp.246–7). The individual then decides whether Chapter 7 or Chapter 13 bankruptcy is most appropriate for them, and submits a petition for bankruptcy to the court. The petition will contain details of the debtor's debts, assets and any income that they have. To file for bankruptcy the debtor is also required to pay a fee of around \$275.[5] Once a petition has been received, the court will appoint a trustee to manage bankruptcy proceedings – somewhat similar in principle to the role of the Official Receiver/Licensed Insolvency Practitioner in the UK.

5.5.1 Chapter 7 bankruptcy

Under the Bankruptcy Abuse Prevention Act 2005, a debtor can only petition for Chapter 7 bankruptcy if they meet one of two income based criteria. The first is that they have an income below the median income of the state where they file. The second criteria is that their disposable monthly income after reasonable living expenses have been taken into account is less than \$166. If they earn more than the state median, or they have more than \$166 of monthly disposable income, then they must file under Chapter 13 (The American Bar Association 2006, p.223).

Chapter 7 bankruptcy is similar in principle to personal insolvency in the UK. From the date that the bankruptcy petition is filed the debtor's assets come under remit of the courts. Once a petition has been filed the court will appoint a Bankruptcy Trustee. The Trustee will be responsible for disposing of the debtors assets in order to pay their outstanding creditors. As in the UK, essential items (up to a certain value) such as clothes, furniture and tools/books required by someone to carry out their profession, are exempted from bankruptcy proceedings. Within federal law definitions of permissible exemptions are provided, but many states also have their own laws specifying additional assets that can be exempted, over and above that specified by federal law.

Discharge from Chapter 7 bankruptcy is relatively quick. Typically, the entire process takes only 4–6 months from the date of filing (The American Bar Association 2006, p.213). After discharge most debts are written-off. However, certain debts are not discharged. These include student loans, court fines, child support payments and unpaid income tax.

5.5.2 Chapter 13 bankruptcy

If a debtor has significant disposable income they can file for Chapter 13 bankruptcy. This is somewhat similar in principle to an IVA in the UK. Along with the bankruptcy petition and details of their assets, a debtor must also submit a payment plan, detailing how much they will pay their (unsecured) creditors over a period of between three and five years, usually in regular monthly installments. After the payment plan has been completed the bankruptcy is discharged, with any remaining unsecured debts written-off. Under US law the repayments proposed by the debtor must result in unsecured creditors receiving at least as much as they would have received if the debtor had filed for Chapter 7 bankruptcy instead. This is to ensure that the repayment plan put forward by the debtor is reasonable. Creditors also have the right to raise objections to the proposed repayment plan if they believe that the proposed repayments do not constitute a significantly large proportion of the debtor's disposable income. If the creditors agree to the debtor's repayment plan, then the court will then make the final decision whether the proposed repayment plan is acceptable.

Once a repayment plan has been confirmed, it is the duty of the debtor to ensure that all repayments are met. If payments are not made then the situation can return to as it was before the bankruptcy petition was made, with collections action taken and repossession of the debtor's property if they have secured debts. If the debtors circumstances change and they are unable to meet their repayments (for example they lose their job), then they may be able to convert to Chapter 7 bankruptcy.

5.6 Chapter summary

The key legislation covering consumer credit in the UK are the Consumer Credit Acts 1974 and 2006. The Acts covers most non-mortgage credit agreements between individuals and commercial credit providers. The Acts specify, amongst other things, the form that a credit agreement must take and the rights an individual has to cancel the agreement. The *Consumer Credit (Advertisement) Regulations 2004* cover the format and content that all material advertising credit must contain. This includes all credit agreements, not just those regulated by the Acts.

The Data Protection Act 1998 is a general piece of legislation that empowers individuals by giving them control over how information about them is used. From a consumer credit perspective, the two most important aspects of the Act are first, the right of an individual to view any data a lender holds about them, and second, for any inaccuracies in this data to be corrected.

The law covering bankruptcy (personal insolvency) in is laid down in the Enterprise Act 2002.

In the US the major federal legislation covering consumer credit is the Consumer Credit Protection Act 1968. The Act comprises of six sub-chapters, each of which covers a specific area of legislation. These are:

1. The Truth in Lending Act
2. Garnishment Restrictions
3. The Fair Credit Reporting Act
4. The Equal Credit Opportunity Act
5. The Fair Debt Collection Practices Act
6. The Electronic Funds Transfer Act

Bankruptcy in the US is covered by the Federal Bankruptcy Code 1978 and the Bankruptcy Abuse Prevention Act 2005.

5.7 Recommended sources of further information

Brumby, F., McTear, A., Williams, C. and Border, R. (2004). *Personal Insolvency*. Cavendish Publishing. Written in plain English, this provides a simple introduction to the process of being declared bankrupt in the UK and the consequences for individuals of doing so.

Dobson, P. (2003). *Sale of Goods and Consumer Credit*. Sweet & Maxwell. Provides a clearly written in-depth analysis of the UK Consumer Credit Act 1974 (but not the more recent 2006 Act). Suitable for both legal experts and the casual reader.

Jasper, M. C. (2006). *Consumer Rights Law*. Oceana. This book provides an easy to read guide for the layperson on consumer rights law in the US. It covers many different subjects in addition to laws on consumer credit, such as banking regulation, health care rights and tenant rights. The appendices also contain a very useful summary of state usury (interest rate) laws and debt collection statutes.

The American Bar Association (2006). *Guide to Credit and Bankruptcy*, Random House. Another well-written book, describing in simple terms the main legislation relating to consumer credit and bankruptcy in the US.

6

The Economics of Credit and its Marketing

At its simplest economics can be described as the science of production and consumption. It is concerned with the supply and demand of goods and services, how these goods are produced, priced, sold and utilized, and the interactions and interdependencies that arise between different goods and services. Economics is a hugely diverse subject covering the financial management of nation states, companies, households and a host of other areas, and it can sometimes be unclear where economics as a subject ends and other disciplines begin, or even whether these subjects are merely sub-specialisms within the wider economics field.

The study of economics is often sub-divided into macro economics and micro economics. Macro economics relates to factors having a global or national impact that affect society at large. Micro economics is concerned with more local issues operating at personal and/or organizational levels. From a credit perspective, a reasonable example of the difference is the effect of interest rates. The base rate of interest (the cost of borrowing from a central bank, such as the Bank of England in the UK) is a macro economic factor. The interest rate charged by an individual lender for its credit products is a micro economic one. A change in the base rate will affect just about everyone in one way or another, with knock-on effects to house prices, manufacturing output, inflation and other national economic indicators. A change in a single lender's interest rate will only directly affect that lender and its customers. There may be some secondary effects seen in relation to the lender's immediate competitors, if as a result of the rate change, customers switch lenders. However, the effect of unilateral action by one lender will not generally result in any significant consequences in wider society.

While acknowledging the importance of the macro economic environment, the focus here is primarily on micro economic factors affecting individual lenders and their customers; that is, the costs and revenues associated with the provision and use of credit products and their contribution to profits. The complexities of the supply and demand of credit within the wider economy and its impact on the economic cycle will not be considered here.

The term marketing has a dual meaning. To the person on the street it usually has narrow connotations and is synonymous with 'advertising' or 'product promotion.' Marketing in its true sense is the science of sales, covering the full product cycle involved in the generation of those sales. This includes issues of production, pricing and distribution as well as promotional activity to stimulate demand. Therefore, these aspects also need to be considered in any discussion regarding the economics of credit provision.

The rest of this chapter is split into four parts. The first two parts describe the ways lenders earn an income from the credit they provide and the costs that they incur in doing so. Part three covers the advertising and promotion of credit. The final part covers capital requirements and securitization.

6.1   Sources of income

6.1.1   Arrangement and account management fees

Arrangement fees (often advertised as an administrative fee or documentation fee) are charged for setting up a new credit agreement. Arrangement fees are most commonly associated with mortgages and other secured lending agreements, and with some sub-prime agreements. This is because the process of setting up these types of credit agreement tends to be more complex and labour intensive than for other types of credit. For example, with mortgages there is a requirement to assess the value of the property against which the mortgage is secured, and to liaise with the borrower's legal representative over transfer of the title to the property. While there is a cost associated with the creation of any credit agreement, there is no legal requirement that fees are representative of costs. Therefore, the fees charged often bear little relation to the true cost of account set-up or account management, and many lenders will charge very high arrangement fees to offset the low interest rates they advertise in promotional literature. For example, fees charged by mainstream UK mortgage providers range from zero to well over $10,000, with an average fee of around $1,650 (Moneyfacts 2007).

Annual fees are associated with card/charge accounts, and serve two purposes. First, they are a source of revenue. Second, they encourage dormant account holders, who no longer make use of their accounts, to close them. Dormant accounts are loss making because they incur the cost of maintaining them, but generate no revenue. Annual fees for credit cards have become less common in the 2000s, but where charged are commonly in the region of $20–$100. Charge cards attract higher annual fees; some charge as little as $80, but some of the more exclusive cards command fees in excess of $500.

6.1.2 Interest charges

As defined in Chapter 2, interest is a charge proportional to the amount borrowed and the term of the agreement. In theory, the calculation of interest is not difficult. In practice, interest can be calculated in a number of different ways and these are discussed in Appendix A.

For most revolving credit products, interest is only charged if the customer does not pay off the outstanding balance in full each month. Kempson (2002, p.4) reports figures from the Credit Card Research Group in the UK, that between 1995 and 2001 between 72 and 77 percent of credit card customers revolved their balances. More recent figures suggested that only 32 percent of UK customers tended to maintain a revolving credit balance (MORI Market Dynamics 2004). Evans and Schmalensee (2005, pp.217–18) reported that in the US in the early-2000s about 56 percent of customers revolved their balances, which is somewhat lower than their previous estimate of 60–75 percent from 1998 (Evans and Schmalensee 1999, p.211). The reason for the large differences between these figures may be due to the method of reporting. If figures include those who have not used their cards in the last month or who keep a card just in case of emergencies, then a lower figure will result than considering only those who use their cards on a regular basis. Many lenders consider a card account to be 'active' for several years after account activity has ceased because it is easier and cheaper for them to try and reactivate a dormant account than recruiting a new customer from scratch. It is questionable whether a customer who has not used a credit card for many months (and who may have destroyed the card when it was no longer of any use to them) would agree with this definition.

A second issue is whether figures relate to people, accounts or balances. The statement balance on revolving accounts tends to be higher than for non-revolving accounts. Therefore, the proportion of balances that revolve will be higher than the proportion of accounts that revolve. It is also important to differentiate between the proportion of people who maintain a revolving credit balance and the proportion of accounts that revolve. If everyone has an average of say, four credit cards, and each person maintains a revolving credit balance on just one card, then the proportion of people maintaining a revolving credit balance is 100 percent. However, the proportion of accounts that revolve is only 25 percent.

6.1.3 Transaction fees

For card accounts, transaction fees are routinely charged for balance transfers, cash advances and credit card cheques. In Europe and the US fees are usually between 2 and 4 percent of the value of the balance transfer, cash advance or cheque, subject to a minimum fee of between $5 and $10. This is in addition to interest which usually begins to accrue as soon as a transaction occurs. Figures from the British Bankers' Association (2008) suggest that in an average year, about 6 percent of credit card turnover (MasterCard and VISA) is due to cash withdrawals and about 10 percent is due to balance transfers.

6.1.4 Late payment fees, penalty charges and early redemption fees

When a borrower fails to make a scheduled repayment, most credit providers charge a late payment fee, in theory to cover the administrative costs of dealing with delinquent cases. However, when a payment has not been received by the due date, many lenders will wait several days before taking action, such as issuing a reminder letter. Therefore, if the borrower is only a few days late with a payment, a lender may take no action, yet still charge the customer a late payment fee. In most cases fees are applied automatically, requiring no manual intervention and costing almost nothing to apply. Even if action is taken, with a letter being issued as part of an automatic account management process, the cost will be no more than a few cents.

Human involvement in arrears processing only tends to occur in cases where the account reaches a state of serious delinquency (payment is 60+ days past the due date) or where the customer is deemed to be high risk due to a history of arrears. However, even in these cases, a typical reminder call or customized letter will only incur a cost of around $5–$6. For a lender operating a modern and efficient account management system, collections and debt recovery costs only become significant after multiple attempts to contact the customer have been made and/or the account reaches a status such that legal action or the use of third party debt collectors is required. On this basis, many collections and debt recovery functions are seen as profit centres, although most lenders would dispute this, arguing that their fees are representative of their costs. Debt collection costs within the credit industry are not generally available, but an interesting insight into the true cost of debt recovery action is given in figures produced by OFWAT, the UK water regulator. This reported that the average cost of debt collection action taken against households in arrears with water bills was only $4.76 (Cox 2003, pp.2–3).

Until 2006, UK lenders routinely charged late payment fees of $30–$50 for credit cards and personal loans, but after intervention by the Office of Fair Trading, a cap of $24 was introduced (Office of Fair Trading 2006). More recently, the Office of Fair Trading has taken legal action to limit the fees charged for unauthorized overdrafts, which can run to hundreds of dollars a month if someone makes several unauthorized transactions.[1]

Figures reported by Kempson (2002, pp.9 & 28) indicate that 8 percent of people with access to a credit facility are in arrears at any one time[2] and my experience of credit card and mail order companies would support this figure. A further observation from Kempson's figures is that arrears tend to be lower for fixed term credit commitments, such as mortgages and personal loans, than for revolving credit products such as credit cards. Figures for the number who are charged other types of fees and charges for things such as cancelled cheques and exceeding the credit limit, are difficult to obtain, but probably occur at a relatively low level compared to the number of late payment fees charged, perhaps affecting no more than 1 or 2 percent of accounts each month. Taking these figures together, it could be inferred that on average between 8 and 10 percent of credit accounts are subject to some type of late payment fee or penalty charge each month.

Many lenders charge an early settlement fee (early redemption fee) for repaying a loan before the date specified within the credit agreement. In the UK since May 2005, all new credit agreements that are regulated by the Consumer Credit Act are subject to the *Consumer Credit (Early Settlement) Regulations 2004* (2004b). These limit the amount of any settlement fee to roughly one month's interest charge and replaces the previous 'Rule of 78' method of calculating the outstanding interest to be paid, which is still applied in some countries.

Mortgage lenders in the UK have more leeway in the redemption penalties they can charge because mortgages are excluded from the early settlement regulations. Redemption penalties are commonly applied to discount and fixed rate mortgages based on a percentage of the amount repaid and the length of time since the agreement was made. So for someone who takes out a mortgage with a fixed rate of interest for three years, the penalty charge may be structured to be 4 percent of the amount borrowed if the mortgage is redeemed in the first year of the agreement, 3 percent in the second year and 2 percent in the third. After the end of the third year the borrower can redeem the mortgage without penalty.

6.1.5 Insurance

Payment protection insurance is sold to borrowers to cover credit repayments if, due to a change in circumstances, they are no longer in a position to repay their debt. Although the terms and conditions of individual policies vary, most cover repayments if the borrower becomes unemployed through illness and/or redundancy. For personal loans insurance premiums are usually added to the initial amount borrowed and then paid along with the regular repayments. For revolving credit products, such as credit cards and mail order accounts, a fee is charged each month based on the value of the outstanding balance. Insurance for mortgage products usually comes in the form of income protection insurance or critical illness cover. This is arranged independently of the mortgage and is designed to provide a fixed income for the borrower, who then decides how to spend it. This enables the insurance policy to be continued as old mortgages are redeemed and new mortgages taken out, or even to continue when the mortgage has been repaid in full.

The profitability of credit insurance products is potentially huge. Typical market rates for credit card payment protection insurance are between 70 and 80 cents per $100 of the account balance each month. This may sound like a small amount, but for a customer maintaining a $5,000 balance over the course of a year and paying 70 cents for $100 of cover, the cost will be $420 a year (12 * $0.70 * $5,000 / 100). This is equivalent to an additional 8.4 percent on the interest rate, and for a low rate card can represent a more than doubling of the revenue generated from interest charges alone. For personal loans, payment protection insurance will add around 10–20 percent to the repayments of a typical loan.

A feature in *The Guardian* newspaper alleged that for Barclays, one of the UK's largest banks with substantial commercial as well as consumer interests, 10 percent of its entire worldwide profits were accounted for by credit insurance charged to just two million of its personal customers on consumer credit products. It also claimed that while

Barclays' customers paid around $700 million in insurance premiums, only around $180 million was paid out (Cotell 2004). Even accounting for overheads, this represents a huge profit margin.[3] As the article also went on to say, the Barclays' situation was not atypical. Other UK lenders make similar profit margins on their insurance products and a later article in *The Guardian* reported a similar situation for insurance products offered by HSBC (Levene 2004). This level of margin is not restricted to the UK. Peterson (2004, pp.183–8) reports that in the US the loss ratio (the proportion of premiums paid by customers that are then paid out to meet insurance claims) for the credit insurance market is only 34.2 percent. This compared to car, health and life insurance where average loss ratios are in excess of 65 percent, and in some cases as high as 90 percent.

Another complaint is that many insurance policies are not comprehensive, and that restrictions on claims are not made clear when polices are promoted to customers. Payment protection plans are often limited in the time over which they cover repayments. Twelve months is the norm, which means that in many cases some, or even most, of the debt will remain outstanding when the cover ends. Many also exclude certain medical conditions (lower back pain for example) or only pay out for a defined list of 'critical illnesses.' Cover for those in non-standard employment is also patchy, with some policies excluding those on temporary contracts or who are self-employed.

Another form of insurance is card protection. This protects the account holder from loss should their card(s) be lost, stolen or fraudulently used. While these types of policies tend to offer some protection and peace of mind, those without insurance generally have only limited liability against malicious use, as long as they report that the security of the account has been compromised as soon as they become aware of it. Card protection insurance is typically charged as an annual fixed fee and a single policy can cover all of the card products maintained by an individual. Fees of between $25 and $50 per annum are common for standard policies. More expensive policies, offering alert services and regular updates about the status of someone's credit report from a credit bureau (via text and/or e-mail) cost upwards of $120 per annum.

In the UK mortgage market, lenders often insist borrowers take out a Mortgage Indemnity Guarantee (MIG) if the mortgage represents more than a certain percentage of the property value. A MIG insures that in the event that a property is repossessed, the lender recovers the full amount owing. One feature of MIGs is that although they are paid for by the borrower, they only benefit the lender. If the borrower has their home repossessed and the revenue from the sale of the property does not cover the outstanding debt in full, the insurer will cover the loss incurred by the lender and then pursue the borrower for the difference.

The MIG fee is calculated as a percentage of the mortgage above the MIG threshold, which is usually defined as a percentage of the property value. If the MIG threshold was 90 percent of the property value and the MIG fee was 7.5 percent, then for a property valued at $400,000 with a $380,000 mortgage the MIG fee would be calculated as:

Amount above MIG threshold = $380,000 − ($400,000 * 90%) = $20,000
MIG fee = $20,000 * 7.5% = $1,500

6.1.6 Merchant and interchange fees

Merchant fees and interchange fees are generated from card transactions. For cards belonging to the VISA and MasterCard networks, a

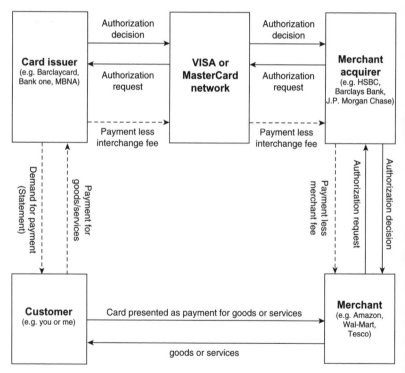

Figure 6.1 The relationship between customers, merchants and card issuers

Note: Full arrows represent activities that occur during a credit card transaction. Dotted arrows represent activities that occur sometime after the transaction has occurred.

merchant who accepts a credit card as payment does not have a direct relationship with the card issuer. As shown in Figure 6.1, a third party bank, referred to as a merchant acquirer, acts as an intermediary between merchants and card issuers.

When a customer presents a merchant with a credit or charge card as a means of payment, the merchant passes details of the card and the proposed transaction to the merchant acquirer, who passes the details to the customer's card issuer via the VISA or MasterCard computer network. If the card issuer confirms that the customer's account is satisfactory, then the transaction is authorized, and the merchant is notified that the transaction can proceed.

After the transaction has been completed, the card issuer pays the merchant acquirer the cost of the transaction, less the interchange fee. The merchant acquirer in turn pays the merchant less the merchant fee. Therefore, in order for the merchant acquirer to make a profit, the merchant fee must be greater than the interchange fee. The VISA and MasterCard computer networks act as intermediaries for these processes, managing the flow of information between merchant acquirers and card issuers, as well as the transfer of funds once transactions have occurred.

If a merchant wishes to accept cards from one of the card networks they will enter into an agreement with a merchant acquirer. In return for the merchant fee, the merchant acquirer will provide the necessary equipment to process card payments and manage the relationship between the network and the different card issuers, and guarantees payment to the merchant.[4] This protects the merchant from losses due to fraud or the customer who, for whatever reason, refuses to pay. In addition, the merchant will receive payment promptly, usually within one or two working days of the transaction occurring.

In theory a merchant acquirer can negotiate the interchange fee individually with each of the card issuers using the VISA and Master-Card networks. In practice, a standard fee is charged across each network and in many cases banks act in a dual capacity as card issuers and merchant acquirers, and it is in their interest for interchange fees to be as high as possible. Interchange fees are country specific, but on average, are between 0.5 and 1.5 percent of the value of each transaction. Both VISA and MasterCard publish details of their interchange fees on their websites (www.mastercard.com and www.visa.com). Interchange fees have come down in recent years, but there is pressure for interchange fees to be reduced further, and in a number of countries they have been the subject of debate as to whether they breach anti-competition legislation. In the UK, interchange fees have been referred to the Office of Fair Trading (Office of Fair Trading 2003) and at the time of writing investigations are still ongoing. In Australia, a report by the Reserve Bank of Australia concluded that the charging structure for interchange fees stifled competition and acted against the public interest (Reserve Bank of Australia 2001, pp.115–16). The Australian Authorities have subsequently legislated to limit the interchange fees that can be charged (Reserve Bank of Australia 2006).[5] In the US, merchants have successfully taken legal action, leading to reductions in the charges levied by the major card networks (Morbin 2003).

The merchant fee is negotiated between individual merchants and merchant acquirers, and averages between 1.5 and 2.0 percent for the two main networks (Evans and Schmalensee 2005, p.260). However, large merchants such as supermarkets or retail chains, tend to be able to negotiate fees as low as 1 percent, while small merchants can pay as much as 4 percent.

VISA and MasterCard were originally set up and managed as joint ventures, controlled by representatives elected by member organizations who were either merchant acquirers, card issuers or both. In the mid-2000s both organizations were partially sold off, with former members now major, but not sole, shareholders.[6] Both networks are supported by transaction fees that are used to maintain and promote the network. Figures provided by Evans and Schmalensee (2005, p.260) suggest that transaction fees are equivalent to between 0.05–0.10 percent of the value of each card transaction that occurs. Fees are paid by merchant acquirers and card issuers, therefore the total fee paid to the card network is double this figure; that is, between 0.1 and 0.2 percent of the value of each transaction.

For single card networks such as American Express, the card issuer negotiates directly with merchants. There is no need for a separate merchant acquirer. This provides advantages in that there is a lower processing (and hence cost) overhead, and transactions can move more quickly around the system. The disadvantage is that the merchant can only negotiate with a single issuer.

6.2 The costs of providing credit

6.2.1 Infrastructure and overheads

Infrastructure covers the fixed systems, processes and resources that need to be in place to allow an organization to function as intended. If a new credit provider were planning to set up operations next year, the infrastructure would be all those things needing to be in place before it could begin trading. This would include customer contact systems to manage communications to/from customers, the mechanisms for processing new credit applications, systems for the management of accounts once an account has been opened, and a collections and debt recovery function. There will also be head office functions to support general business operation, such as marketing, IT, personnel, accounting and finance and legal. For retail credit and mail order, there will also be a need to integrate credit and retail operations to insure that appropriate credit account processing takes place when a retail transaction occurs. For example, the account management system will need to be matched with the stock and pricing databases, so that when a purchase takes place the correct amount is credited to the account and details of the purchased item(s) appear on the customer's statement. Infrastructure and overheads can generally be described as falling into one of the following categories:

- Capital expenditure: The cost of major items, such as land or buildings, which have the potential to retain a proportion of their value over time.
- Depreciation: This represents the loss in value of assets as they age and wear out. Depreciation usually applies to things such as buildings, vehicles, IT and so on; that is, things that were purchased as a capital expenditure.
- Operational expenditure: Covering day-to-day expenses and running costs, such as utility bills, rent, salaries, stationary and so on.

When someone applies for credit, there is an initial cost associated with processing their application, and this cost applies regardless of whether or not the application is accepted. In most cases there will also be the cost of purchasing a credit report from a credit reference agency. Costs for credit reports are negotiated on a one-to-one basis. Therefore different organizations pay different amounts for the credit reports they require. However, for a very large organization requesting millions of credit reports a year, the typical cost of a credit report might be no more than a few cents. For smaller organizations, perhaps requesting no more than a few hundred reports per year, the cost may be $5–$10 dollars or more for each report.

Once an application has been accepted in principle a variety of tasks must be undertaken which incurs further costs. Documentation, including a credit agreement, must be produced and delivered to the customer. If credit has been arranged remotely, there is a need to process and store returned agreements signed by the customer, and for contacting customers if they fail to return the agreement within a certain timeframe. For card accounts, cards and PIN numbers need to be produced and dispatched, usually separately for security reasons. The card holder is then required to activate the card before it can be used, requiring further contact with the lender.

Ideally, costs would be allocated at an individual account level and differentiation made between fixed and variable costs. Some organizations do attempt to do this, but many find it difficult to do so – they simply do not maintain the necessary level of accounting detail. Alternatively, the internal political situation may make it difficult to allocate the true costs to the appropriate departments and processes. On this basis, working on an average cost per account basis is a sensible option.

For unsecured products processed without face-to-face contact (via mail, the phone or the internet) application processing costs are probably in the range of $10–$30 for each new customer. If a personal consultation is required, which is common for loans processed through branch networks or retail credit arranged in store, then these costs can be significantly higher, perhaps of the order of $40–$100 per application. For mortgage lending there are additional costs for liaising with third parties, such as solicitors and surveyors, which can result in typical costs of $200–$400 for each new mortgage.

Once an account has been opened it needs to be managed and monitored on an ongoing basis. The account management costs for operationally simple products such as a personal loan tends to be low, perhaps no more than $20 per customer per annum. Once an account has been opened there is little to do except process payments, issue an annual statement of account and chase late payers.

For more complex products, such as card or mail order accounts, costs will be higher. Transactions can occur many times a month and there may be frequent customer contact via monthly statements and customer queries over balances, purchases and other transactions, requiring large numbers of people, IT and other resources to facilitate. Account management costs probably average between $40 and $60 per account per annum for a typical revolving credit portfolio comprising one to two million active customer accounts.

6.2.2   Cost of funds

In some respects a credit product can be thought of in the same terms as any other manufactured product; albeit one without physical form.

Lenders need to obtain raw funds and then process it into neat packages of personal loans, credit cards, mortgages and so on, that can then be provided to customers. The raw material is money and like any raw material a supply needs to be established before it can be worked into the finished product. The cost of funds is the cost of obtaining this money.

There are generally two sources of funds available to lenders. Deposits held in current accounts and savings accounts, and the money markets (also known as the Interbank market) which facilitate commercial lending between banks and other large financial organizations. Both sources of funds have inherent costs associated with them. Account holders expect to receive interest on their deposits and money borrowed from a commercial lender attracts interest. The cost of funds acquired through the interbank market is typically at or close to the base rate of interest set by the central bank. However, due to the speculative nature of commercial money markets, the actual rates charged for commercial loans depends very much on the term of the loan, risk of borrower default, how the market believes the supply and demand for money will change over time, and market liquidity (the amount of money organizations are willing to lend). If it is believed that the money supply will increase or decrease in relation to future demand, then lending rates will tend to change in line with this expectation. For example, in the credit crunch of 2007/8 the supply of funds was severely limited as banks became unwilling to lend to one another. The result was a sharp rise in the cost of funds, despite central bank intervention to lower interest rates.

The main benchmark of the interest rates charged in the Interbank market is the London Interbank Offered Rate (LIBOR), which is calculated by the British Banking Association (BBA) on a daily basis. Separate LIBOR rates are calculated for loans of different terms, ranging from overnight borrowing to a maximum of 12 months. It is important to note that a LIBOR rate is not the specific interest rate that any one institution charges for its loans, but represents an average rate compiled from a panel of major banking institutions. The BBA calculates LIBOR for several economic regions including Australia, Canada, the Euro zone, Japan the UK and the US.

The interest paid to account holders is often lower than interest charged for commercial loans obtained via the Interbank market, but the administrative costs of dealing with a large number of individual accounts incurs a significant overhead which must be factored into the overall cost. In practice, many financial institutions acquire funds from both individual savers and the money markets to varying degrees.

Figures provided by Evans and Schmalensee (2005, p.224) suggested that for credit cards in the US the cost of funds represented around 30 percent of the total cost of credit provision.

6.2.3   Bad debt and write-off (charge-off)

When a customer has been in default for a considerable period of time (usually somewhere between six and 12 months without making a payment) the loan is classified as bad debt. The debt will then be written-off (charged-off). This means the lender assumes that the debt will never be repaid, and therefore, their assets need to be reduced (written down) by the amount of the bad debt. The amount written-off then appears as a loss within the organization's profit and loss account. In the UK in the mid–late-2000s, write-off rates for outstanding credit card debt averaged around 6 percent a year; that is, of every \$100 of money lent \$6 was not repaid and therefore written-off.[7] For other types of unsecured lending average write-off rates were about 3.5 percent.[8] For mortgages, average write-off rates were a fraction of 1 percent (Bank of England 2008, p.30). Write-off rates for mortgages tend to be much lower than for other types of borrowing because the lender can normally recover the debt through the sale of the property against which it is secured.

The amount of write-off experienced by an individual lender can vary enormously. For low risk personal loans and credit cards, where perhaps 60 percent or more of applicants are declined, bad debt can be lower than 1 percent. For organizations operating at the more risky end of the market write-off levels can be as high as 15 percent, and even higher write-off rates are associated with some sub-prime lending operations.

Figures provided by Evans and Schmalensee (2005, p.224) for VISA credit card issuers in the US, indicated that bad debt (including provision) accounted on average for 37 percent of the cost of supplying credit in the early-2000s. The amount of bad debt written-off by US credit card issuers in this period was in the region of 4.5–5.5 percent (The Federal Reserve Board 2005).

6.2.4   Fraud

Fraud is a high profile issue, particularly in card and retail credit markets. Common types of credit related fraud include:

* Identity theft: This is where an individual uses another person's details to obtain credit.

- First party fraud: This occurs when the applicant applies for credit in their own name, but falsifies some of the information requested. For example, their age or income.
- Security compromization and account takeover: This is when an unauthorized individual obtains access to account details and/or passwords. The most common manifestation of this type of fraud is the theft and use of credit card details. Account takeover takes things a step further. The fraudster gains sufficient information to pass security checks, enabling them to change account details. For example, a fraudster may contact the card provider and tell them that they have moved address. A short time later they report that they have lost their card. Consequently, a new card will be dispatched to the address given by the fraudster.

One problem is that some types of fraud are difficult to detect, especially if there is no victim to highlight the crime, as is the case with first party fraud. In these cases there is a reasonable chance that the fraud will not come to light and the account, if it becomes delinquent, will be processed by the organization's normal debt recovery procedures, finishing up as a case of bad debt. This means that while figures for total bad debt can be known precisely, the specific proportion due to fraud can only ever be estimated. In the US in 2006, the estimated value of fraudulent card transactions was in excess of $3.5 billion (Experian 2007). In the UK, card fraud was estimated to be $856 million, representing 0.13 percent of all card transactions (APACS 2007). This figure represents a relatively small component of the overall cost of operating a credit business, but if considerable time and effort were not spent countering fraudulent activity, losses due to fraud would be much greater.

6.2.5 Provision (and impairment charges)

It can be expected that some customers who are currently meeting their repayments will experience repayment difficulties in the future, resulting in some or all of their debts being written-off. This means it is over-optimistic to base estimates of future profitability on the expectation that all outstanding debts will be repaid. Provision is an amount set aside against future bad debts, accounted for in the present, allowing a more realistic estimate of profitability to be arrived at. Making provisions is an acknowledgement that the asset value of outstanding loans reported on an organization's balance sheet is less than the amount stated (McNab and Wynn 2004, p.147). In some ways provision can be considered analogous to depreciation, which represents the loss in value of an asset, such as a building or vehicle, over time (Wood and Sangster 1999, p.213).

At the beginning of each financial year organizations estimate the level of provision appropriate for their portfolio of debts. This estimate is then used as an input to their profit and loss forecast for that year, and is usually described in the accounts as a 'provision for impaired loans'. An impaired loan is a debt where it is believed that some or all of the debt won't be repaid. To some extent all debts are impaired. This is because no matter how creditworthy someone is, there is always a chance, however small, that the debt won't be repaid. However, most provisions for impaired loans result from customers who are demonstrably more likely to default than average. For example, they have a long history of missed payments and/or are currently in arrears. An important point to remember is that a provision reported in an organization's accounts is not a known quantity, but an estimate of a cost that is expected to be incurred at some point in the future. Therefore, provision estimates need to be reviewed on a regular basis (usually monthly or quarterly) and any changes used to update the profit and loss forecast.

If no new credit is advanced, the value of write-off plus provisions should remain constant for a given cohort of debt. As time progresses the amount written-off will increase while provision decreases. Eventually, all debts will have been repaid or written-off, with zero provision. However, credit granting institutions are continually advancing new credit, and so the overall provision level will never decline to zero. Instead, the value of provisions will fluctuate as the size of the portfolio varies and updates are made to estimates of the likelihood of each risk (each loan) defaulting.

Provision is only an estimate of future write-off. So whenever a debt that has been provided for is written-off, a corresponding amount of provision is released. This means that the total value of provisions is reduced by the amount of provision that was originally set aside for the debt. If the actual amount written-off is different from the value of provision originally allocated, then the difference is added into the profit and loss account. Take the case where a provision of $450 was made for a $1,000 loan because it was believed that there was a 45 percent chance that the loan would be written-off. If the entire $1,000 is written-off then the total write-off will increase by $1,000, the value of provisions will decrease by $450 and the overall increase in losses will be $550 ($1,000 – $450). Conversely, if the loan is repaid in full, then the provision would also reduce by $450, but there would be no increase in write-off. Therefore, reported losses would decrease by $450; that is, profit would increase by $450.

International accounting standard IAS39 lays down guidelines for how impaired loans should be accounted for within organizational accounts.[9] One particular requirement is that provisions for impaired loans should be calculated on the basis of net present value, using the contractual rate of interest specified within the credit agreement. This means that provision calculations must be adjusted to take into account the repayment schedule and the interest rate specified in the agreement.

Net present value is a way of thinking about how much future income is worth in today's terms, taking into account things like inflation and/or cost of funds/lost investment potential. In simple terms, the value of a sum of money in today's terms, is worth less the further into the future you have to go before you get it. One way to think about net present value is to ask yourself the following question: if someone promises to give you $1,000 in a year's time, how much would you be willing to accept if you were offered an alternative cash amount today? If you knew that you could take the money and put it the bank earning interest at say, 5 percent per annum, then the net present value of $1,000 in a year, would be $952.38. This is calculated as $1,000/(1 + 0.05) or working the other way, if you put $952.38 into a bank account today, it would be worth $1,000 in a year's time if interest was paid at a rate of 5 percent. The general formula for calculating net present value is:

$$NPV = A / (1 + P)^N$$

where A is the amount, P is the interest rate per unit time and N is the number of time periods ahead for which the net present value is calculated. So if we wanted to know what the net present value of $1,000 was in three years' time, with an annual interest rate of 7 percent, the calculation would be:

$$NPV = \$1{,}000/(1 + 0.07)^3 = \$816.30$$

IAS39 requires provision to be calculated on a net present value basis, taking into account the value of the debt, the repayment schedule and the contractual rate of interest specified in the credit agreement. So if a company offers two different types of loan, one with an interest rate of 12.49 percent and another with an interest rate of 9.9 percent, each rate must be used for customers with the respective loans in the net present value calculation. The following is an example of net present value applied

Table 6.1   Customer repayment schedule

Month	Outstanding balance ($)	Interest added ($)	Payment ($)	Post payment balance ($)
1	20,000.00	144.16	494.38	19,649.78
2	19,649.78	141.64	494.38	19,297.04
3	19,297.04	139.09	494.38	18,941.75
...	...	...	...	...
...	...	...	...	...
23	12,494.58	90.06	494.38	12,090.26
24	12,090.26	87.15	494.38	11,683.03
25	11,683.03	84.21	494.38	11,272.86
...	...	...	...	...
...	...	...	...	...
47	978.17	7.05	494.38	490.84
48	490.84	3.54	494.38	0.00
Total		**3,730.24**	**23,730.24**	

Note: Interest added = outstanding balance * (1 + contractual interest rate)$^{1/12}$

to provisions under IAS39, for a loan agreement. Imagine that a customer has borrowed $20,000 to be repaid in 48 equal monthly installments, with a contractual rate of interest of 9 percent. After making 24 payments, the customer misses a payment, entering a state of default and the account is classified as impaired. Details of the customer's repayment schedule, interest charges and outstanding balance are shown in Table 6.1.

From Table 6.1, after the customer has made 24 repayments, the outstanding balance at the start of month 25 is $11,683.03. From past experience, the bank estimates that it is likely to recover 90 percent of the outstanding debt, with 10 percent of the debt being written-off. Therefore, in this case the bank expects to receive 90 percent of the $11.683.03 owing; that is, $10,514.73. This amount is then subject to the net present value calculation over the two remaining years of the loan. $10,514.73 / (1.09)^2 = $8,850.04. The provision is then calculated as the difference between the amount owing and the net present value of the expected loan repayments: $11,683.03 – $8,850.04 = $2,832.99.

6.3   Advertising and promotion

Most lenders promote their products to potential customers in the belief that they can convince them their product is the best one for them and to persuade them to apply for it. To do this they utilize a range of promotional mechanisms.

Mass media communicate with general populations, using broad channels such as TV advertising, billboards, internet pop-ups, newspaper adverts and magazine inserts to get the message across. Direct marketing aims to contact specific households or individuals on a one-to-one basis. This is often a mailing, but can also be a telephone call, e-mail, text message or home visit.

Target marketing is the science/art of matching promotional activity to the audiences to which the product is best suited and which will yield the greatest returns. With mass media, a successful target marketing campaign will need to identify the types of people with whom the product will appeal and the types of media that these people encounter. For example, a company planning a TV advertising campaign, which has established that its product appeals mainly to the over fifties, might look to identify TV shows that the over fifties watch and position their adverts in the commercial breaks of these shows.

The most common approach to direct marketing is the use of database marketing techniques. Marketers will trawl through their organization's customer databases, publicly available data, and privately purchased databases in order to identify desirable individuals who are likely to respond to promotional activity and be profitable customers.

The response rate is the proportion of people who respond to promotional activity by applying for the product. Response rates to mass media promotions are typically between 0.01 and 0.05 percent and for direct marketing between 1 and 2 percent (Tapp 2004, p.303).

For all types of marketing campaign, there will be costs associated with the planning of the campaign strategy, which can involve significant numbers of people, both internally within the organization and externally via third party advertising agencies. Other functions, such as IT and customer contact centres also need to be involved to ensue sufficient resources are in place to deal with the demand generated. For a mass media campaign, other costs will include the production of the advert(s) and the purchasing of advertising space/time. For target marketing, the main costs are the production of the list of customers to contact and the cost of contacting those customers via the chosen channel(s).

The actual costs of these activities varies enormously by lender, product and target audience, but to put them in perspective, consider the following examples of two different marketing campaigns.

Example 1. A bank decides to undertake a TV advertising campaign for one of its credit cards. The total cost to create, produce and air the campaign is $560,000, and the ad is seen by 20 million adults. Five thousand people respond to the campaign by applying for the card – a response rate of 0.025 percent. Of the 5,000 who apply, a significant proportion are subsequently declined because they are uncreditworthy; that is, they are not considered to be desirable customers on the grounds of low expected profitability or high likelihood of default. For this example it is assumed that 20 percent are declined for this reason,[10] resulting in 4,000 new customers. Therefore, the average promotional cost for each new customer is $140 ($560,000/4,000).

Example 2. Consider a direct mailing campaign for a personal loan. 500,000 prospective customers are selected from a mailing list, the cost per mailing is $1.00 and campaign management costs are $130,000. Therefore, the total campaign cost is $630,000. 10,000 people respond – a response rate of 2 percent. As for example 1, some who respond will have their applications declined because they are uncreditworthy. However, many (but not all) uncreditworthy cases will have been identified prior to mailing, and therefore, excluded from the campaign. Consequently, relatively few applicants will be declined. Assuming a 10 percent reject rate, 9,000 will have their applications accepted. The average promotional cost per customer is therefore $70 ($630,000/9,000).

In practice, most organizations use a combination of promotional activities, utilizing mass media to raise general product awareness and brand affinity, followed by targeted campaigns to encourage individual applications. Tapp (2004, p.303) estimates that the average cost of recruiting a new customer from direct mailing campaigns is between $60 and $140 per customer. Tapp also quotes figures for a major (unnamed) provider of personal loans for which recruitment costs varied from $24 to over $1,200 for a single customer, with an average cost of $500. Figures provided by Evans and Schmalensee suggest that for US credit card providers the average solicitation cost is only $25 (Evans and Schmalensee 2005, p.225). One reason that these costs can vary so much is that the response rates for different groups within the population can vary enormously. Another reason is the way in which costs are allocated between different business functions and the accounting practices being used within different organizations.

A common task for a marketer is to determine the response rates for different population segments based on test mailings. Consider a credit card company that has decided to offer a card targeted at 'sexy young professionals' to be marketed via a direct mail campaign. A mailing list containing personal details of 100,000 individuals, selected at random,

Table 6.2 Response rate analysis

Population segment	Description	Number mailed	Number of responders	Response rate	Cost per response
1	Single females earning >$90,000, aged 26–40	980	31	3.16%	$31.61
2	Male home owners earning >$90,000, aged 26–45	2,553	49	1.92%	$52.10
3	Single or cohabiting without children, aged 22–25	16,874	212	1.26%	$79.59
4	Inner city renters aged 26–49, earning $50,000–$90,000	6,521	65	1.00%	$100.32
5	Aged 26–49, earning $35,000–$49,999	11,004	96	0.87%	$114.63
6	Aged 22–44, earning <$35,000	15,778	83	0.53%	$190.10
7	Aged >=55	19,765	101	0.51%	$195.69
8	Male students aged <22	2,509	11	0.44%	$228.09
9	Female students aged <22	2,450	8	0.33%	$306.25
10	All others segments	21,566	44	0.20%	$490.14
Total		**100,000**	**700**	0.70%	**$142.86**

Note: Cost of each mailing is assumed to be $1.00. Therefore, cost per response is calculated as number mailed * $1.00/number of responders.

is used in an experimental mailing. Of those that were mailed 700 respond – a response rate of 0.7 percent. Statistical analysis is then undertaken to determine the type of individuals that were most likely to respond (the methods employed in this type of analysis are similar to those applied in credit scoring, which is discussed in Chapter 7). The results of this analysis are shown in Table 6.2.

Table 6.3   Contribution analysis by population segment

Pop seg.	Description	Number mailed	Number of responders	Response rate	Cost per response	Average contribution per response
1	Single females earning >$90,000, aged 26–40	980	31	3.16%	$31.61	$–40.21
2	Male home owners earning >$90,000, aged 26–45	2,553	49	1.92%	$52.10	$31.52
3	Single or cohabiting without children, aged 22–25	16,874	212	1.26%	$79.59	$–24.24
4	Inner city renters aged 26–49, earning $50,000–$90,000	6,521	65	1.00%	$100.32	$132.61
5	Aged 26–49, earning $35,000–$49,999	11,004	96	0.87%	$114.63	$83.13
6	Aged 22–44, earning <$35,000	15,778	83	0.53%	$190.10	$43.30
7	Aged >=55	19,765	101	0.51%	$195.69	$–20.65
8	Male students aged <22	2,509	11	0.44%	$228.09	$–21.46
9	Female students aged <22	2,450	8	0.33%	$306.25	$–156.66
10	All others segments	21,566	44	0.20%	$490.14	$–410.10
Total		100,000	700	0.70%	$142.86	

If it is deemed that the maximum cost for which a customer can be recruited profitably is say $150, then from Table 6.2 only segments one through five should be targeted. If sufficient funds are available, all individuals in these segments can be targeted. In practice, most organizations have a fixed marketing budget, allowing them to target a fixed number of people. In this case, the ideal would be to mail only those falling into the highest response/lowest cost segment, which in this case is segment one – single females, earning more than $90,000 and aged 26–40. However, if there are insufficient numbers available in this group then they will also target the second segment, then the third and so on, until their budget has been exhausted, or no further profitable cases can be identified.

At one time a marketing department may have worked in isolation and based much of its activity solely on the basis of response rates and recruitment costs. In today's well-run organization, marketers work in conjunction with credit and finance professionals to consider other dimensions of customer behaviour such as the risk of default and the estimated revenues that different customer groups are likely to generate. Continuing with the example of Table 6.2, if the results from the test mailing also included the revenues and costs generated by the responders, it would be possible to calculate a measure of each account's contribution to profits. If we assume that this information has been obtained, then Table 6.2 could be adapted to produce Table 6.3.

From Table 6.3 a different picture now emerges. The most desirable groups are now 2, 4, 5 and 6; that is, those where the average contribution is positive.

There is a problem with producing this type of analysis. The time taken to determine the response rate to a test mailing is usually of the order of one to two months. All that is required is to send out the mailing, then wait and see how many are returned. However, determining the contribution from these responses is dependent on the time horizon over which the organization measures customer contribution, which can be anything up to five years or more. Therefore, it would be necessary to wait this length of time after responses had been received before producing actual contribution figures. In practice, revenue, bad debt and other components of contribution are estimated. If the credit provider has a well-established business it can use estimates based on similar accounts that have been on its books for a number of years. For new entrants to the market, figures may be based either on 'best guess' by industry experts or information purchased from third party data providers, such as credit reference agencies.

6.3.1 The special case of mail order catalogues

For traditional mail order catalogue businesses, customer recruitment is a two stage process. In the first stage promotional activity is undertaken to encourage individuals to apply for a copy of the company's catalogue. Having received a catalogue, there is no obligation for the individual to then order anything from it. Therefore, in the second stage, promotional activity is targeted at those who have received the catalogue in order to encourage them to place an order.

With some catalogues having in excess of 1,000 colour pages, catalogue production costs are not trivial. If only 20 percent of catalogues lead to an order being placed and an account opened, and each catalogue costs $10 to produce, the additional catalogue cost for one new account will be $50 ($10/20%). One might expect goods ordered via a mail order catalogue to be cheaper than corresponding items on sale in a retail outlet, given the reduced overheads that result from not having physical stores. However, the total cost of recruiting individuals who typically spend only a few tens or hundreds of dollars, is one reason why goods purchased via mail order can be relatively expensive.

6.3.2 Offers and incentives

Many credit products come with 'promotional wrappers' – features and offers that are ancillary to the credit being provided but designed to differentiate it from its competitors and to tempt people into becoming customers.

For revolving credit products where the amount of credit advanced is not set when the credit facility is granted, rewards to encourage spending and/or the establishment of a revolving (and hence interest-bearing) account balance is the goal. Cash back rewards customers for spending by returning to them a percentage of what they have spent, usually by making a payment to the account each month. So for a customer who spends $2,000 on a credit card with a 2 percent cash back incentive, the card issuer will credit the card account with $40.

A related scheme is the use of loyalty points. Points are awarded each time the customer spends, which can then be exchanged for certain goods or services. Loyalty point schemes are less attractive to customers than equivalent value cash back schemes because points can only be exchanged for a limited range of goods. On the other hand, they have the advantage that the monetary value of the goods exchanged for reward points is usually less than the cost of the goods paid for by the card issuer. For example, loyalty points earned by American Express Nectar Credit Card customers in the UK, had a monetary value that could be used towards the purchase of goods at a wide range of stores including Amazon and Sainsbury's supermarkets. The cost of these goods to these retailers would have been somewhat lower than that paid by the customer, with the difference representing overheads and profit margin. Therefore, the cost of offering loyalty points, are in theory, lower than that for equivalent cash back schemes.

Many card providers offer customers an introductory interest rate for a number of months, with zero rate offers having become popular during the early-2000s. Balance transfers, where a borrower transfers debt from one credit product to another, can be attractive for both card issuers and their customers. For the customer, they allow debt from another credit agreement to be transferred automatically to the new product, allowing them to obtain more favorable terms for repaying their debt. For the card issuer, a balance transfer is a fast way for the customer to establish a sizable balance, which if it revolves will generate a significant income stream.

One side effect of the widespread use of low or zero rate introductory rates in conjunction with balance transfer facilities, is the practice of card surfing. A borrower will look to acquire a new card every time the introductory rate expires. In this way they can maintain a credit balance at little or no cost for a considerable period of time. Not surprisingly, credit providers do not tend to make money from these types of customers.

Payment holidays are offered for a variety of credit products including mortgages, loans and credit cards. A payment holiday allows the customer to miss one or more repayments without becoming delinquent. Sometimes payment holidays are built-in to the original credit offer, with the customer able to take one or more holidays at a time of their own choosing. In other situations they may be offered by the lender from time to time on an *ad-hoc* basis to encourage customer loyalty. In the short term a payment holiday will have a negative impact on cash flow due to repayments being delayed. However, taking a long term view, most lenders continue to charge interest over the term of the payment holiday and therefore a payment holiday will increase the total revenue generated over the life of the credit agreement.

Buy Now Pay Later (BNPL) is a feature of retail credit and mail order and can be considered analogous to a zero rate introductory credit card offer. Credit repayments are deferred for a number of months after which the customer begins paying as normal. A somewhat controversial alternative to BNPL is Buy Now Charge Later (BNCL). During the period of deferment, interest accrues even though the customer is making no payments (similar to a payment holiday). Therefore, the customer's balance may have grown significantly before loan repayments commence. The cost of BNPL and BNCL is represented in the cost of funds. If the cost of funds is 6 percent per year and the BNPL period is 4 months, then the cost of funds to provide the BNPL facility will be 2 percent of the value of the goods (6% * 4/12).

A further promotional lever for store card providers and mail order retailers is the offer of a discount on the first purchase. This is often around 10 percent of the purchase price for cards and between 10 and 20 percent for mail order. In some situations, a free gift, such as a toaster, kettle or MP3 player may be offered instead of, or as an alternative to, a discount.

6.3.3   Retention and attrition

Customers are not particularly loyal in credit markets. If a better offer comes along, most have no qualms about taking up the new product at the expense of their existing ones – the customer is said to attrite. Attrition is a particularly pronounced feature in card and mail order markets, but is also prevalent in the UK mortgage market, where short term fixed and discount rate offers are prolific.

The problem of attrition is often understated and overshadowed by the drive to acquire new customers. However, retaining profitable customers and preventing attrition can have big impacts on an organization's profitability. Reichheld (2001, p.36) quotes figures for the credit card industry where increasing retention rates by 5 percent, from say 90 to 95 percent per annum, leads to a 75 percent increase in profit over the lifetime of accounts. There are a number of reasons why increasing retention can have such a pronounced effect. First, the credit provider already has a relationship with the customer, with knowledge of their past behaviour when using the product. Therefore, marketing activity can be much more effectively targeted towards specific customer behaviours and the customer is much more likely to be interested in the lender's offers than the population at large. Second, the recruitment cost has already been expended when the customer was first recruited. Therefore, if a customer can be retained, this saves the lender the cost of recruiting a new customer from scratch. Third, customers of long standing, who do not have a history of default, are much less likely to default in the future than new customers. Therefore, the costs associated with bad debt and write-off are much reduced. Finally, long serving customers tend to generate higher revenues than new customers, either because they have built up large interest-bearing balances, or because they have moved to the lender's standard terms which are much more profitable than the introductory terms provided to new customers.

To reduce attrition, a lender will have in place a customer contact strategy based on actual and predicted customer behaviours. They will know from past experience the types of behaviour that indicate a customer may soon attrite and the actions that will prevent it. Profitable customers who they believe are more likely to attrite will be targeted with beneficial terms or special offers designed to keep them loyal. For example, if customer spending on a credit card is seen to reduce over time, then this may indicate that the customer is making greater use of a rival product. Therefore, the lender may have a policy in place to reduce the interest rate on the card for a period of time, and this could be communicated via the next statement or as a one-off communication such as an e-mail or telephone call. In this case the contact with the customer could also be used to promote any other products and services on offer.

Smart lenders will also know which customer groups are loss making and will actually encourage attrition for these types of customer. There are a number of ways of doing this, such as increasing the interest rate or other charges made for running the account or by excluding individuals from benefits offered across the wider customer base.

6.3.4   Cross-selling and up-selling

Most credit providers offer a range of financial products and services, and many credit users have more than one credit product. However, customers typically apply for credit on a piecemeal basis, perhaps applying for a credit card one month, a personal loan the next. Consequently, one goal for credit providers is to secure the largest possible 'share of wallet' from each customer; that is, to be the provider for as many of the customer's credit requirements as possible.

Cross-selling is where a customer who applies for one product is targeted for another one that they may also be interested in. Perhaps the most common example of cross-selling is the offer of a credit card to a personal loan or mortgage customer.

Up-selling is where it is believed that a better version of the product could be provided. For example, a customer with a high income and who is a good credit risk may apply for a standard credit card, when the lender would be quite willing to offer them a prestigious platinum card with a far higher credit limit. Another example would be to offer a customer who applied for a personal loan of say, $17,000 to buy a new car, a loan for a higher amount, say $20,000, by tempting them to spend on the next model up, or to use the additional funds to purchase something else such as a holiday.

6.4 Capital requirements

As discussed in section 6.2.5, there are always going to be some borrowers who fail to meet their repayment obligations, resulting in the write-off of some or all of their debts. To account for these losses organizations make provisions, setting aside funds to cover write-off expected to occur in the future. A core principle of provision calculation is the idea of expected loss – it's a 'best guess' of how much write-off will occur. Provision does not take into account unforeseen events that may cause losses to be greater (or less than) expected. So if interest rates rise unexpectedly and the economy falters, bad debt losses are likely to be higher than the amount provisioned for due people finding it more difficult to meet the increased interest charges on their loans. If an organization does not have sufficient funds (capital) to cover the additional losses, then it may face financial difficulty, possibly becoming insolvent. It therefore makes sense to put some additional capital aside to act as a safety net, just in case something unexpected occurs. This is especially important for deposit taking institutions that provide current account and savings products to ensure that depositors don't lose their funds when an organization encounters financial difficulty. The amount of extra capital that the regulatory authorities require an organization to set aside is termed its capital requirement.

The Basel II capital accord is an international agreement drawn up by the bank of international settlements based in Basel, Switzerland, and is implemented independently within each country's regulatory framework. The accord describes the way in which banking organizations must calculate the capital requirements they need to keep their risk of insolvency below acceptable levels. At the time of writing the accord is due to be implemented in all OECD countries by 2009. The accord is based on three core principles referred to as 'Pillars':

- Pillar 1. Minimum capital requirements. Pillar 1 concerns the capital required to cover unexpected losses to an organization's assets. For retail banking institutions the main assets used to calculate capital requirements are their credit portfolios. However, losses linked to other type of assets are also covered by capital requirements. For example, reductions in land/building values, devaluation of foreign currency holdings, and losses resulting from natural disasters and terrorism.

- Pillar 2. Regulatory response. This covers the role of banking regulators to ensure organizations maintain sufficient capital. Regulators are required to audit how organizations make their assessments of risk and hence their capital requirements. Regulators may specify that additional capital is needed to cover risks that an organization has not considered, or to address any shortcomings with the methods or data used in the capital requirements calculations.
- Pillar 3. Disclosure. This is concerned with the information that an organization must release to the market regarding its calculation of the risks it faces, and how it has calculated its capital requirements.

The full accord is long and complex (so complex that some people are now suggesting that a simpler capital requirements framework may be required). In addition, the accord is implemented independently within each region and therefore subject to differing interpretations depending where in the world an organization is based. Therefore, the rest of the discussion presented here is limited to only the most general principles of accord within the scope of capital requirements for credit risk; that is, consumer credit portfolios with the first pillar.

6.4.1   What is capital?

Capital is the value of assets, less any liabilities (Smullen and Hand 2008). Capital that can be used to meet capital requirements is categorized as the sum of tier I (core) and tier II (supplementary) capital. Tier I is the most important, and covers liquid assets that are readily available to cover losses (such as cash sitting in a bank account). It consists of shareholder equity and retained profits (Howells and Bain 2004, p.389), and is calculated as:

(The original value of shares issued) +
(Accumulated net profits after dividends have been paid) −
(Losses that have been incurred)

So if an organization issued $10,000 worth of shares, and then made net profits (after dividend payments) of $2,000 and $3,000 in the first two years of trading and a loss of $500 in the third, then the overall tier I capital would be $14,500.

Tier II covers a wide range of other assets that regulators allow to be included as capital, but are not so readily accessible as tier I. An example of tier II capital is a revaluated asset. A revaluated asset is something that has increased in value since its original purchase. For example, an office building may have been built on a cheap green field site many years ago and the value of the land has subsequently risen. The increase in land value would be classified as tier II capital. For the purpose of calculating capital requirements, at least 50 percent of an organizations capital must be tier I.

6.4.2　Assets, risk and risk weighted assets

Organizations have many different assets. The portfolio of debts held by a bank is an asset, as is cash, property, inventory, shares, foreign currency reserves, patent rights and so on. These assets are subject to risk; that is, there is a chance that something will happen resulting in an asset being devalued. The BASEL accord classifies risks into three types:

1. Credit risk. This covers losses that might arise due to debts being written-off. Six different categories of credit risk are defined by the accord. These are corporate, banks, equity, retail, project finance and sovereigns (Gup 2004). Consumer credit, including mortgages, personal loans and credit cards are included within the retail credit category.
2. Operational risk. Operational risk is the loss that could arise from internal or external events that may adversely affect an organization. An external event might be a natural disaster, lawsuit or an act of terrorism. An internal event could be a catastrophic failure of the organizations IT systems or industrial action taken by employees.
3. Market risk. This is the loss associated with changes in the value of financial instruments such as stock options, futures and foreign currency.

For some assets only a proportion of the asset may be at risk. Therefore, only a part of the asset's value is considered when deciding how much capital is required – the asset is said to be 'risk weighted'. Consider a building that's worth $10 million, including the land it's built on. Assume that if the building didn't exist, then the land would be worth $4 million and that for the sake of argument the land itself is not subject to any risk of devaluation, so whatever happens the land will always be worth $4 million. Therefore, although the building as it stands is worth $10 million, if it was completely destroyed only 60 percent of the building's value would be lost; i.e. $6 million. Therefore, an appropriate risk weight for the office building would be 60 percent and the asset would be described as having a risk weighted value of $6 million (Finlay 2008).

6.4.3 The Capital Ratio

The Capital Ratio is the key measure used to determine if an organization is maintaining sufficient capital. It is calculated as:

Capital Ratio = Total Capital / Total Value of Risk Weighted Assets

where the Total Value of Risk Weighted Assets includes credit risk, operational risk and market risk. Organizations must maintain sufficient capital such that the Capital Ratio is 8 percent or more. To put it another way, the total capital must be greater than or equal to the total value of risk weighted assets multiplied by 8 percent.

6.4.4 The standardized approach

The Basel II accord allows organizations to use one of three methods to calculate credit risk. These are:

- Standardized
- Foundation IRB
- Advanced IRB

The simplest is the standardized approach. Risk weights for each asset type are set by the regulatory authorities. For mortgage lending the risk weight is 0.35, so only 35 percent of the value of a mortgage portfolio

Table 6.4   Capital requirement calculation using the standardized approach

Asset	Asset value $m	Risk weight	Risk weighted asset value $m
Mortgages	10,500	0.35	3,675
Unsecured personal loans	2,100	0.75	1,575
Secured personal loans	560	0.75	420
Credit cards	3,800	0.75	2,100
Total	16,690		7,770
Capital requirement	621.6		

is considered. This is because the property can be repossessed and sold to recover the debt in cases of default and therefore the risk to the lender is small. So why are mortgages given a risk weight of 35 percent and not zero? The risk weight reflects the 'worst case scenario' in which property values fall considerably. Even if the economy enters recession and houses prices fall, it is unlikely that they will fall by more than 65 percent. Other types of consumer borrowing (credit cards, loans and so on) are allocated a risk weight of 75 percent.[11] Table 6.4 illustrates the capital calculation using the standardized approach.

In Table 6.4 the bank has a mortgage portfolio with a value of $10,500 million, which has a risk weighted asset value of $3,675. Likewise, the total value of all risk weighted assets is $7,770 million. Therefore, the capital requirement is $621.6 million ($7,770m * 8%).

6.4.5   IRB approaches

The standardized approach is a 'one size fits all' methodology. It is deliberately conservative in order to minimize the risk of organizations having insufficient capital. If an organization has a good quality consumer credit portfolio with a very low risk of defaults, then the standardized approach will result in more capital held than is required. The foundation IRB and advanced IRB approaches provide a more flexible framework that allows organizations to generate their own assessment of credit risk. The regulatory risk weightings used for the standardized approach are replaced by an organization's internal assessment of risk weighted asset value. The calculation of risk weighted asset value is based on three components.

- The probability of default (PD). This is the likelihood that a customer will be in arrears with their repayments in 12 months' time.
- The exposure at default (EAD). This is the amount of the outstanding debt at the point when an account defaults. The EAD includes the current balance, plus any additional credit that may potentially be advanced prior to default, less any expected payments made by the customer before default.
- The loss given default (LGD). This is the proportion of the exposure at default that is expected to be written-off, less any recoveries that occur after write-off has occurred. For example, from litigation or the sale of the debt to a third party debt collection company.

The expected loss (EL) over a 12 month period is then calculated as:

$$EL = PD * EAD * LGD$$

So the expected loss is the probability that a loan defaults, multiplied by the value of the debt at the time when default occurs, multiplied by the proportion of the default value that is eventually written-off. In theory EL should be a similar amount to that which an organization has provisioned for, but in practice the two values will differ due to the different methods of calculation that are applied for provision and capital requirements respectively. As an example of the EL calculation, consider a credit card customer for whom the following estimates have been made:

- The expected probability of default within the next 12 months is 3 percent (PD = 3%).
- The expected balance on the card should the customer default is estimated to be $8,000 (EAD = $8,000).
- Should the customer default, the organization expects to recover 40 percent of the debt via collections and debt recovery. The remaining 60 percent is expected to be written-off (LGD = 60%).

the expected loss will be 3% * $8,000 * 60% = $144. To arrive at a capital requirements figure, the expected loss figure is adjusted to take into account the worst case scenario'. This is defined as the risk that is likely to occur only once in every 1,000 years (99.9 percent chance that it won't occur in any one year). The expected loss figure is multiplied by a suitable factor to generate a capital requirements value. So if the required factor was say, 3,[12] then the amount of capital required to be put aside would be $144 * 3 = $432. This compares with $480 (8% * $8,000 * 75%) that would be required using the standardized approach.

To apply the foundation IRB approach, organizations calculate their own estimates of PD. The regulatory authorities then provide the other two measures; that is, EAD and LGD. To calculate PD the accord requires accounts to be grouped into a number of risk grades. The average probability of default is then calculated for each grade, based on historic default rates within each grade over a period of five years or so. All accounts currently within each risk grade are then assumed to have the same probability of defaulting. It is up to each organization to decide how it should assign risk grades, but organizations must be able to demonstrate to the regulatory authorities that their method is sound. The most common approach is to use statistically derived scoring models of customer repayment behaviour (similar to those discussed in Chapter 7).[13] Each account is assigned a score representative of the risk that the account represents, and these scores are then used to assign accounts to appropriate risk grades.[14]

With the advanced IRB approach organizations provide their own estimates for all three components; that is, PD, EAD and LGD, with various statistical modelling techniques used to generate EAD and LGD.

It is important to note that the regulatory authorities lay down strict requirements about how each component of expected loss is calculated and stressed, and this requires organizations to hold large amounts of very detailed historic information about the behaviour of their credit portfolios if they wish to apply an IRB approach. The cost of upgrading IT systems to meet the requirements of advanced IRB can be very extensive and take a considerable period of time to complete. Therefore, while in theory the advanced IRB approach may result in lower capital requirements, many organizations have simply chosen to adopt the standardized or foundation IRB approach for reasons of operational simplicity.

See the BASEL committees guidance notice (Bank for International Settlements 2005) for a more complete description of calculating credit risk using IRB approaches.

6.5 Securitization

Securitization is a way to use illiquid assets to raise new capital quickly. At the same time it facilitates removing (potentially risky) assets from the balance sheet – hence offering a quick way of reducing an organization's capital requirement. By illiquid I mean an asset, such as a portfolio of credit cards or personal loans, that has value, but the value can not be realized easily. For example, it is possible for a lender to sell all or part of its personal loan portfolio to another organization. However, there is no pre-existing market in personal loan portfolios. Therefore, such a sale would require the lender to seek potential buyers and enter into negotiation with them. This is a long winded and costly exercise, with no guarantee that at the end of the process a suitable buyer will be found.

Securitization of consumer credit portfolios became increasingly popular in the 1990s and 2000s, with many organizations using it as an easy way to raise new capital that could be used to fund further lending. The basic process of securitizing an asset is as follows:

1. An organization (termed the originator) sets up a fund or trust that is a separate legal entity. This fund is referred to as a Special Purpose Vehicle (SPV). As separate legal entities the originator has no liability for any losses that the SPV incurs.
2. The originator sells the assets it wants to securitize to the SPV. This provides funds that the originator can lend to new customers.
3. The SPV sells bonds to investors. Net revenues generated by the asset are distributed amongst the bondholders.
4. The SPV pays the originator fees to maintain the securitized assets. In the case of consumer credit portfolios, this covers things like processing payments, issuing statements, chasing late payers and so on.

From a customer perspective, the securitization process is completely invisible. They will continue to deal with the originator in the same manner as they have always done, and the SPV has no involvement in the day to day management of individual customer accounts.

The bonds issued by SPVs generate regular income for bondholders, but are themselves tradable instruments. If the value of securitized assets rise, maybe because the default rates within a portfolio are lower than expected, resulting in greater income for the bondholder, then the value of the bonds will rise and the bondholder may profit from the sale of the bond to someone else. However, the converse is also true. If the value of securitized assets fall, then bondholders are left nursing a potential loss. This is one of the key features of the US subprime mortgage collapse that occurred in the US in 2006/7 and the worldwide credit crunch that followed. Mortgage providers securitized large amounts of poor quality sub-prime mortgages, whose value was widely overrated. When the US housing market collapsed the value of securitized assets fell dramatically, leaving bond holders with substantial losses.

6.6   Chapter summary

Credit providers generate revenue from a number of sources, which include:

- Arrangement and annual fees.
- Interest.

- Interchange fees.
- Insurance products which include:
  - Income protection.
  - Critical illness cover.
  - Payment protection.
  - Card protection.
  - Mortgage indemnity insurance.
- Late fees and penalty charges.

While interest is perhaps the cost foremost in the minds of borrowers, for many credit providers a significant part of their profits comes from other sources, particularly the selling of insurance and the charging of late fees and penalty charges. These additional charges tend to feature less in advertising material than interest rates, and are generally given little attention by consumers. Therefore, many lenders see increasing existing charges or introducing new ones as a better way to increase revenues than increasing interest rates. The major costs incurred by credit providers in supplying their products are:

- Cost of funds.
- Bad debt (and provision).
- Fraud.
- Promotion and advertising, including the costs of incentives such as loyalty points, interest-free periods and discount offers. This also includes targeting existing customers to retain their business and thus reduce the incidence of attrition.
- Application processing.
- Infrastructure costs comprising, capital expenditure, depreciation and day to day running costs.

Of these costs, the two most significant by far are the cost of funds and the cost of bad debt. Between them they can account for more than 70 percent of the total cost of credit provision for some credit products.

6.7   Suggested sources of further information

Evans, D. and Schmalensee R. (2005). *Paying With Plastic. The Digital Revolution in Buying and Borrowing*. The MIT Press. This book provides a lot of information about the cost structure for card accounts and the economics of operating credit card and charge card accounts in the US.

Tapp, A. (2004). *Principles of Direct and Database Marketing*. FT Prentice Hall. Tapp provides a comprehensive introduction to database marketing – the prospecting technique most widely used by financial service providers. The book includes many practical examples and case studies, many of which relate to consumer credit.

Bank for International Settlements (2005). *An Explanatory Note on the BASEL II IRB Risk Weight Functions*. Basel. This provides a guide to calculating credit risk for BASEL II using the two IRB approaches.

7
Credit Granting Decisions

In an ideal world, every borrower would repay their debts on time and lenders would earn a living from the interest and other income earned over the lifetime of the relationship. In the real world however, there is an inherent risk that a borrower will not repay the credit advanced to them. This could be for any one of a number of reasons, ranging from poor financial management or loss of employment, to family breakdown or death. A credit business will only be profitable if the return from those that repay their debts exceeds the losses where default has occurred. Therefore, when someone applies for credit, a lender needs to be able evaluate their creditworthiness, and only lend to them if there is a good chance that they will repay the loan.

In this chapter the methods used by commercial lending organizations to evaluate creditworthiness are discussed. The first part of the chapter describes how creditworthiness is defined. The second part of the chapter compares and contrasts the two main methods that are used to assess creditworthiness: judgemental decision making and credit scoring.

7.1 The creditworthy customer

In the insurance market it is impossible to determine categorically whether the property or life insured will result in a claim. An actuary will make an estimate of the likelihood of a claim being made based on their experience of a large number of past claims. The same principle applies to credit. Presented with a single person's details, it is impossible to say with certainty whether or not they will repay any credit advanced to them. Therefore, credit managers attempt to estimate the likelihood of repayment. Applications from people who have a good chance of repaying the loan, and hence make a positive contribution to profits, are accepted. Those deemed to be too high a risk are declined and are of no further interest at that point in time.

The decision to grant credit (or insurance) can be viewed as a forecasting problem, no different in principle from predicting what the weather will be like tomorrow or the level of interest rates this time next year. In the case of weather forecasting, meteorologists gather and analyse historical information about air pressure, wind patterns, temperature and so on, in order to establish how conditions on one day affect conditions on another. They then use information about these types of relationships to forecast the weather tomorrow or next week, based on the readings taken today. In the credit granting case, credit managers gather information about the demographics of individuals, their current financial situation and previous credit history and use this to make predictions about future repayment behaviour.

In credit granting the term risk is used to refer to the relationship between the expected return from customers who repay the credit advanced to them and the losses that result from those that do not. Acceptable risk is where the overall expected return is positive; that is, the expected return from those that repay their debts outweighs losses from those that default. Consider the case of a bank offering personal loans. If a loan is repaid in full the bank makes a return on its investment equal to 8 percent of the original loan amount. Should a borrower default, the bank incurs a 100 percent loss – the entire loan is written-off.[1] Imagine that someone applies to the bank for a loan of $10,000. If they repay the loan, then the bank will make a return on its investment equal to:

$$\$10,000 * 8\% = \$800.$$

but if they default then the loss incurred by the bank will be equal to:

$$\$10,000 * 100\% = \$10,000.$$

Should the bank grant the loan in this situation? Assume that by using information that is known about the applicant the bank can estimate that the risk or odds that the individual will default on the loan is say 19:1; that is, out of 20 similar individuals 19 would be expected to repay the loan and one would be expected to default. In this case, the return that the bank can expect to make can be calculated as:

$800 * 19   = $15,200 –   (Total expected return)
$10,000 * 1   = $10,000   (Total expected loss)
  = $ 5,200
$5,200/(19 + 1)   = $260   (Average expected return per loan)

So for a single loan of $10,000 the bank will either make $800 or lose $10,000, but averaged over a large number of similar loans, the expected return will be $260 per loan. Being a positive amount the risk is acceptable – the bank should grant the loan. But what if the odds calculated by the bank were lower than 19:1? Obviously, there will be a point below which the bank will not expect to make a return on their investment, and in these situations any loan applications should be declined. The break even or cut-off odds are the odds where the expected return will be zero. If the odds of the applicant defaulting are less than the cut-off odds then the expected return will be negative and the application should be declined. If the odds are higher than the cut-off odds then the expected return will be positive and the application should be accepted. The cut-off odds for the loan example are given by:

$$\text{Cut-off odds} = \frac{\text{Expected loss (from a customer who defaults)}}{\text{Expected return (from a customer who repays)}}$$
$$= \$10,000/\$800 = 12.5{:}1$$

So the bank should accept loan applications where the odds are above 12.5:1 (these customers are creditworthy) and reject applications where the odds are below 12.5:1 (these customers are uncreditworthy). Although all mainstream lenders use similar information in the decision making process, such as the applicant's occupational status, type of residence, income and so on, each has their own method of calculating the associated odds, with some being better at it than others. Different organizations also operate at different levels of profitability, have different cost bases and different management and accounting practices. Therefore, for any one individual, the assessment of the odds and expected return will vary between lenders and even between different products offered by the same lender. This is why some people find that they can obtain credit from one lender, but not from another. When a lender talks about whether or not someone is creditworthy, what they mean is that the odds of default that they have calculated for that individual are above or below the cut-off odds that they use to make lending decisions.

In practice, the cut-off odds used by different lenders range from less than 2:1 in the sub-prime sections of the market, to over 40:1 for the choicest credit cards and personal loans. Although it is difficult to quote precise figures, the average cut-off odds in the unsecured lending market are probably in the region of 10:1. What this means is that for groups where the average odds are below this level, say 8:1, eight potential customers who would have repaid the loan profitably will be rejected for every one default case that's rejected. From a lender's point of view this is a reasonable policy because they will lose money if they accept applications with odds at this level. From a societal perspective, this is the main reason that only about 5 percent of the UK population has a proven record of serious arrears (Experian 2005), but around 20 percent are denied credit by mainstream lending institutions (Whyley and Brooker 2004, p.10).

7.2 The application for credit

In order to be able to make any quantifiable assessment of risk, a lender needs to obtain information about the applicant, just as weather forecasters require meteorological data to make their predictions. The primary source of this information comes from the answers given by the applicant during the application process. This can come from a variety of channels, such as the internet or a paper application form, but regardless of its source, the applicant generally provides the lender with the same information. Part of a typical paper-based personal loan application form is shown in Figure 7.1.

Beyond the basic details required to open and run the account, such as name, address, loan amount requested and so on, the majority of the other questions are asked because they are useful for assessing the applicant's risk. From a marketing perspective the key objective is to provide the most seamless interface possible between the applicant's desire for the product and the credit agreement being signed – the less questions asked the better. On the other hand, a credit risk professional will always be interested in asking additional questions that will provide a better estimate of the applicant's risk. Therefore, in many organizations there exists a balance of forces between the credit and marketing functions in determining the number and type of questions presented to the applicant.

What is perhaps surprising is how constant and homogeneous the questions asked by lenders have remained over time, across products

Blueberry Bank
Personal Loan Application Form

Please tell us about yourself

First name:		Home phone number:	
Surname:		Work phone number:	
Address:		Mobile:	
		e-mail address:	@
	Postcode		
Date of Birth: (DD/MM/YYYY)	/ /	Nationality:	

What is your residential status? Owner ☐ Private tenant ☐ Council tenant ☐ Living with parents/relatives ☐

If you own your own home, what is the approximate value of your home? £ [ ] Outstanding mortgage £ [ ]

Time living at current address (YY/MM) [/] Previous address if less than 3 years [ ]

Time living at previous address if less than 3 years at current address (YY/MM) [/]

Postcode [ ]

Are you: Married ☐ Single ☐ Widowed ☐ Cohabiting ☐ Divorced/Separated ☐

Number of children [ ] How many cars are there in your household [ ] Total annual milage (approx) [ ]

Please tell us about your emploment and financial status

Employment status: Full-time ☐ Part-time ☐ Unemployed ☐ Retired ☐ Homemaker ☐ Student ☐

Are you: Self employed ☐ In temporary employment ☐ In permanent employment ☐

Employer's name:		Employer's phone number:	
Employer's address:		Time in current Employment (YY/MM)	
	Postcode	Gross annual income: (Including overtime and bonuses)	£
Your occupation		Partners annual income: (Including overtime and bonuses)	£

How much do you pay each month for your mortage/rent/board? £ [ ]

How much council tax do you pay each month? £ [ ]

How much do you pay for utilities each month (gas, electricity and water)? £ [ ]

Do you have a credit card (Y/N) [ ] How many do you have? [ ]

Do you have a bank account (Y/N) [ ] How long have you had one (YY/MM)? [/]

Loan details

Amount of loan requested £ [ ] Term of loan (YY/MM) [/]

This is a credit agreement regulated by the Consumer Credit Act 1974. Sign it only if you want to be legally bound by its terms.

Signature of applicant

X

/ /
Date of Signature (DD/MM/YYYY)

Your right to cancel. Once you have signed the agreement, you will have for a short time a right to cancel it. Exact details of how and when you can do this will be sent to you by post by us.

For and on behalf of Blueberry Bank Limited

Figure 7.1 Personal loan application form

and countries. An underwriter from 1950s America would find many common features with the application forms of their time and those used today in the UK and many other countries. Of course there have been some changes and lenders do ask product specific questions. However, one could speculate that although there have been huge strides in the marketing, diversity and complexity of credit products, the characteristics of the borrower which are predictive of risk have remained relatively static and are not necessarily specific to a particular credit product or country.

Having obtained some information about the customer and their circumstances, there are two broad approaches to evaluating the risk of a credit application; judgemental decision making and credit scoring.

7.3 Judgemental decision making

Until the early 1980s the majority of lending decisions where made judgementally on a case-by-case basis by human underwriters, trained to assess the creditworthiness of individuals applying for credit. For high value credit agreements such as a mortgage or an unsecured fixed term loan, this could involve a lengthy face-to-face meeting between the applicant and a representative of the lender, qualified in an underwriting capacity, such as the local branch manager. In the banking sector it was not uncommon for the bank's representative to actually know the borrower and to have personal knowledge of their accounts, employment, family situation and so on. Where an application was made by post, such as for a mail order account, the application would be assessed by a member of the organization's underwriting team. In each case the aim of the underwriter was to come to a somewhat subjective view as to whether or not the individual was creditworthy.

Decisions were made on the basis of the underwriter's personal assessment of the likelihood of the applicant repaying the debt. At the core of the decision making process was the concept of the 'Cs' of credit as described by Savery (1977):

- Capital and Collateral. The assets, such as a home or car, available to be offered as security against the debt.
- Capacity. The ability to meet the agreed loan repayments, taking into account the applicant's existing income and expenditure.
- Character. The intent to repay and general 'respectability' of the applicant.

- Conditions. The general market conditions at the time. This would include the general economic climate as well as the specific conditions of the industry within which an individual was employed.

To establish if each of the Cs were satisfied, an underwriter would examine the information supplied by the applicant, which might then be combined with a credit report from a credit reference agency detailing the applicant's repayment record with other lenders. They would then use their intuition and experience to make a decision.

As credit organizations developed, it was common practice for the accumulated wisdom of the senior underwriters to be distilled into a formal statement of lending practice. The 'Policy' would contain, in the form of a document or manual, the rules underwriters should follow when making lending decisions. Typical policy rules would be along the following lines:

- Do not lend to anyone under 21, unless they have been employed for at least two years with the same employer OR they can provide the guarantee of a parent or guardian.
- Accept all applications from individuals who have obtained credit from the company in the past and whose repayment record was satisfactory.
- The maximum allowable loan for someone earning a salary of between $60,000 and $80,000 is $20,000.

In some organizations the policy would be a simple list of absolutes, such as those who should never be granted credit under any circumstances, and this list might be contained on a single sheet of paper. In others, the policy would be very detailed indeed, running to hundreds of rules dealing with almost any conceivable situation. Although these policy documents lent a certain level of consistency to the practice of underwriting compared to what went before, they tended to be difficult to manage and had a tendency to grow over time as new rules were added, and contradictions between different rules was not unknown. In branch-based networks there were often issues of consistency with some branches using different versions of the policy or interpreting certain aspects of policy in different ways.

The balance between the use of the policy and the underwriters' own judgement would vary enormously between institutions. In some the underwriter was king, with decisions based entirely on their expert opinion. In others, they would act in little more than an administrative capacity, ensuring the policy was followed to the letter and only referring applications to senior underwriters in unusual or ambiguous cases.

7.4 Credit scoring

The later stages of the twentieth century saw credit scoring become the major decision making tool used in consumer credit markets. Today, all major financial institutions in the developed world use credit scoring to make the vast majority of consumer lending decisions, with only small or specialized lenders maintaining a majority judgemental decision making capability (Hand and Henley 1997).

Credit scoring can be defined as: '*any quantitative method, technique or practice used in the granting, management or recovery of consumer credit.*' As such, credit scoring is not a singular technique, nor is it represented by a single objective. Rather, it is the application of a range of analytical techniques concerned with the analysis of large and complex data sets, customized to the specific set of conditions found in the consumer credit environment (Finlay 2006b). Under this definition, there is an argument that the rules contained within an organization's underwriting policy do in fact constitute a credit scoring system that could be implemented within some type of computerized rule base. However, the real power and impact of credit scoring is that whereas judgemental decision making involves making qualitative assessments of credit risk, credit scoring methods use and generate quantitative measures; that is, a number that can be directly interpreted as a measure of creditworthiness, or some other aspect of consumer behaviour. This leads to systems that can be readily automated, resulting in the removal of human involvement from the day-to-day decision making processes. It is the automated nature of credit scoring systems, together with their ability to provide improved estimates of creditworthiness that has had the biggest impact on the way in which credit is granted since information technology was first introduced within financial institutions in the 1960s.

The first investigation into the use of statistical techniques for credit assessment was undertaken by Durand (1941) for the National Bureau of Economic Research in the US, and the first reported commercial use of credit scoring was at the General Finance Corporation in Chicago in 1945, where a system was developed to assess the creditworthiness of personal loan applicants (Wonderlic 1952). However, it took the financial services industry a significant period of time to adopt credit scoring as their major decision making tool and until the early 1960s credit scoring models were not widely used (Myers and Forgy 1963). At the US Senate hearing on redlining (financial exclusion based on address) in 1979, it was estimated by William Fair, president of Fair Isaac & Co., that 20–30 percent of lending decisions in the US made use of credit scoring (U.S. Senate 1979). A 1990 survey reported a figure of 82 percent (Rosenberg and Gleit 1994), indicating the major growth period in the use of credit scoring systems in the US occurred during the 1980s.

Credit scoring models (often referred to as credit scorecards) are used to generate forecasts of future customer behaviour. Given what is known about the customer today, how will they behave in the future? In this respect the objective of a credit scorecard is no different from the judgemental case in that it is based on the same information about the applicant and has the same goal of identifying only those individuals who are likely to be creditworthy. The critical difference is that whereas an underwriter's decision is based on a somewhat subjective view and can take into account aspects of the applicant such as their 'character,' credit scoring is based on mathematical relationships and demonstrates consistent behaviour. Given the same information twice, a credit scoring system will always generate the same estimate of risk on both occasions. In general, this cannot be said to be true for the judgemental method.

Although the methods for generating scorecards can be complex and require a certain level of mathematical grounding, the scorecards generated by most credit scoring techniques are in a form that can be readily interpreted by the layperson. In fact, this is an explicit design feature adopted by many credit scoring practitioners to enable them to explain their results to a senior management that does not necessarily have the technical background required to understand them. An example of a typical scorecard is shown in Figure 7.2.

The basic principle is to assign some rating, or score, to an individual based on the information that is known about them at the time of application. The score is then taken as indicative of the future behaviour of the applicant; that is, the likelihood that the applicant will prove to be an acceptable risk. In general, the higher the score the lower the risk, and therefore the greater the likelihood of the applicant making a positive contribution to profit should the loan be granted.

For the scorecard of Figure 7.2, the points are assigned by taking the constant as the base score, then adding or subtracting the scores for each attribute. Consider an applicant with the following characteristics:

- 38 years old.
- Home owner who has lived at their present address for three years.

- Income of $135,000 per year.
- Self-employed for the last five years.
- Has a credit card.

The initial score would be 900, as represented by the constant. Five points would then be added for the applicant's age, 46 added for being a home owner, nine points deducted for the time at current address and so on, to give a final score of 956. What is important to note is that the score is not reliant on any one attribute but represents the overall contribution from each aspect of the applicant's profile. Therefore, a low score with one attribute (such as being 18–21 years old) can be offset by another (being a home owner for example).

Constant	+900		

Age of applicant		Number of dependents	
18–21	−54	0	0
22–25	−33	1–2	+5
26–29	−7	3+	0
30–34	0		
35–39	+5	**Employment status**	
40–55	+15	Full-time employed	0
56+	+27	Part-time employed	−23
		Self employed	−11
		Homemaker	−21
Residential status		Student	−48
Home owner	+46	Unemployed	−85
Renting	−12		
Living with parents	0		

Time at current address		Time in current employment	
< 1 year	−70	< 1 year	−68
1–2 years	−25	1–2 years	−19
3–5 years	−9	3–4 years	0
6–9 years	0	5–7 years	0
10+ years	+10	6–10 years	0
		11–15 years	+7
		20+ years	+12
Annual income $		Not in employment	0
120,000+	+12		
90,000–119,999	+9	**Do you have a credit card?**	
40,000–89,999	0	Yes	+13
30,000–39,999	−29	No	−39
0–29,999	−49		

Figure 7.2 Example of a credit scorecard

7.4.1   Using the score to make decisions

A sensible question to ask at this point is, what does a score such as 956 actually mean? The usual approach is to observe accounts for a period of time and then to classify them as 'good' or 'bad' credit risks, based on their behaviour over that period. Simplistically, loans that are repaid in full will be classified as good, and those that are written-off will be classified as bad. In practice, however, definitions of good and bad are more subtle. The UK industry guide to credit scoring defines a 'good' account as *'an account where the record of repayment is such that the credit granter would choose to accept the applicant again'* (Finance and Leasing Association 2000), which can be taken to mean that good accounts are those that the lender believes generated a positive contribution to profits, bad those that incurred a loss. In practice, every lender has their own definition of good/bad due to differing overheads, operational procedures and accounting practices, as well as the subjective views of individual credit managers as to what constitutes a good or bad account. However, most definitions of good and bad are along the following lines:

- Good: An account that has been on the books for a reasonable period of time, is currently up-to-date with repayments and has a record of repayment to the repayment schedule. Most lenders will also classify accounts that have missed the odd payment, but which have never been seriously in arrears as good.
- Bad: An account where the customer is in a state of serious arrears, where serious is usually taken to be three months or more behind with repayments. Why three months? Because accounts this far in arrears will nearly always continue to experience repayment problems and will usually end up being written-off eventually.

Earlier in this chapter the odds of a customer defaulting were defined as the ratio of non-default cases to default cases. The good:bad odds are a similar measure, defined as the ratio of good accounts to bad accounts within a population:

$$\text{Good:bad odds} = \frac{(\text{Number of good cases in the population})}{(\text{Number of bad cases in the population})}$$

The good:bad odds is one of the most common measures used by credit professionals when assessing consumer credit portfolios. Most credit scorecards are designed so that each score relates to a specific value of good:bad odds, and the relationship between score and

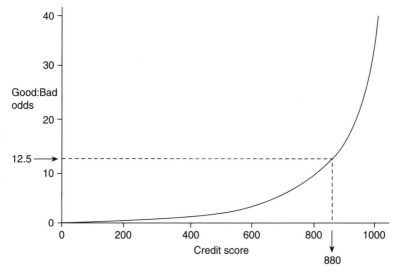

Figure 7.3   Relationship between the good:bad odds and score

good:bad odds is such that the higher the score the higher the odds. So, for example, a score of 500 may equate to good:bad odds of 2:1 and a score of 800 to good:bad odds of 10:1. When a new application is made and receives a credit score, if the good:bad odds associated with that score are below that which the lender deems creditworthy the application will be declined. The decision as to what this score should be is termed the acceptance cut-off strategy. To determine what the acceptance cut-off strategy should be it is necessary to establish the relationship between the score and good:bad odds. The most common way to do this is to calculate the credit score for a large sample of existing accounts for which the good/bad status is already known, and then to plot the relationship between the credit score and the good:bad odds, as shown in Figure 7.3.

Returning to the personal loan example of section 7.1 where the cut-off odds were determined to be 12.5:1, the point where these odds apply is a score of 880. Therefore, the acceptance cut-off strategy is:

- Decline if applicant scores at or below 879.
- Accept if applicant scores at or above 880.

A further report that is widely used is the score distribution report, as shown in Table 7.1.

Table 7.1   A score distribution report

Score interval:		Number of good accounts	Number of bad accounts	Interval good:bad odds	Total number of accounts	Total %
From	To					
0	425	27,709	22,291	1.24	50,000	10%
426	645	36,671	13,329	2.75	50,000	10%
646	732	42,185	7,815	5.40	50,000	10%
733	789	42,983	7,017	6.12	50,000	10%
790	847	44,521	5,479	8.13	50,000	10%
848	895	46,904	3,096	12.55	50,000	10%
896	945	47,624	2,376	20.05	50,000	10%
946	960	48,228	1,772	27.22	50,000	10%
961	981	48,603	1,397	34.79	50,000	10%
982	999	48,806	1,194	40.87	50,000	10%
Total		434,234	65,766	6.41	500,000	100%

Although the score distribution report of Table 7.1 could contain a separate row for every individual score, because the range of scores can be large, scores are usually grouped into several intervals for convenience. The interval odds can then be calculated, as shown in the third column from the right. The score distribution report is used in addition to the graph of the score/odds relationship of Figure 7.3 because it provides additional information, such as the number of accounts at different scores, which is important operationally for establishing how many applicants are likely to be accepted from those that apply. It is also useful where an organization wishes to make decisions regarding the absolute number of applications accepted, or to accept a fixed proportion of those that apply. For example, if it was desired to operate a policy of accepting 70 percent of all new applications, then from Table 7.1 the appropriate action would be to accept all applications scoring 733 or more and decline all those scoring less than 733. This type of strategy is common for new products, where the primary objective is to secure market share. The acceptance of some customer segments that may be loss making is seen as an acceptable short term cost in meeting this objective.

7.4.2 Choosing the outcome period

An important question for the developers of credit scoring systems is, over what outcome period should accounts be observed before the good/bad classification is applied? The obvious answer is to simply wait until the end of the credit agreement. However, in many situations this is not a realistic option. A 20+ year mortgage is common and it is impractical to wait 20 years before observing whether an account is good or bad. For revolving credit products such as credit cards and mail order accounts, there is no fixed end date to the agreement. Accounts remain active for as long as the customer continues to use them or for as long as the lender wishes to trade with the customer. Another issue is that the longer the outcome period the worse any forecast is likely to be. Returning to the weather example, tomorrow's forecast will always be more reliable than the one for next week. Similarly, estimates of credit risk are much more robust over timeframes spanning a year or so compared to those spanning several years. Therefore, the precise choice of outcome period is something of a compromise. It must be long enough to capture general patterns of customer behaviour and yet short enough to be of practical use. In practice, most outcome periods tend to be in the region of 6–24 months and in my experience 9–15 months is the norm for credit cards, mail order and short term lending, while for mortgages and personal loans 12–24 months is more widely applied. While this is not sufficient time to fully evaluate repayment behaviour over the entire term of most credit agreements, it is generally sufficient to gain a reasonable picture of an individual's repayment behaviour.

7.5 Comparing judgemental lending and credit scoring

Human decision making and credit scoring can be compared in a number of areas. The original use of credit scoring was supported by research reporting that a well-constructed credit score gave a better estimate of risk than a judgemental assessment made by an experienced underwriter (Myers and Forgy 1963). Yet there are few, if any, independent studies which can be said to have compared credit scoring and judgemental lending in a truly objective manner in an operational lending environment, for example, by running a credit scoring system and a manually based underwriting system in parallel, with new applications randomly allocated to one method or the other.

Another criticism of the comparisons that have been made is that they have usually been between a newly designed credit scoring system and an existing underwriting system. A fairer comparison would consider reviewing the underwriting guidelines, as contained in the organization's policy, and comparing the revised policy with the new credit scoring system. However, the accumulated research evidence lends support to the view that credit scoring out-performs judgemental lending, and statements made before the US Senate by the Fair Isaac Corporation, one of the industry's leading credit scoring suppliers, asserted that the introduction of a credit scoring system to replace a judgemental one would lead to an increase in the number of accepted applications of the order of 20–30 percent with no increase in the amount of bad debt (Fair Isaac Corporation 2003, p.5). If true, then for large organizations booking billions of dollars of business a year this clearly represents a significant benefit. One way to verify the accuracy of this claim might be to question lenders to determine when credit scoring was introduced within their organizations, and then to examine their financial accounts before and after credit scoring was introduced to see what changes had occurred.

The other and perhaps most significant impact of credit scoring on business processes has been the centralization and automation of the decision making process, particularly for organizations that maintain large branch networks such as the high street banks. With judgemental lending it becomes almost impossible to coordinate operational changes to lending policy. For example, if it is felt that the business should reduce the overall volume of lending by 10 percent, how is this communicated and acted upon by individual underwriters (who may actually be incentivized on the amount of business they underwrite)? With most credit scoring systems this strategy would be implemented centrally by simply adjusting the cut-off strategy upwards by the appropriate amount. In the case of Table 7.1, changing the acceptance rate from 70 to 60 percent would simply result in the cut-off score changing from 732 to 789.

The automated nature of credit scoring systems leads to rapid decision making, allowing a decision about an individual credit application to made in seconds. A credit application today, can be assessed in real time in a store, over the phone or via the internet. In the 1970s you could often expect to wait days or weeks before a decision was made while your credit application sat in an underwriter's in-tray. Automation also leads to lower costs through reduced staffing levels, although some of these savings are offset against the infrastructure costs associated with credit scoring systems and the new breed of professionals required to maintain them.

Credit scoring is consistent and repeatable. For credit practitioners there is the well-known industry tale of the 'Monday morning, Friday afternoon' effect. One lending institution found that their underwriters consistently granted more loans on a Friday afternoon, when they were feeling good about the weekend, than on Monday morning after returning to work. Yet reviews of the loan business found no difference in the quality of applicants at different times of the week. The repeatability aspect also means that if a customer wants to know why they were rejected for credit an objective statement can be given based on the scores in the scorecard. Returning to the scorecard of Figure 7.2, people who have been in their current employment less than 12 months are scored negatively and this can be quoted as a contributing factor for decline, along with any other characteristics that also resulted in a reduced score.

Credit scoring is often quoted as being unprejudiced, with no particular likes or dislikes in terms of race, sex, religion or any other conscious or unconscious feeling that may be expressed by a human assessor. This does not mean credit scoring does not discriminate against certain people, but any discrimination is supported by statistical evidence. There is also the possibility that undesirable discrimination occurs via indirect effects. For example, a credit scorecard may be restricted so not to allocate different scores based on an applicant's gender. However, if people with lower incomes receive negative scores, then women, who in the UK earn significantly less than men across almost all occupational groups and industry sectors (Perfect and Hurrell 2003) will, other things being equal, receive lower scores than their male counterparts. It is also worth noting that there is nothing to prevent a scorecard produced by statistical means being manipulated prior to implementation. For the scorecard in Figure 7.2, if it was felt that people who described their marital status as 'cohabiting' to be undesirable, then a large negative score, say –100, could be allocated for these cases. Whether this type of manipulation is widespread or not is unknown, as there have never been any published audits of commercial credit scoring systems. However, an example of where this type of activity was proposed, was when a representative of a well-known organization for whom a scorecard was being developed, asked me to ensure that the scorecard generated very low scores for anyone of a certain nationality.[2]

The main downside of credit scoring is its reliance upon the information from which the original credit scoring system was constructed. If there are certain types of application that were not considered or not available at the time the system was developed, these cases will not be assessed in an optimal capacity. Often this will affect small groups within the population who are overshadowed by the characteristics of the majority. For example, most credit scoring systems will give low scores to people who have not lived very long at their address, have recently started a new job, rent instead of own, or do not have some previous credit history. While this is a justifiable strategy for the general population, professional people who have moved to another country to take up new employment will possess all of these characteristics and will tend to be declined when they apply for credit due to a low credit score. This is probably not representative of the true risk they represent.

7.6 The case against credit scoring

Although credit scoring is now widely accepted, this was not always the case, and several arguments were put forward against its use. Harter (1974) argued that credit scoring systems were self-perpetuating and biased, with those being rejected for credit being more likely to be rejected when making subsequent applications. The counter argument, presented by Chandler and Coffman (1979), was that one would expect scoring systems to have less bias than judgemental systems because there are at least some attempts, via reject inference (the process of estimating how rejected applications would have behaved if they had been accepted) to adjust for the bias. Empirical evidence from the UK shows that lending increased dramatically between 1990 and 2000, both in terms of amounts borrowed and the number of people with access to a credit facility (Kempson 2002, p.16). Given this was the period when credit scoring became the dominant force in credit assessment in the UK this would tend to discount Harter's arguments.

Capon (1982) argued primarily on moral grounds against the use of *'brute force empiricism...leads to a treatment of the individual applicant in a manner that offends against the traditions of our society'* while others challenged the theoretical assumptions upon which the statistical models used in credit scoring were based (Eisenbeis 1977, 1978).

Chandler and Coffman also discussed the differences between judgemental decision making and empirically derived scoring systems, concluding that credit scoring had a number of advantages over judgemental decision making and that the arguments against the performance and use of credit scoring applied equally to judgemental decision making. The only case they could find for judgemental lending was in exceptional cases, where the credit decision required consideration of factors outside the scope of those employed within the empirical system; that is, some new or exception case arose that the credit scoring system was not designed to deal with.

One might surmise that the real thrust of the argument was not against the use of statistical and mathematical methods in themselves, but against automation and the exclusion of the human element from the decision making process. The arguments between the supporters of judgemental decision making and credit scoring have to all intents and purposes, been won by those favouring credit scoring. However, while credit scoring is the norm, there are always some cases that require manual review. There are also some non-mainstream lenders, particularly in the sub-prime and door-to-door market, who do not apply credit scoring. Thus the role of the underwriter remains, albeit in a specialist or minority capacity, and is likely to do so for the foreseeable future. It is also worth noting that while credit scoring is an accepted practice in many developed countries, in areas where banking systems are less well developed, judgemental decision making is still heavily relied upon.

7.7 Enhancing credit scoring systems with judgemental decision rules (policy rules)

In general, the accuracy of judgemental forecasts tends to be inferior to statistical ones. However, combining the best aspects of judgemental and statistical methods can lead to synergy (Makridakis *et al.* 1998, p.483 & p.503). Therefore, while the empirical evidence tends to support credit scoring as preferable to judgemental decision making – at least from a lender's perspective – credit managers often augment the decisions made by credit scoring models with judgemental decision rules (often referred to as policy rules or score overrides) (Lewis 1992, p.89; Leonard 1998; McNab and Wynn 2004, pp.81–4). In addition, there are some operational situations where certain actions must be taken in respect of an application, regardless of the credit score. In some cases these rules are automatic, leading to some fixed outcome, in others they result in applications being referred for manual review by a human underwriter. These policy rules can occur for a number of reasons which are described in the following sections.

7.7.1 Organizational policy

Many organizations will decide that certain types of credit application should be automatically accepted or declined regardless of the risk profile they represent. A lender may wish to automatically accept all applications from their own employees, or reject all applicants who are unemployed on responsible lending grounds. Alternatively, where the applicant already has the product but applies again, the lender may want to automatically decline a second or subsequent application.[3] In many organizations there is a policy that where the good:bad odds of an application are marginal, being either just above or just below the cut-off point, they will refer the case for manual review to ensure that the 'best' decision is made. The reasons for doing this are somewhat dubious given the demonstrably better performance of credit scoring, and in some respects these types of override rules can be considered as leftovers from the days of judgemental lending and very similar to the rules that would have been contained within an organization's policy document.

7.7.2 Data sufficiency

When insufficient information is available to accurately assess an application, the application may be held in a pending state while further information is collected. One of the most common overrides of this type is to confirm the identity and/or address of the applicant. If the lender is unable to automatically obtain independent confirmation of name and address (by consulting a credit reference agency for example) they will ask the applicant to provide some further evidence that they are who they say they are; for example, by asking to see a copy of a recent utility bill or pay slip bearing the applicant's name and address. If the applicant is unable to provide this then they are declined no matter how good their credit score.

7.7.3 Expert knowledge

Credit scoring models are developed based on the known characteristics of existing customers. However, there may be some characteristics that are believed to be predictive of risk, but which are not possessed by any of the lender's existing customers. For example, people who have recently been declared bankrupt tend to have a very high probability of default if granted credit again. Therefore, because their applications are always rejected, there will be no cases of bankruptcy within the sample used to develop the scorecard. Consequently, recent bankruptcies will not feature within any statistically derived scoring model. However, a credit professional with wider industry experience will know that the risk profile of recent bankrupts is very poor. Therefore, a rule will be implemented to reject all applications from people who have recently been declared bankrupt, regardless of their other attributes.

7.7.4 Legal requirements

There are times when a lending decision is made on legal grounds. In the UK, a lender cannot automatically decline an applicant based on information obtained from a credit reference agency if the individual has challenged the accuracy of the information held by registering a 'notice of correction.' In this case the application must be reviewed manually. Another case is where an application is made by someone under 18 years of age. Legally, they cannot be held responsible for any debts they incur. Therefore, while not illegal to advance funds to them, most lenders will not do so because they cannot take any action to recover the debt should the account fall into arrears.

7.8 Pricing for risk

This chapter opened with a discussion of acceptable risk and the break-even odds above which a customer should be accepted, based on the ratio of expected loss to expected return. In household and motor insurance markets, with which credit granting shares many analogies, the concept of a single cut-off strategy has been superseded by the concept of pricing for risk. An insurer will establish the price for insurance after determining the risk associated with the individual. Consequently, those who are most likely to make a claim pay more for their insurance. Only in a very few cases, where the risk of a claim is almost certain, will applications be declined. In the consumer credit market the traditional practice has been the opposite. A lender sets the interest rate (price) of the product first, and then accepts applications from those who have a risk profile which suggests that they will be profitable at that price. The reasons for these differences between these two risk markets are difficult to fathom, but the fact that in many countries there is a legal requirement to include interest rate and repayment information in marketing literature is probably a contributory factor. However, credit markets are changing. American Express moved to a tiered pricing structure in 1991 (Cate *et al.* 2003, p.17) and many lenders now operate pricing for risk strategies. The derivation of pricing for risk strategies can be seen as a natural evolution of the acceptance cut-off strategies discussed previously in relation to Figure 7.3 and Table 7.1. Table 7.2 demonstrates how these cut-off strategies can be adapted to cater for the pricing for risk scenario.

The interest rates quoted in Table 7.2 can be used to illustrate that a small increase in interest rate can lead to a very large increase in revenue. If after costs, the profit margin on a loan charging interest at 8.9 percent is say 1 percent, then increasing the interest rate by 1 percent to 9.9 percent will in theory double the return (assuming sales volumes are maintained). Applying these figures to our example, the returns generated

Table 7.2 Pricing for risk strategies

Score interval: From	To	Number of good accounts	Number of bad accounts	Interval good:bad odds	Total number of accounts	Total %	Pricing strategy
0	425	27,709	22,291	1.24	50,000	10%	Decline
426	645	36,671	13,329	2.75	50,000	10%	Offer high
646	732	42,185	7,815	5.40	50,000	10%	interest rate
733	789	42,983	7,017	6.12	50,000	10%	(12.9%)
790	847	44,521	5,479	8.13	50,000	10%	
848	895	46,904	3,096	12.55	50,000	10%	Offer standard
896	945	47,624	2,376	20.05	50,000	10%	interest rate
946	960	48,228	1,772	27.22	50,000	10%	(9.9%)
961	981	48,603	1,397	34.79	50,000	10%	Offer low
982	999	48,806	1,194	40.87	50,000	10%	interest rate (8.9%)
Total		434,234	65,766	6.41	500,000	100%	

from the lowest scoring group where interest rates are 12.9 percent are in theory 400 percent higher than those where the interest rate is 8.9 percent. In practice, this gain will be offset by greater bad debt, but it means that the quality (the good:bad odds) of applicants that are accepted for the product at an interest rate of 12.9 percent can be many times worse than those where the interest rate is 8.9 percent. In theory, it should be possible to offer credit to any group of people on this basis. Even if the chance of default is extremely high, if the interest rate is high enough it should be possible to make a return on investment averaged over a large number of similarly risky individuals. In practice, the rate at which interest would need to be charged on the most risky groups in society could be 100 percent or more, where the chance of default could be as high as one in two or worse (good/bad odds of 1:1 or less). Most lenders are also aware of their duty to act as responsible lenders and if it is believed there is a significant chance of someone defaulting on money you are asked to lend them, it is hard to argue that granting such a request is a responsible thing to do.

One consequence that can be expected from the wider use of pricing for risk is an increase in the volume and proportion of bad debt seen by lenders as they extend credit to more risky sections of the population. Likewise, one would also expect to see a corresponding increase in the number of court cases and bankruptcies as these higher risk individuals default and are subsequently litigated against to recover the debt.

7.9   Credit scoring models of profitability

Instead of building simple models to predict whether someone will be a 'good' or 'bad' credit risk, some lenders try to predict how much profit contribution each customer will make (Thomas *et al.* 2005). The decision to accept or decline someone is then based directly on the profitability estimate that results. Applicants the model predicts will generate a positive contribution to profit are accepted and everyone else is declined. This is regardless of whether or not they are likely to default – the only question is whether or not they generate enough contribution before default occurs. This would seem like an obvious approach, but it is not popular, and most lenders continue to base their decision making on models that predict simple binary behaviours such as default/non-default. Why? One argument against building profitability models is that it is very difficult to gather enough information to accurately assess the profitability of individual customers. At a portfolio level generating measures of profitability is straight forward. Given cost and revenue information, such as the payments received, debt written-off, marketing expenditure and so on, it is easy to calculate portfolio profitability. However, at the level of an individual credit agreement, the analysis becomes more complex, requiring more information to be maintained (Hopper and Lewis 1992). Take the case of a credit card where there may have been hundreds of transactions per annum. Generating an accurate and precise view of profitability means keeping detailed records of each transaction, taking into account the different interest rates charged at different points in time for cash advances as opposed to retail purchases, account charges and late fees as well as marketing and operational costs. Historically, lenders did not have the IT or reporting infrastructures in place to be able to do this, and while information systems have improved markedly, many organizations still struggle to define an accurate and robust definition of the profitable customer.

One can counter the lack of information argument by adopting the position that full and accurate information is not a requirement for developing usable (although not optimal) models of customer profit-ability. One can think about customer information as lying along an 'information spectrum'. At one end of the spectrum very little is known about customer behaviour, perhaps nothing more than the final default/non-default (good/bad) status. In this situation, a lender will build models and make decisions on the basis of this limited information; that is, models of good/bad behaviour. At the other end of the spectrum, where everything possible is known about customer behaviour, a lender should use this information to build models of financial behaviour and make informed decisions on the basis of profitability estimates – the question as to whether or not an individual defaults becomes irrelevant.[4] If the true situation is somewhere in the middle – which is probably the case for many mainstream lending institutions in the early part of the 21st century – then the best strategy should be to incorporate whatever information is available into the modelling/decision making process, to provide the best possible approximation to the organizations financial objectives, even if this is not as much information as the lender would ideally like to have.

The second line of reasoning against developing models of profit-ability is that they tend to give poor results (Lucas 2001), and do not provide enough benefit over standard credit scoring models of good/bad payer behaviour to justify their development and use. Lucas's main argument is that profit measures are very sensitive to events that occur over the forecast horizon, whereas eventual delinquency status is much more robust. For example, it could be argued that increasing the credit limit on a revolving credit product, such as a credit card, will have little or no effect on the eventual delinquency (good/bad) status of accounts, but profitability will be highly correlated with the limit increase if cus-tomers makes use of the additional credit facility. Therefore, the rela-tionship between the customer profile at the start of the outcome period and the profit generated by the end of the outcome period will be weak. Taking this argument further, one might conclude that the more action taken to control the customer over the outcome period, by varying the interest rate, the credit limit or other account features, the worse any forecast of customer profitability will be. This has led some to suggest that simple forecasting may be inappropriate, and a dynamic approach that simulates the effect of different actions by lenders over time should be applied (Crowder *et al.* 2005). However, it can also be argued that if a customer's current borrowing is unconstrained by the existing terms of a credit offer, the profitability generated from the cus-tomer will be invariant to any action taken to extend more credit or otherwise alter the terms of the agreement. Therefore, the relative[5] profitability of each customer will be no more sensitive to the lender's actions than the good/bad payer status (Finlay, S. M. 2008). This will be especially true if the lender's current lending strategy has evolved over many years, and is therefore close to optimal. The effect of new strategies applied to accounts acts only to maintain the current status quo, not to provide any large changes to the relative profitability of individual customers. The estimated 68 percent of credit card users who pay off their balances each month (MORI Market Dynamics 2004) and hence pay no interest, comes to mind as a group whose relative contribution is likely to be static regardless of the interest rate or credit limit strategies applied to them. Research by Finlay, S. M. (2008) supports this view. He demonstrated that good predictive models of a simple contribution function, based on revenues, bad debt and delinquency status could be constructed using standard forecasting methods, and that such models outperform standard models of good/bad behaviour, in terms of their ability to identify accounts that contributed the most to profit.

Another argument against modelling profitability is the 'share of wallet' issue (Lucas 2001). A lender's share of a customer's total borrowing requirement (and hence the profit they make from them) will be dependent upon the actions of other lenders with whom the customer also has a financial relationship. Given that lenders do not tend to have information about the marketing and operational strategies of their competitors, a credit scoring model designed to predict the financial behaviour of accounts will inevitably generate poor forecasts due to this lack of information. This may be true for some customers, but again if we consider the credit card case where most customers do not maintain a revolving credit balance, the offers and incentives put forward by the competition, such as low interest rates, balance transfer options, high credit limits etc. are unlikely to prove attractive to the majority of a lender's book. Anecdotal evidence of this is presented by considering the case of Barclaycard. For many years Barclaycard was the major provider of VISA credit cards in the UK. A huge wave of competition arrived in the late 1980s and early 1990s, and today, the UK market is an extremely competitive one. However, despite many competitors offering far superior product terms than Barclaycard (in terms of interest rates and credit limits) Barclaycard has retained its position as the market leader. The success of new entrants in the market can largely be attributed to the growth in the market – not from acquiring business from Barclaycard.

What must also be recognized when discussing 'share of wallet' is the difference between accounts and customers, and the difference between forecasting individual behaviour and forecasting portfolio behaviour. If an individual is in the market for say, a credit card, mortgage and an unsecured personal loan, then the actions taken by different lenders to attract that customer may be very influential on the eventual outcome as to which products the customer chooses from which lenders, and hence the share of wallet each lender obtains. However, at the account level the actual credit usage of the customer may be very similar regardless of the product they choose. So, if an individual has a credit card with one lender, whether or not they choose to then take out a mortgage with the same lender or a different lender, will have little impact on their credit card usage.

The case could also be put that credit managers over estimate the impact of their account management decisions on customer behaviour in relation to other areas of the business. If changes in the customer services department result a marked increase/decrease in service levels, then this may be a far more important factor in changing customer behaviour in terms of attrition rates, cross sell opportunities etc. than the actions controlled by the credit department – such as altering the fee structure, changing credit limits or increasing the APR.

7.10 Behavioural scoring

The term application scoring is applied to the sub-set of credit scoring models used to forecast the behaviour of individuals when applying for new credit products, with the most common decision being whether to accept or reject the application based on the estimated good:bad odds. However, once an applicant is accepted and becomes a customer, the decision making process is not over, and there may be many additional decision points during the lifetime of the product. The term behavioural scoring encompasses the sub-set of credit scoring models applied to existing customer accounts in order to change or modify the terms of a product or the way in which the relationship between the lender and borrower is managed. This includes account management decisions, such as credit line increases, card renewal, pre-screening for cross-selling and up-selling of products and changes to the APR, as well as collections and debt recovery scoring applied to delinquent accounts to determine what action to take to recover the debt.

The basic principles of behavioural scoring are the same as for application scoring. Given what is known about the customer today, how will they behave in future? In practice, the information upon which forecasts of existing customer behaviour are made is much richer than for new applications because it includes all the information held by the lender about the past behaviour of the account, and for products such as credit cards, even when, where and what type of expenditures occurred. A common example of the use of behavioural scoring is the decision to raise a customer's credit line, either automatically when the account cycles each month or when a line increase is requested by the customer. The lender will recalculate the good:bad odds using the additional and more recent data available, and if the odds have improved, then an appropriate increase in credit limit will be granted.

7.11   The impact of credit scoring

The introduction of credit scoring systems to replace judgemental underwriting has had a major impact on the organizational structure of many institutions. In providing a centralized decision making capability, the power of those working in local branches is much diminished. Looking at the UK situation, the 1980s saw significant job losses in the banking industry as branch networks were rationalized and individual branches moved away from credit assessment and account management towards a sales and customer services orientation. While credit scoring was only a part of this process, it was undoubtedly a significant contributor, particularly when combined with the advances in computing and deregulation that occurred at that time.

The introduction of credit scoring in the UK faced some opposition from employees and unions who, with some justification, saw credit scoring as a threat to their livelihoods. At an individual level many, if not most, underwriters believed credit scoring was inferior to their own judgement and would always identify the exception cases where the credit scoring system was obviously wrong (in their opinion). It is worth noting that this type of resistance to mechanically derived forecasting tools is a general problem and is not restricted to the financial services industry. Experts in a particular field always believe that they can make better forecasts than mechanical approaches, regardless of the true situation. With hindsight it is no surprise that many early credit scoring systems failed to deliver the promised benefits because their operational implementation was too lax, allowing staff to override any decisions they did not agree with, resulting in a situation little different from that which existed prior to the introduction of credit scoring. Ironically, in some systems this level of openness was actually a design feature, with the intent of facilitating the acceptance of credit scoring into the workplace by allowing people to retain the ultimate decision making responsibility.

While credit scoring systems have sometimes been derided for their cold and 'inhuman' approach to customer assessment, there have been many hidden benefits that have not been as widely publicized as perhaps they deserve. With organizational change behind them, the improved decision making capability of credit scoring has meant that credit granters can be more precise in their estimates of risk and it is reasonable to conclude that this has been a factor in more people being in a position to obtain more credit, more quickly and more easily than ever before.

Credit scoring systems by their mechanically derived nature do not, if developed properly, demonstrate the prejudices that were undoubtedly expressed consciously or unconsciously by some underwriters against people from certain sections of society. This is not to say that well-designed credit scoring systems don't display bias, but where discrimination does exist this is not a conscious design feature and is supported by statistical evidence. Very little research has been conducted into the bias expressed by credit scoring systems, but what work has been undertaken has concluded there is not much support for the argument that discrimination exists (Avery *et al.* 2000). Another conclusion is that even if credit scoring systems do display bias which might be considered in some way unfair or unethical, it is of a lower order than what went before.

On the negative side, as Kempson *et al.* (2000, p.17) noted, the greater accuracy and consistency offered by credit scoring systems also means that those who cannot gain access to credit face greater financial exclusion. For those that have difficulty obtaining credit the situation is further exacerbated because one side effect of credit scoring has been that different lenders now tend to use very similar credit scoring systems and data. So perhaps in respect of the self-perpetuation theory, Harter (1974) did have a point after all.

7.12   Chapter summary

In this chapter the decision making processes used to assess individuals when they apply for credit have been explored. Lenders attempt to forecast the likelihood that a potential customer will be a 'good' or 'bad' risk and make lending decisions based on this prediction, with good and bad acting as approximations to profitable and non profitable respectively. Every lender has different overheads and operates at a different level of profitability. Therefore, a customer who is deemed creditworthy by one lender, may be not be considered creditworthy by another.

At one time lending decisions were made purely on the basis of an underwriter's subjective assessment of an individual's creditworthiness. Today, judgemental decision making is very much the exception, with most lending decisions being based on credit scoring – the application of mathematically derived forecasts of future repayment behaviour. While credit scoring is not perfect, it displays a number of benefits over and above the judgemental alternative:

- It provides a more accurate assessment of risk.
- The application of credit scoring within automated decision systems has led to faster and more efficient processing of credit applications, which can be managed easily via a centralized control function.
- Credit scoring is consistent and repeatable.
- Credit scoring does not tend to display the unjustified prejudices that human underwriters sometimes expressed against certain sections of society.

7.13   Suggested sources of further information

Lewis, E. M. (1992). *An Introduction to Credit Scoring*. Athena Press. This was the first book to describe in detail the principles and practices behind the development of credit scorecards and is arguably still one of the best books on the subject. It does not enter into the detailed mathematics of credit scoring, instead it focuses on the practical issues involved in the development of credit scoring models, such as data collection, the definition of goods and bads and the operational issues involved in implementing scorecards within a lender's IT systems.

Thomas, L. C., Edelman, D. B. and Crook, J. N. (2002). *Credit Scoring and Its Applications*. Siam. This book provides a comprehensive review of the mathematical theory underpinning the various techniques used in credit scoring, as well as the practical issues involved in the development of credit scorecards. It also comprehensively covers all significant academic literature relating to credit scoring prior to its publication.

Siddiqi, N. (2005). *Credit Risk Scorecards*. John Wiley & Sons. Well written and very readable. This book provides a detailed guide about how credit scoring models are constructed in practice by practitioners working within the financial services industry.

8
Credit Reference Agencies

Since the earliest times lenders have realized that if an individual had a poor credit history with one lender, then there was a good chance they would default on loans taken out with another. The converse was also true. Those with a good history of repayment tended to be good customers again in the future. It therefore made sense for lenders to follow a 'you show me yours and I'll show you mine' policy of sharing information about the repayment behaviour of their customers. In many markets the idea of sharing information with competitors is considered a rather unwise thing to do. However, the accepted wisdom within the credit industry is that the benefits of obtaining customer information from many other lenders far outweighs any loss that might result from sharing information about your own.

In this chapter we focus on the way lending institutions share customer data, and in particular, the role of credit reference agencies in this process. A credit reference agency (also known as a consumer reporting agency or a credit bureau) is an organization that collects, owns or controls access to information about the financial status of individuals or other financial entities (such as limited companies). When someone applies for credit, the organization to which they apply will ask them for information about themselves and their financial circumstances, but they will also request a credit report (credit reference) from a credit reference agency. The credit reference agency will interrogate its databases and relevant information about the applicant will be returned to the lender. The lender will then incorporate this information into its decision making process.

8.1   The history of credit reference agencies

The first organizations set up specifically to share information about debtors were mutual trade protection organizations. These arose in the

UK in the early 1800s and were principally concerned with trade credit, allowing members to share details of bad debts, fraud and attempted fraud that they had experienced. Most were locally based organizations, operating in one town or district. The London Association for the Protection of Trade, which was to eventually evolve into the first national credit reference agency in the UK, was formed in 1842, becoming Infolink in 1987 (Greig 1992, p.11 & pp.336–7). However, the modern UK credit reference agencies emerged at the end of the 1970s, growing out of the internal data sharing systems of the large mail order catalogue companies (Competition Commission 1997). It might seem surprising that mail order data provided the basis for credit reference agencies in the UK, but in the late 1970s credit cards and personal loans were much less common than they are today, and mail order was the preferred medium of unsecured lending for many people. GUS Home Shopping, for example, had far more credit customers than the largest banks and building societies. Consequently, its computer systems were state of the art and geared to dealing with hundreds of thousands of customer transactions a day – an ideal foundation for a credit reference agency.

Experian (formally CCN) was formed in 1980 (Experian 2008). It was originally a wholly owned subsidiary of the GUS group, which was the largest mail order catalogue retailer in the UK at the time. GUS bought the US credit reference agency Experian (formally TRW) in 1996 and merged it with CCN to form the Experian group. Experian was eventually spun off as a separate company in 2005. The UK arm of Equifax, the American based credit reference agency, was created sometime around 1990 as a joint venture between Equifax and the UK retailer Next (using the customer database of Gratton, Next's mail order subsidiary). Next subsequently sold its share of the venture to Equifax in 1991. Equifax went on to acquire Infolink in 1994 (Jentzsch 2007, p.100). The UK's third credit reference agency, Callcredit, was formed in 2001 and is a wholly owned subsidiary of the Skipton Building Society.

In the US, mutual trade protection organizations were also being formed during the early–mid 1800s. The first commercial credit reference agencies, providing credit reports to paying subscribers, appeared in the 1830s and 1840s (Norris 1978, p.10) and organizations providing consumer credit referencing services appeared around 20 years later (Jentzsch 2007, p.64). At one time there were over 2,200 organizations offering credit reference services in the US. Originally these operated mainly within individual towns, cities, counties or states; but by 1996 this had coalesced into the three national agencies in the market today;

Equifax, Experian and TransUnion (Cate *et al.* 2003, p.3). Equifax is the largest credit reference agency in the US. The company began by offering its credit services in 1899 to local businesses in Atlanta Georgia, but soon branched out to provide insurance rating services as well as credit reports. Prior to the Second World War the company's credit referencing business suffered mixed fortunes, but grew rapidly from the 1950s onwards (Grant 2007, pp.177–83). Experian was originally the customer information division of the industrial conglomerate TWR, and was spun off as a separate business in mid-1960s. The TransUnion credit reference agency was created in 1969 when the company took a strategic decision to enter the credit referencing market and acquired the Credit Bureau of Cook County (CBCC). This then formed the basis of the world's first fully automated online credit referencing system (TransUnion 2008).

8.2 Information held by credit reference agencies

The type of information maintained by credit reference agencies around the world is broadly the same. However, the precise information held by individual credit reference agencies varies from country to country due to local legislation and industry agreements that dictate the uses to which information can be put. The main discussion therefore begins with the operation of credit reference agencies in the UK. The differences between the UK, US and other national situations are discussed towards the end of the chapter. All three of the UK's credit reference agencies hold the following types of information:

1. Public information, accessible to the general public. For example, the Electoral Roll can be viewed by anyone at their local library, and everyone has access to local and national telephone directories.
2. Private information, supplied by financials services companies, utility suppliers and other organizations. This information is not accessible to the general public.
3. Derived information, that the credit reference agencies have created from a variety of public and private sources. These provide profiles of customer behaviours at individual, household and postcode levels.

Each of these categories is discussed in more detail in the following sections.

8.3   Public information

8.3.1   Court judgements, bankruptcies and repossessions

Anyone who is taken to court and found liable for unpaid debts will have a County Court Judgement (CCJ) registered against them. CCJs and the more serious cases of bankruptcy are publicly available information, maintained on a national register by Registry Trust Limited on behalf of the Lord Chancellor's Department. A copy of the register is supplied to the credit reference agencies who maintain records of all CCJs and bankruptcies for a period of six years. The information held covers:

- When the judgement or bankruptcy occurred.
- The value of the judgement or bankruptcy.
- Whether or not the judgement or bankruptcy has been satisfied; that is, whether or not the debt has been paid in accordance with the court's ruling.

The presence of a CCJ or bankruptcy on an individual's credit record is one of the strongest indicators of future risk and almost inevitably leads to an individual being declined credit by mainstream credit providers, especially if the debt was recent or for a high value.

Repossession of someone's home does not necessarily result in a CCJ or bankruptcy, but most credit providers view repossession with a similar level of caution and highly indicative of risk. The Council of Mortgage Lenders provides details of all repossessions of residential properties to the credit reference agencies, including cases where voluntary repossession has occurred.

8.3.2   The Electoral (Voters) Roll

The Electoral (Voters) Roll contains details of all adults registered to vote in UK elections. The roll is captured in full each year, with monthly updates to allow people who have moved home to remain registered. The Electoral Roll is published in two forms. The full register is available for credit vetting and identity verification. The limited version excludes people who have indicated that they do not wish their details to be used for commercial purposes, and is primarily used by commercial organizations for the production of mailing lists.

Credit reference agencies maintain historic as well as current versions of the Electoral Roll. This is because it can be useful for identity verification purposes to be able to confirm if someone was registered at their previous address, or that they used to be registered at their current address, but are not registered there now.

8.4 Private information

8.4.1 Shared customer account data

The largest files held by credit reference agencies are those containing customer account information. Each month, organizations provide the credit reference agencies with the following details about their customers' accounts:

- Personal details for identity purposes (account number, name, date of birth, address and so on).
- The type of product (for example, loan, credit card or mortgage).
- The date the credit agreement commenced.
- The term of the credit agreement (if appropriate).
- The credit line (if appropriate).
- The outstanding balance.
- The current arrears status (up-to-date, 30/60/90 days past due and so on).
- Historic arrears status for up to 47 months; that is, the balance and arrears status one month, two months, three months ago and so on.
- A range of indicators to highlight certain situations or special cases. For example, where the account closed with a good repayment record, where there is some dispute with the customer, or where the customer has entered into a payment arrangement with the lender.

When a credit agreement is terminated and the lender stops supplying account details, information about the account is maintained by the credit reference agency for up to six years. Therefore, when a credit search is performed, the status of completed credit agreements can be reported.

What is important to emphasize is the very limited nature of the information provided to the credit reference agencies. Detailed transactional information about how customers use a product, what was bought, where and for how much is not provided. Product features, such as the interest rate being charged, the length of any interest-free period and any annual charge or loyalty schemes are also withheld, as is security information such as pin numbers and card expiry dates.

The Standing Committee on Reciprocity (SCOR) exists as an industry body comprising representatives from the financial services industry and the credit reference agencies. The purpose of SCOR is to define the 'rules of reciprocity' specifying the information lenders and credit reference agencies agree to share and the uses to which shared information can be put. The rules only allow full account information (meaning information about good paying accounts as well as those that are delinquent) to be used for the purposes of identity verification and credit vetting. Details of good payment performance cannot be used for marketing purposes to target customers from rival organizations; for example, in a mailing campaign to attract low risk credit card holders who maintain high balances (and hence a very profitable customer segment). However, the use of derogatory credit information is allowed for the purpose of pre-screening mailing lists to de-select those individuals with a history of serious arrears (three months or more behind in their payments). This is in line with the concept of responsible lending by not encouraging further borrowing by individuals who have a proven record of financial difficulty.

Lenders are not obliged to provide credit reference agencies with information, but it is to their advantage to do so as the reciprocity rules laid down by SCOR dictate that information provided by one lender is only accessible by other institutions if they themselves provide the same level of information in return. For example, a lender who simply contributes information about the derogatory accounts in their portfolio will only be allowed access to the derogatory information provided by other lenders, with positive information about good paying accounts being withheld. If a lender decides not to contribute any of its customer information at all, they will be denied access to all shared information contributed by other lenders. However, they will still be able to perform a credit search to access other types of information collected from other sources, such as public information about CCJs, bankruptcies and the Electoral Roll.

8.4.2 Credit searches

Every time a credit search is performed a record of the search is logged by the credit reference agency. When another search is initiated at a later date, the new search will report any previous credit searches that have been made. People for whom there have been many credit searches in a short period of time (say five or more over a six month period) tend to have a more risky profile than average. This is not to say they are declined automatically, but that the act of seeking a lot of credit in a short period of time has a negative impact on their overall risk rating, as represented by the credit scores used by most lenders. In some cases this penalizes people who shop around making tentative applications for a number of products, each one resulting in a credit search being recorded. Until the early 2000s this problem was particularly acute in residential mortgage markets because two credit searches would be performed; one when the preliminary application was made and another when the customer was ready to progress with a property purchase. In recent years lenders have had the capacity to inform the credit reference agencies as to what type of search is being performed (enquiry/identity verification or full search). Only the full searches are reported when a subsequent credit search is made. The information about credit searches is limited to:

- The date the search was performed.
- The type of product applied for (for example, mortgage, personal loan or credit card).
- The organization that requested the search.

The outcome of the search (whether the application was eventually accepted or declined) is not recorded by the credit reference agencies. Search information is updated on a daily basis and is held for a period of at least 12 months.

8.4.3   Credit Industry Fraud Avoidance Scheme (CIFAS)

The Credit Industry Fraud Avoidance Scheme (CIFAS) is an industry funded organization that maintains details of known and suspected cases of fraud reported to it by member organizations. Copies of the CIFAS database are made available to the credit reference agencies. Therefore, when a credit search is undertaken by a CIFAS member, then if the subject of the credit search has a CIFAS record – indicating that the individual has previously been suspected of acting fraudulently – this will be reported as part of the search. It is important to note that the majority of CIFAS information relates to cases of suspected fraud that were declined before any fraudulent act was committed, not where proven cases of fraud have occurred. Therefore, lenders are obliged not to use CIFAS information as the sole reason to decline an application. Rather, a CIFAS indicator returned as part of a credit search should lead to the application being referred for further investigation.

8.4.4   Gone Away Information Network (GAIN)

The Gone Away Information Network (GAIN), which is managed by CIFAS, records cases where people in arrears have moved address without informing the lender. If at some point in the future the individual's new address comes to light then GAIN will flag up the case and alert the lender with whom the original default occurred, allowing them to pursue the individual for the debt. GAIN works by detecting when the absent borrower inadvertently makes their new address known and relies upon member organizations providing details of their customers' addresses and changes of address. Consider the case of an individual who has a credit card from one lender and a personal loan from another. When the individual moves address they stop repaying the loan and fall into arrears. When the loan company makes attempts to recover the debt, they discover the individual is no longer resident at their original address and inform GAIN of their 'gone away' customer. Then, if the individual has maintained their relationship with the credit card company, the credit card company will pass on the change of address details to GAIN, who in turn inform the loan company.

8.4.5 Notice of correction

The Consumer Credit Act 1974 and the Data Protection Act 1998 give anyone in the UK the right to receive a copy of any information about them held by a credit reference agency. If the information is incorrect, then the credit reference agency is legally obliged to correct it. However, if the information is believed to be correct, an individual still has the right to record a short 'notice of correction' statement against the item, stating why they think the information is incorrect and/or detailing any special circumstances they believe should be taken into consideration if they apply for credit in the future. If a notice of correction is present on a credit report a lender must review the application manually before making a final decision. However, lenders are under no obligation to make different decisions from the ones they would have made if the notice of correction had not existed.

8.5 Derived information

8.5.1 Geo-demographic and socio-economic data

A large number of public and private surveys are undertaken in the UK each year, capturing information about individuals' and households' behaviours, preferences and lifestyles. Some are undertaken on behalf of the government, some by well-known institutions such as MORI and some on behalf of the credit reference agencies. Records of all UK directors, incomes by region, census data and an array of other information is also publicly available. Credit reference agencies have combined this information with credit data to produce demographic measures at individual, household and postcode levels. For example, Experian's MOSAIC classifies each postcode (representing about 20 households) into one of 60 or so classifications with titles such as 'sprawling sup-topia' and 'middle rung families' giving information about the socio-economic profile of the people who live in these areas. While the primary use of these types of classification tools are for marketing purposes, to identify population segments most amenable to different products and services, they have also been found to provide some additional insight into the risk profile of individuals.

8.5.2   Credit scores

In maintaining large and diverse databases about the current and historical behaviour of individuals, credit reference agencies are well positioned to construct generic scorecards (also referred to as bureau scorecards). These generate individual scores representing the risk profile of an individual. An example of a bureau score would be a score that provides an estimate of the likelihood of a credit card applicant defaulting within the next 12 months, that could be used by any credit card provider to help them decide whether or not someone applying for a new card was creditworthy. Due to the amount and diversity of information held by the credit reference agencies, these scores are usually more accurate than a credit score that an individual lender could construct using only their own customer databases, and many lenders will use them either in conjunction with, or instead of, the credit scores generated by their own in-house scorecards. Bureau scores are also of particular worth to lenders in start-up situations where they do not have sufficient account information available to construct their own scorecards.

Information about individuals can change daily as updates are made to the databases maintained by the credit reference agencies. Consequently, bureau scores are not always maintained within a credit reference database, but generated dynamically as and when a client organization requests it. One side effect of the dynamic nature of these scores is that there is no requirement for a credit reference agency to provide them under data protection legislation, if they only exist at the point in time that a lender requests them. However, the individual does have some recourse because lenders who use bureau scores will tend to store them within their own IT systems and should report them to the individual upon a request being made under the Data Protection Act.

8.6 Performing a credit search: matching applicant and credit reference data

When a credit search is made, the standard method of enquiry is via a computerized data link. The applicant's details will be entered into the lender's application processing system, which then transmits the name, address and date of birth of the applicant electronically to one or more of the credit reference agencies to commence the search process.

Whereas in countries such as the United States and Norway, social security numbers are widely used to uniquely identify an individual, in the UK there is no reliable national identity number. The nearest potential equivalent is the National Insurance Number, which in theory is unique to every individual. However, there are approximately 21 million more numbers in circulation than there are people in the population and these additional numbers are widely used by fraudsters (Watt 1999). Therefore, when an organization requests a credit search, the search is based on the name, address and date of birth of the applicant.

The matching algorithms used by the credit reference agencies are generally very good and are continually refined; however, the matching process can be complex and there can be ambiguities resulting in incorrect data being associated with an individual. Figure 8.1 demonstrates the type of differences that can occur.

Common sense would suggest that it is probably the case that all of these records belong to the same Steven Finlay, but it is impossible to be 100 percent certain. When dealing with tens or hundreds of millions of individual records some cases are bound to arise where data will be incorrectly matched. Mismatches arise for two reasons. First, data coming from different sources may be captured in different formats. Second, data can be incorrectly keyed by data entry staff. While the number of mismatches is probably very low in percentage terms, with around 140 million credit searches being performed each year in the

Mr Steven M Finlay	Mr Stephen N Finlay	Mr Steven M Finlay
11 Greenfield Drive	11 Greenfield Drive	11a Greenfield road
Allerton		Allerton
Liverpool	Liverpool	Liverpool
L10 4EL	L10 4EL	
DOB 12/05/1973	DOB 05/12/1973	DOB 05/12/1937

Figure 8.1   Differences in name and address data

UK (Callcredit 2001), it only takes a very small percentage of errors to lead to a significant absolute number of cases being reported.

Cases of people having difficulty obtaining credit or being pursued for debts that are not theirs due to incorrect name/address matching are reported from time to time in the press and it is reasonable to assume that the number of reported cases is only a small proportion of the actual cases where errors have occurred. This is due to two reasons. First, it is probable that most disputes over data are resolved without recourse to the media. Second, people are only likely to become aware of errors in their credit record when it results in an application for credit being rejected: there is little incentive to check one's credit record if everything is fine. One option for credit reference agencies would be to tighten their matching criteria. However, if the matching criteria are too tight, correct information may be discarded because of minor differences between the information provided by the lender and that held by the credit reference agency. Credit reference agencies are therefore always sitting on a knife edge between being too strict and not reporting data that actually belongs to the individual (and which may actually improve the individual's credit rating) and being too relaxed and matching data which belongs to another individual with similar details.

Once data has been collated it is returned, usually electronically, to the lender. The data is then available to be used within the lender's decision making systems. The entire search process usually takes only a few seconds and is completely transparent to the applicant who may be making an application in real time in a branch, over the phone or via the internet.

8.6.1 No trace cases

If an individual is not on the Electoral Roll and does not have any previous history of credit, a credit search will not return any information about them. There is said to be 'no trace' of the individual at the address. This probably occurs in 3–5 percent of all credit searches. No trace cases sometimes lead to further information being sought by the lender, via some form of manual processing to confirm the applicant's address, or to obtain references and then for an underwriter to make an assessment of the application. Alternatively, the application may be declined automatically, as some lenders take the view that having no information about an individual is correlated with a high risk of default or, do not consider it worth the time and effort (and hence cost) to sift through these cases manually.

8.6.2 Previous addresses, linked addresses and joint applications

Credit reference data is matched to an individual on the basis of the person's name, address and date of birth. Therefore, if a person moves home, all existing credit data will become disassociated from the individual and will not be reported as part of a credit search undertaken at the new address. This situation is partly rectified by the individual informing lenders with whom they have existing credit relationships of their new address, because each lender will in turn pass the details on to the credit reference agencies. However, given that institutions only provide account information on a monthly basis, it could be several weeks before a credit reference agency records the address change. There is also the issue of old credit agreements, accounts in default and county court judgements, which the applicant is unlikely to inform the lender about and thus remain registered at the old address. Therefore, a credit search performed shortly after a change of address (which is common after a house move when people seek to fund the purchase of new fixtures and fittings) may still not result in a full credit report being produced. Common practice is to request that the applicant provides details of their previous address(es) if they have moved within the last three years (three years is a rather arbitrary, but widely used period of time) and for credit searches to be performed at these addresses. The information from all the applicants' addresses is then pooled and provided to the lender as a single credit report.

If an individual fails to declare a previous address on the application form, but has recorded an address change with at least one lender with whom they have an existing relationship, or have had their Electoral Roll record updated, the credit reference agency is able to create an address link. An address link is a record of an address change and the old and new addresses. Once this link has been established it is then possible to retrieve all credit data relating to both addresses, even if the applicant does not disclose their old address as part of a new credit application.

If a credit application is made in two or more joint names, it is normal practice to initiate a separate credit search for each applicant and to consider the joint information returned. It is therefore possible that for a single application for credit where there are two applicants who have moved home several times, what on the surface appears to be a single credit search actually consists of a number of subsidiary searches which are amalgamated to produce a single credit report. This has costing implications as lenders may be charged for each subsidiary search performed.

8.6.3   Third party data

Data about individuals other than the applicant that is used to make decisions about the applicant, is termed third party data. At one time credit reference agencies reported data at a household level. If a person moved into a house where a current or previous occupant had a poor credit record, the new resident would be associated with this information and would be likely to experience difficulty obtaining credit. Thankfully, this practice was discontinued many years ago. However, until 2004 it was still permissible to use information about anyone with the same surname who lived at the applicant's address, regardless of whether a financial association existed between them. While this might seem reasonable in some cases, such as a husband and wife, it raised issues about other associations. Should a son or daughter be disadvantaged when seeking credit because of the parents' debts, or indeed vice versa? Or what about the case of two unrelated people with the same surname renting rooms in the same house? The use of most third party data was eventually deemed unlawful under the Data Protection Act 1998 and by October 2004 all organizations should have discontinued using the majority of third party data within their decision making systems. Today, the use of third party data is only permissible in a limited set of circumstances that can be represented diagrammatically, as shown in Figure 8.2.

Firstly, following the left hand branch of Figure 8.2, if an individual applying for credit chooses to 'opt in' (for example via a check box on the application form) the data returned by the credit reference agency will include data about other individuals living at the applicant's address with whom there exists a known financial association; that is, some current or historic record of a joint credit agreement or a joint credit application. This is regardless of whether the two people are related or share the same surname. If two friends buy a house together and share the mortgage, and one of them applies for a mail order catalogue account and opts in, the credit report would also contain the full credit history of the other person (the associated third party). This will include not just details of the shared mortgage, but any other credit commitments they have held, either individually or jointly, at any time in the past.

If a credit report returns only very limited data about an individual, the individual is said to have a 'thin credit file'.[1] If on the basis of this limited data the lender would decline the application, the lender is then permitted to use information about other people with the same surname living at the applicant's address, regardless of whether or not

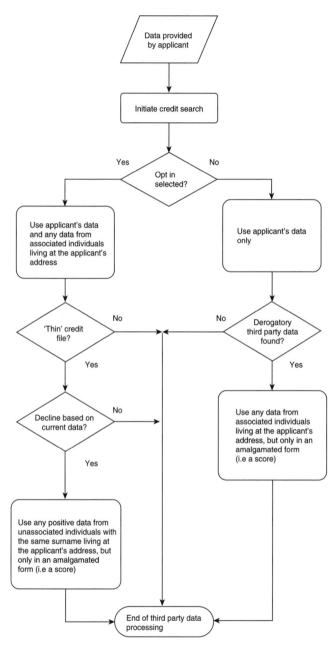

Figure 8.2 Logic for the use of third party data

a proven financial association exists; that is, if the lender finds positive information about other family members living with the applicant, this can be used to change a preliminary decision to decline the application to one to accept it. However, because the information relates to financially unassociated individuals, it is only allowed to be used in an amalgamated form, such as a credit score. Lenders are not allowed to look at the specific details of the unassociated individual's account history, only some overall measure of how the information impacts on the applicant's risk profile.

If on the other hand, the applicant declines to 'opt in' (or a lender does not ask the question) the logic shown in the right hand branch of Figure 8.2 is followed. The applicant is asked to confirm that to the best of their knowledge they are not financially associated with anyone living at their address who has a previous history of serious arrears, default or bankruptcy and the lender is only allowed to use information relating to the applicant to make their decision. The exception to this is if the credit reference agency reports that, despite the applicant's denial, derogatory information about a financially associated person at the applicant's address does exist. In this case, only derogatory information relating to the associated individual can be used, and again, only in an amalgamated form such as a credit score. Therefore, given that in the 'opt out' case only derogatory third party data can be used, it can be assumed lenders will only use this data to override a preliminary decision to accept an application to one to decline it. Information relating to other individuals at the address with the same surname, where no financial association exists, cannot be used in any form if the opt-in option is not selected.

It is worth noting that while it can be argued that the exclusion of unassociated third party data is a good thing from privacy and civil liberties perspectives, if an applicant is classified as a no trace case, knowing that other family members living with the applicant have good repayment histories is likely to improve the individual's credit score and hence their ability to obtain credit.

8.7 US credit reference agencies

The US the credit referencing market is dominated by three organizations. Equifax, Experian and TransUnion. As in the UK, all three organizations are commercial concerns looking to maximize their return from the sale of their services. Many smaller organizations still describe themselves as credit reference agencies, but these do not hold credit reference data themselves. Instead, they act in an intermediary capacity negotiating the collection and supply of data between lenders and the three main players.

The operation of credit reference agencies is regulated by the Fair Credit Reporting Act of 1970 (Amended 1996 & 2003) and the Equal Credit Opportunity Act 1974 (Amended 1976) which were introduced to deal with the way in which the credit reference agencies collect, maintain and report on consumer credit information and the type of data that can be used in the credit granting process. The information held by the US agencies is more comprehensive than in any other country. All major lenders contribute fully to the credit reference agencies and where organizations have tried to prevent or limit the supply of data, legislative action has been threatened to force them to do so (Lee 2003). The data held by the credit reference agencies is broadly consistent with that held in the UK in terms of shared customer data, bankruptcies, credit searches and so on, but there are also a number of additional items of data which include:

- Current and previous employer details.
- Salary details.
- Tax liens (a tax demand which lays claim to an individual's assets in lieu of unpaid taxes).
- Residential status.
- Name of spouse.
- Phone number(s).
- Drivers license number.
- Social security number.

The presence of a social security number assists in the matching processes and should in theory reduce incidents of mismatched information. With a richer collection of information available, and no limitations on the use of third party data, the predictive power of bureau scores is very good and they are relied upon by lenders to a greater extent than in the UK. The most common of these are the FICO scores developed by the Fair Isaacs Corporation that are applied across the databases of all three credit reference agencies.

Account information about individuals is held by the credit reference agencies for seven years and details of bankruptcy can be legally held for up to ten years.

Unlike the UK there are no restrictions on the use of full credit data for marketing purposes. Consequently, there is a prevalence of pre-approved credit offers, with credit providers promoting their products to customers with the guarantee of acceptance. This is possible because the information used in credit vetting is the same as that available to marketers when the pre-approval offer is made. A full credit report is produced at the time the marketing campaign is instigated and only those who would be accepted for the product are targeted.

8.8   Other national situations

Credit reference agencies providing consumer credit reports exist in over 70 countries, and new ones are being established every year in regions where they do not currently exist. Most privately operated credit reference agencies in the world are owned by Equifax, Experian or Trans-Union, who can be viewed as global information companies. However, in a few countries such as Finland and Greece, credit reference agencies are run as industry joint ventures (Jentzsch 2007, p.83). In some countries credit reference agencies are also operated by governments or central banks as publicly managed services.

Miller (2003, pp.29–33) carried out surveys of public and privately operated credit reference agencies. These reported that in 77 countries with at least one credit reference agency, in 41 cases a public credit reference agency existed and in 44 cases there was at least one privately owned credit reference agency. In some cases public and private agencies co-existed, such as in Germany and Brazil. Miller also observed that public agencies tended to be more limited in the information they provided. They tended to focus on arrears or default cases and often excluded details of loans below some minimum value. In some cases public agencies only held details about current account status and no information about the historical status of accounts. Privately run agencies were reported to be more likely to maintain detailed account information, including details of good repayment behaviour. However, in most cases publicly maintained agencies provided their information for free, being supported in their activities either by general taxation or by industry contribution.

In the main, consumer credit markets are less well developed than in the US or UK and this is reflected in the amount of information that is maintained by the credit reference agencies and the services they provide. In some countries, such as Australia, Denmark, Finland and France, only 'negative' information concerning serious arrears and default accounts is shared with the agencies, effectively providing a screening service to enable lenders to identify those with a poor repayment history, but not allowing more subtle distinctions to be made between borrowers with a good record of repayment. This restricts the capacity to apply complex customer segmentation strategies, such as pricing for risk.

8.9 The role of credit reference agencies in credit granting decisions

Credit reference agencies maintain publicly that they act purely as providers of information, with all decisions about whether an individual is accepted or declined for credit being entirely the responsibility of the lender. While this position is factually correct, it is worth pausing to think about the types of information provided by credit reference agencies. In particular their bureau scores, which provide measures of an applicant's likelihood of default.

The constituents of the bureau scores and the details as to what features of the applicant lead to high or low scores, are determined entirely by the statistical analysts in the credit reference agency's employ. The financial institutions that use bureau scores have no say about how they are constructed, and all they see is the final score, not the components that comprise it. Therefore, if certain types of applicant receive very low bureau scores[2] that are passed on to the lender, the only logical decision the lender can make is to decline them. One could argue that those who are heavily reliant upon bureau scores are only going through the motions of making a decision. In effect, the decision has been made by the credit reference agency in all but name.

It is also a widely held belief that credit reference agencies maintain blacklists, with any individual who appears on the list being unable to obtain credit. Again, in a strict sense this is not true. However, some items of information are so predictive of bad risk that any individual who has that characteristic will undoubtedly be declined by any mainstream lender. For example, in the author's experience someone who has had a court judgement for unpaid debts of more than $1,000 within the last 12 months would almost certainly fall into this category.

8.10 Using credit reference data to re-evaluate existing customers

Many lenders reassess accounts at the monthly cycle point when customer statements are produced, in order to make decisions about changes to credit lines, interest rates, or the marketing of additional products and services. Any new offers or account changes can then be communicated to the customers with their monthly statement letter. Credit reference data may be incorporated into this decision process, often in the form of a credit score. A lender will provide a file of accounts, on a daily or monthly basis, to which the credit reference agency attaches relevant information and credit scores. Of particular interest are cases where a customer has a good repayment record with them, but where there is evidence of current payment problems with other lenders. In this situation the lender will be unlikely to want to offer a customer an increased credit facility or market new products to them.

Another area where credit reference data is of use is within debt collection departments. If the only debt the customer has is to you, then there is arguably more scope for taking time to recover overdue payments and managing the customer back to being a good and profitable source of business. On the other hand, if the customer also has other debts, it may be prudent to try and recover as much money as quickly as possible before other lenders start making demands, or to tailor the collections activity in such a way as to make it more appealing for them to repay your debt rather than that owing to other creditors.

8.11   Infrastructure requirements for credit reference agency operation

Experian UK holds more than 400 million separate records (Experian 2005) covering the UK's 46+ million adults – an average of about nine records per person. However, as noted earlier, the amount of data held in each of these records is relatively low. Even the records of customer account history contain only a few dozen entries about the status of month-end balances and arrears. To put it another way, the average credit report contains less information than is contained in this paragraph. Taking 100 bytes of information as the average amount of space required to store a credit record using efficient storage mechanisms, a credit reference database containing 400 million records would require around 40 gigabytes[3] of storage space.

Storage requirements are only one aspect of database design. Other issues include the volume, frequency and type of transactions being processed. With around 100 major organizations (and numerous smaller ones) making around 140 million credit searches a year in the UK, a credit reference agency with 50 percent of this market would need to process an average of three requests for credit reports per second,[4] with each search resulting in an average of about 900 (9 * 100) bytes of data being generated and supplied to the lender; although at peak times, such as mid-afternoon on Saturday or in the run up to Christmas, demand could be expected to be several times higher. Data links between lenders and the credit reference agencies can be via a dedicated communication link, which is common for volume users making thousands of search requests a day, or through a standard internet connection.

Updates to credit reference agency databases tend to be instigated as batch processes on a nightly basis when search demand is low and spare processing capacity is available, which is common practice for many operational databases. Most of the data within a credit reference database is static, and only about a quarter of records on the database represent active account records that are updated when new balance and arrears information is provided each month. Therefore, only about 100 million of the 400 million records in the database will be subject to change in any given month and these changes will occur throughout the month, not just at month end.

A credit search facility is seen as critical to the financial services industry. Therefore, reliability and downtime must be kept to a minimum. 24 hour support staffing and dual site disaster recovery capability are required, as is monitoring and maintenance of the data links between the credit reference agency and its clients. In support of its services, a credit reference agency also requires a data management function (tape library) to manage and monitor data as it is collated from different sources and a customer services facility to deal with sales, the setting up of new client data links, client queries, fault resolution and to manage queries from the press and general public. A statistical analysis unit is also required to monitor and report upon the data held by the agency and to develop generic credit scores from the raw credit data.

8.12   The myth of complexity

Credit reference databases are often represented in the media as massive data stores containing huge amounts of highly detailed personal information. There is no doubt that these databases are large, and when computerized credit reference databases were originally developed in the 1960s and 1970s they may well have been amongst the most massive commercial databases in existence. However, comparison to databases maintained in other areas suggest credit reference databases are orders of magnitude smaller in size and complexity than the largest commercial databases in existence today. Fernandez (2003, p.344) asserts that commercial databases of 100 gigabytes are common and Hand *et al.*

(2001, p.19) describe an 11 terabyte[5] database of retail customer transactions and a telecoms company database processing 300 million transactions per day.

Where observers may be confused is the difference between the financial information provided for credit assessment, and other information held by credit reference agencies for other purposes. Credit reference agencies, by their nature, have IT infrastructures that are suitable for handling business information from a variety of different sources in different formats and database structures. They are used to dealing with differing types of information and know how to integrate it in a usable, business friendly format. They have used this technological pragmatism to amass information relating to a range of other uses, not directly connected to the consumer credit market. For example, both Experian and Equifax hold census data and large quantities of consumer survey data. This has been used to provide database marketing services to a wide range of organizations, enabling them to target people with a high propensity to use their products and services.

So while the overall volume of data maintained by organizations such as Experian and Equifax is growing ever larger, the credit referencing component is becoming an increasingly smaller part of the credit reference agencies' wider commercial operations. To some extent the title 'credit reference agency' is a misnomer – 'information conglomerate' is perhaps a more apt term to describe these organizations and their activities. Where observers perhaps have some right to be concerned is with the moves credit reference agencies have made to integrate and combine information from across their business interests and the uses to which such information might be put. For UK and other European nationals there are safeguards in the form of data protection legislation. However, legislation in other countries varies, and can be weaker and more patchy in the protection it affords.

8.13 Secondary uses of credit reference data

Credit reference agencies have come to realize that data initially used for credit assessment is useful for a variety of other purposes, particularly those relating to the 'character' and identity of individuals. Identity verification is perhaps the most prominent area where credit data is proving to be of worth. In the US credit reference agencies provide identity verification services in support of the USA Patriot Act 2003, requiring financial services companies to verify the identities of their customers. For credit card lending in the UK a separate source of verification of name and address is a mandatory requirement under money laundering regulations. At one time this would have meant providing a recent utility bill, bank statement or similar document, but today a credit reference agency can provide this verification by matching an applicant's details to the Electoral Roll or to credit accounts held by the individual.

Many organizations ask for a credit report when considering someone for a job posting, particularly in the financial services industry where the financial probity of the employees is seen to reflect on the company. This practice has been established in the US for many years and is becoming increasingly common in the UK and elsewhere.

In the US insurance market, credit data is routinely used in assessing the likelihood and magnitude of claims, since there is a proven correlation between the risk of default on a credit product and the risk of making an insurance claim and/or the size of the claim (Kellison *et al.* 2003). Why this should be the case is somewhat unclear, but one might hypothesize that the 'character' component of credit assessment, considering the willingness and intent to repay, is closely aligned with the honesty and care people display in other aspects of their lives. For example, they are less careful drivers and have more accidents, or they make claims against property which has been deliberately damaged, or where a real claim has occurred there is a tendency to inflate the value of the claim. In the UK the use of credit data for insurance is relatively limited, in part due to the Standing Committee on Reciprocity agreement which limits the sharing of data to contributing organizations – a limitation not present in the US. However, public information, such as details of county court judgements and bankruptcy, are increasingly being used by UK insurers to estimate measures of risk.

8.14 The impact of credit reference agencies

Credit reference agencies have undoubtedly had a major impact on the range, diversity and pricing of consumer credit products. For the lender, they provide a more comprehensive picture of the individual's ability to repay debt than would ever be available from the lender's own files. Consequently, the volume of bad debt experienced is much reduced and a wider range of products can be offered to more people. In particular, lenders can afford to offer credit to individuals with whom they have had no previous relationship, but with whom they can establish that a good relationship has existed with another lender.

To quantify the benefit credit reference data provides, Miller (2003, p.52) questioned lenders from a number of different countries and reported that without access to credit reference data, lenders believed default levels would be at least 25 percent higher, and that the time taken to process credit applications would increase considerably. More quantitative work by Barron and Staten (2000) simulated the difference in loan acceptance rates between US and Australian lenders for a 4 percent delinquency rate. They concluded that the additional data available to US lenders, but disallowed through legislation in Australia, allowed them to acquire 11 percent more business than their Australian counterparts on a like-for-like basis. However, this does not necessarily translate to an 11 percent increase in profit. The additional 11 percent may represent marginal cases that previously would have just been declined, but are now just deemed acceptable.

Credit reference data is also very important to new entrants in consumer credit markets, particularly where there is insufficient information for them to construct their own credit scores. This means they are protected to some extent from the increased bad debt that is associated with a young portfolio after a new product is launched. As Shaffer (1998) describes, new credit products tend to attract a disproportionate number of high risk applications from individuals who have previously been rejected by other lenders, or who have fraudulent intent, and who view the new lender as an easy target. Being able to accurately evaluate individuals in this situation, by reviewing their past behaviour with other lenders, reduces bad debt and start-up costs and hence eases the path for new entrants into the market.

For individuals with a good credit history, the improved ability of lenders to discriminate through the use of credit reference data has had a positive impact on product pricing. Reduced levels of bad debt means lenders can operate at lower margins and offer better priced products than would be the case without full knowledge of the individual's previous credit history. However, there is an argument that social and financial exclusion have become more of a problem, especially when credit reference data is combined with credit scoring. If credit reference information about an individual is available, then a lender is in a situation to evaluate that information, determine the risk and make an appropriate lending decision. However, if no information is held by a credit reference agency (the no trace case) lenders will in many cases decline the application. Thus having good a credit history generally leads to the ability to obtain further credit, but obtaining credit for the first time can prove difficult.

8.15   Chapter summary

Credit reference agencies collect and manage information about the credit histories of individuals and their ability to repay debt. When a lender assesses a new application for credit, they will usually carry out a credit search to obtain this information and then use it in conjunction with their own data to make the lending decision.

The information maintained by credit reference agencies in different countries depends on local market conditions and national legislation. However, most credit reference databases contain details of bankruptcies and the current delinquency status of accounts. Those in more developed markets, such as the US and UK, contain more comprehensive information about individual accounts; for example, credit lines and an ongoing record of historic repayment behaviour over several years.

The amount of financial information held by credit reference agencies about individuals, even in the US, is fairly limited. They do not supply information about individual financial transactions or purchasing preferences for the purpose of credit vetting.

The information provided by credit reference agencies greatly improves the ability of lenders to assess the risks associated with both new and existing customers. Without access to credit reference data, the volume of delinquency and bad debt suffered by lenders would undoubtedly be greater than it is, and access to credit by the general public would be significantly lower and more difficult to obtain.

The commercial organizations that maintain credit reference data have in the late 1990s and 2000s extended the scope of their operations to cover almost any commercial purpose requiring personal or geo-demographic information and the differences between credit data and other data held by these organizations is becoming increasingly blurred. In particular, credit reference agencies are providing services to governments, marketers, insurers and employers for a range of purposes, such as target marketing, employee vetting, insurance assessment and identity verification.

8.16   Suggested sources of further information

Miller, M. J. (ed.) (2003). *Credit Reporting Systems and the International Economy.* MIT Press. Miller collates information about public and private credit reference agencies from around the world, describing the types of information they hold and the relationships between credit reference agencies, governments and financial institutions. The book also covers much of the academic literature about the value and impact of credit reporting systems to financial organizations and national economies.

Jentzsch, N. (2007). *Financial Privacy. An International Comparison of Credit Reporting Systems*. This book provides a wealth of information about the history and economic impact of credit reporting systems, with particular emphasis on the US, UK and Germany. It covers much of the same material as Miller, but is arguably a little more up to date.

9
Credit Management

Credit management is about the day-to-day activities required to run a modern consumer credit business. In this chapter the activities of the different business functions responsible for credit management, and the systems and processes they employ to manage customer relationships, are introduced within the context of the credit lifecycle. The credit lifecycle represents the different stages in the life of a credit product, as shown in Figure 9.1.

Some contact usually occurs between an individual and a lender prior to a credit agreement being entered into – via promotional activity or an enquiry from the individual. However, the relationship proper only begins at the recruitment phase, when a lender receives a credit application, decides to accept it, and a credit agreement is signed by the customer. The lender then creates some form of account record to hold information about the current and historic status of the agreement. The account record will be used as the basis of the account management phase of the lifecycle as repayments are made, further credit advanced and other products and services are marketed to the customer. For some small lenders account records may be paper based, but for all major credit granting institutions account records will be maintained within some sort of computerized system.

If a customer breaches the terms of the agreement, causing their account to becoming delinquent, collections action will be taken in an attempt to nurse the account back to a healthy up-to-date status. If this fails, the account enters debt recovery, where the objective is to recover as much of the outstanding debt as possible before terminating the agreement.

The life of a credit product ends in one of two ways. Either the agreement ends naturally when all outstanding debt has been repaid and the account is closed, or if collections and debt recovery action fail to

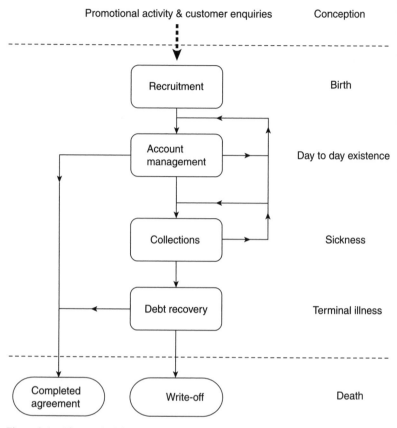

Figure 9.1   The credit lifecycle

bring a delinquent account back into line, the outstanding debt is written-off or sold to a third party debt collector.

Figure 9.1 shows that there are four major areas of credit management that a credit operation must deal with; recruitment of new customers, account management, collections and debt recovery. Each of these are discussed in turn in the next four sections. In the fifth and final section the roles played by different organizational functions in managing credit agreements across the credit lifecycle are discussed.

9.1   Recruitment

In order to convert a credit applicant into a new customer during the recruitment phase a number of processes need to be undertaken.

Information about the applicant needs to be collected, a lending decision made and the administrative tasks performed that are required to finalize the agreement and open an account. For all major lenders an application processing system, as shown in Figure 9.2, will be at the heart of their recruitment process.

In Figure 9.2, the data management unit controls the flow of data between different areas as the application progresses. Data collected from the applicant by the operational areas will need to be matched to the company's databases of existing customers, pending applications

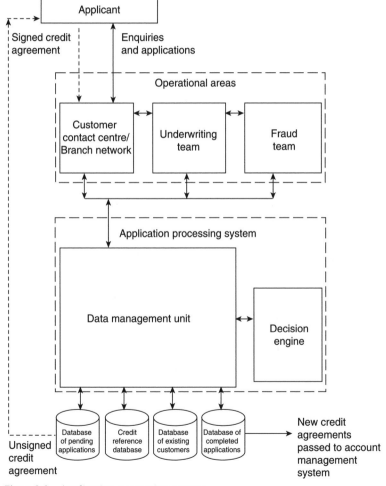

Figure 9.2 Application processing system

and completed applications. If a credit report is required, then the data management unit will manage the process of obtaining one from a credit reference agency and processing the data returned. New data fields will also be derived. For example, the applicant's age will be calculated from their date of birth and the application date to ensure that credit is not advanced to people who are under 18.

The decision engine is a piece of specialist software that processes data passed to it by the data management unit and then applies decision making rules to the application. These decisions are then acted upon by the operational areas. The decision engine might, for example, decide that not only should a telephone applicant be accepted because of their high credit score, but because the credit score is so good, the customer should be up-sold from a gold to a platinum version of the product. A decision code would be assigned and passed to the customer contact centre, via the data management unit. The telephone operator's screen would then be programmed to display a suitable message prompting the operator to ask the applicant if they would be interested in the platinum rather than gold version of the product. Alternatively, the decision engine may identify cases that need to be assessed manually by the underwriting team, or suspected cases of fraud that need to be dealt with by the fraud team.

While the decision to lend can be made very quickly in principle, supporting processes that must be undertaken before funds can be released to the customer can take a considerable period of time to complete. Therefore, the system caters for applications to be held in a pending state. For postal, phone and internet applications, a credit agreement may need to be sent to the customer, who then signs and returns it.[1] This could take several days or weeks and, in some cases, may never be completed if the applicant decides they no longer want the product they applied for. If the application is completed, the details of the application will be archived for future analysis, or used to spot repeat applications by the same individual in the future. Where the application has been accepted and a credit agreement signed, details are passed to the account management system where an account record is created and the relationship managed on an ongoing basis.

9.1.1   The credit granting decision process

To the customer the decision to grant credit can appear straightforward, often made in real time in a few seconds. However, behind the scenes the decision granting process is more complex, involving a number of separate steps and multiple decision points that are con-

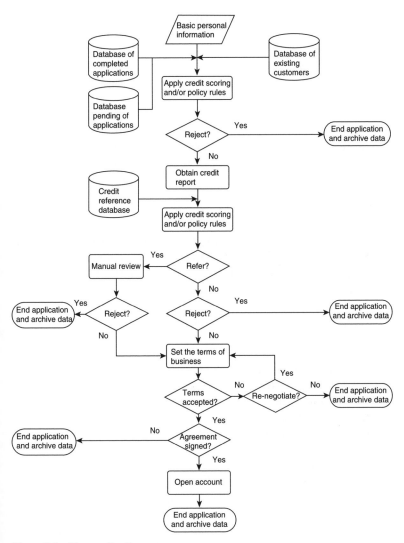

Figure 9.3 The application process

trolled by the logic contained within the decision engine. A typical
credit granting decision process is shown in Figure 9.3.

Once a lender has gathered basic personal information from the
applicant via a customer contact centre or the branch network, it is
matched against the databases of pending and completed applications,
and existing customers, to see if there has been any type of previous

relationship with the customer. The application will then undergo a preliminary credit scoring process and/or some simple policy rules will be applied. The decision engine is then in a position to make a preliminary accept/reject decision. Common reasons for rejecting applications at this stage are that they have a low credit score and/or they fail one or more of the following policy rules:

- The applicant's income is below the lender's minimum threshold.
- The applicant has provided an overseas address (which may put the applicant outside the jurisdiction of the region in which the organization operates).
- The applicant has had a previous credit agreement with the lender that was not repaid satisfactorily.
- The applicant already has the product.
- The applicant is applying for the product again, within a short space of time. This is often indicative of an attempt to obtain credit fraudulently. Therefore, many lenders will automatically decline a new credit application if insufficient time has elapsed since a previous application.
- The applicant is under 18 years of age.
- The applicant is not in permanent employment.

If the application is rejected, the details will be archived within the database of completed applications for subsequent analysis at a later date. If the application passes the preliminary screen, a credit report will be sought from a credit reference agency. The application then undergoes a second decision process that sees the application credit scored for a second time and further policy rules applied. If necessary the application will be referred for manual review, otherwise a final decision to accept or reject the application will be made automatically. Reasons for rejecting an application at this stage include:

- A low credit score, based on the applicant's full details, including those obtained from a credit report supplied by a credit reference agency.
- The presence of specific items of derogatory data within the credit report. For example, a bankruptcy or a case of serious delinquency with another lender within the last 12 months.
- The credit report is blank. The credit reference agency is unable to find any information about the individual's previous credit history and there is no record of them being registered on the Electoral Roll at their stated address.

- The applicant's existing credit commitments are too high.
- The applicant has made many previous applications for credit with other lenders in a short period of time.
- A case of attempted fraud is suspected, based on information provided by the credit reference agency.

In some cases it will be necessary to refer the application, regardless of the credit score, for review by a human assessor. Common reasons for referral are suspected fraud, missing information or identity verification.

If the lender decides the application is acceptable, the next stage is to set the terms of business under which they are willing to enter into an agreement with the applicant; that is, what interest rate, credit line, loan amount and so on, to allow the customer. At this point, those who are believed to be good candidates for cross-sell or up-sell opportunities for other products and services will also be identified. The terms of business are then communicated back to the customer. With the increasing prevalence of pricing for risk policies, these terms may well be different from the terms previously encountered by the applicant within any promotional material. Therefore, some level of explanation may be required to explain to the applicant why they are being offered different terms than those they applied for. Alternatively, the customer may have applied for more credit than the lender is willing to grant, or desire the agreement to run over a timescale that is unacceptable. If this is the case, it may be necessary for the lender and the applicant to renegotiate the amount and/or term of the credit to be advanced.

If the applicant accepts the terms of the agreement then they must authorize it by physically signing it or, in the case of electronic documents, providing a suitable electronic signature. The signed agreement is then returned to the lender. Therefore, if an application has been made remotely there will often be a requirement to send the agreement to the applicant for signing and await its return. If no response is received within a reasonable period of time, follow-up activity, such as a reminder letter, may be initiated to encourage the applicant to sign and return the agreement. Only when a signed credit agreement has been received should an account be opened and funds advanced; otherwise, there is no legal recourse should the borrower default.

Figure 9.3 represents a typical application process applicable for most types of mainstream credit. In practice, a number of variations to this process are adopted. Some lenders do not bother with the preliminary screen, always seeking a full credit report from a credit reference agency before making any decision. While this increases costs because more applicants are credit searched, having full information about all applications can be valuable for assessing the profile of customers in future and in particular, for developing more robust credit scoring models. In addition, having a single data collection and decision point results in a simpler and more easily managed process that may result in lower overall costs than a two stage process.

Others take the view that credit reference data is more important than personal data captured from an application form, and begin by only asking the applicant the most basic identity information such as name, address and date of birth in order to be in a position to ask for a credit report from a credit reference agency. If the credit score and policy rules based on the credit report are satisfactory, they proceed to solicit further information from the applicant, such as their income, residential status and occupation, before (optionally) scoring the application for a second time. This approach has the advantage of reducing the amount of time spent processing applications from people with whom the lender is not prepared to deal with on the basis of their previous credit history, or conversely, speeding up the application process for individuals who have such a good credit history that their personal information is deemed unimportant and need not be asked for.

Different recruitment channels may require different processes to be applied to some applications. For example, if an application results from a direct mail campaign, where the majority of the applicant's personal details are already known, there is little point in having a two stage process because those who would be declined due to their income, age, having an overseas address and so on, would have already been excluded from the mail shot. The lender will proceed directly with a credit report and then make their decision. However, this logic may not be applicable for applications received from the internet or in response to a mass media campaign, where relatively little is known about the applicant before they apply, requiring a two stage process to be undertaken.

For organizations offering a range of different credit products the application processing system is usually engineered to be able to cope with the different products on offer. So where an organization offers both credit cards and personal loans, the system would be configured to establish at the beginning of the application process the type of product being applied for and to treat the application appropriately. Typically, this will mean slight variations in the information provided by the applicant and the application of different credit scores and terms of business within the decision engine. This type of multiple product capability is also commonly found within the other systems maintained by lenders, such as those for account management and debt recovery.

9.1.2 Setting the terms of business

The terms of business allocated within the decision engine usually involve setting one or more of the following parameters:

- The interest rate(s) the customer will be charged.
- For fixed term credit agreements:
  o The maximum loan amount.
  o The minimum acceptable repayment period.
  o The maximum acceptable repayment period.
  o The amount of any deposit (for retail loans and hire-purchase).
- For revolving credit agreements:
  o The type of account offered (for example gold or platinum).
  o The credit line (and shadow limit).
  o The time until account renewal.
  o Whether or not to charge an annual fee.

In setting the terms of business, lenders usually refer to a number of different aspects of the credit application, including:

- Credit score(s).
- Personal income.
- Household income.
- Past credit history.
- Existing credit commitments (number of products and/or balances).
- Existing non-credit commitments (for example, household bills, rent, local taxes and school fees).
- Whether the customer is new to the lender or an existing customer.
- Those applicants flagged as having a 'VIP' status; for example employees of the lending organization and their families.

However, there is no reason why any other information that is known about the applicant could not be used to set the terms of business. If it was decided to allocate different credit lines to individuals based on their residential status or occupation, for example, this would be possible. The way in which this data is normally used is within some form of hierarchal decision tree, with the terms of business set at the root nodes of the tree, as shown in Figure 9.4.

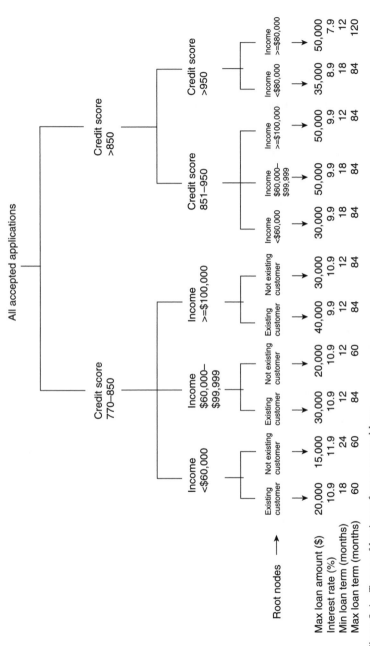

Figure 9.4 Terms of business for a personal loan

In Figure 9.4, if the applicant:

> Has a credit score of between 770 and 850 AND
> has an income of between $60,000 and $99,999 AND
> is an existing customer

then the maximum loan amount would be $30,000 and the interest rate on the loan would be 10.9 percent. The minimum term over which the loan would be advanced is 12 months and the maximum 84 months.

A large organization with several different credit products may have decision trees containing hundreds or even thousands of different terms of business, and managing these can be a non-trivial and time consuming task. The terms can also be determined by the use of formulas, rather than fixed values. Therefore, if a lender uses income multipliers, which is common for mortgage lending and setting the credit limits for credit cards, these can also be applied. For example, if it had been decided that the maximum loan advance should be equal to 40 percent of gross income, the maximum loan figure of $30,000 could be replaced by the formula:

> Gross personal income * 0.4.

So if the applicant earned $60,000 the maximum loan would be $24,000, and if they earned $99,999 it would be $40,000.

A key question is, how is the decision tree and associated terms of business defined? For a lender offering a new product, without information about previous customer behaviour, the answer is to define each branch in the tree and the terms of business based on expert opinion; that is, they will make an educated guess based on their previous experience, or what has been gleaned about the terms of business offered by competitors.

Once a credit portfolio is established, the most common strategy to refine the terms of business is trial and error, based on what is termed the champion/challenger approach. Within any given group of customers, a small percentage are randomly assigned to a challenger subgroup that is used to test some proposed new terms of business. The majority of accounts continue to have the existing terms of business applied to them and are referred to as the champion group. After the new terms of business have been applied to the challenger group for a period of time, the performance of the two groups is compared. If the challengers outperform the champions, the challenger terms of business are then also applied to the champion group. The process is then repeated with a new challenger. Consider the previous example quoted in relation to Figure 9.4. A lender may believe that customer profitability is constrained by the $30,000 loan limit imposed on existing customers earning between $60,000 and $99,999. They decide that they want to see if a $40,000 limit would be better. A $40,000 limit is introduced for 5 percent of all new customers in this group, with the $30,000 limit retained for the remaining 95 percent. After observing accounts for 12 months the performance of the two groups are evaluated. The average contribution per loan is found to be higher for the challenger group and therefore, the $40,000 limit to is applied to all new accounts in future.

One drawback of the champion/challenger approach is the time taken to evaluate challengers. One solution is to have many challengers running in competition. For example, assigning 80 percent of cases to the champion and 2.5 percent to each of eight challengers. Another (riskier) option is to base performance measures on short outcome periods – assuming that if the challenger outperforms the champion in the short term, this will also be the case in the long term.

Another problem is that some of the time the challenger group(s) will perform less well than the champion. Therefore, the optimal terms are not being applied across the entire portfolio. Consequently, there is a desire to keep challenger groups as small as possible.

One would expect statistical forecasting methods would overcome these problems, allowing the optimal terms of business to be determined by analysing the historical behaviour of accounts, which can then be implemented quickly – not dissimilar in principle to the way in which credit scorecards are developed. While it is believed some organizations do attempt to do this, the problem of choosing the best terms to offer customers has proven remarkably resilient to accurate prediction.

9.1.3 Shadow limits

An almost universal strategy adopted by revolving credit providers is the use of shadow limits. When the terms of business are assigned, two credit lines are set. The lower credit line is communicated to the customer as the maximum amount they can borrow. The second credit line, the shadow limit, is the actual amount of credit the lender is willing to grant. The shadow limit is then used in one of two ways:

1. If the customer spends beyond their allotted credit line, they are allowed to continue spending up to their shadow limit, although they may incur penalty fees for breaching their formal credit limit.

2. If the customer contacts the lender and requests an increase to their credit line, the credit line may be extended by any amount up to the shadow limit without the need to undertake a detailed review of the current status of the account.

9.1.4 Application fraud

Fraud is a serious concern for many lenders and most large credit granting institutions will have a dedicated fraud team to deal with cases of known or suspected fraud that are passed to it by other employees or which have been flagged automatically by the organizations systems. The most common type of fraud encountered during application processing is first party fraud, where the applicant falsifies their own details to improve their credit rating and/or the amount of credit they can obtain. Lenders are able to identify this type of fraud in one of three ways:

1. Discrepancies in the data supplied by the applicant. A 20-year-old who reports their time in current employment as 15 years is an obvious suspect.
2. Inaccuracies in the data supplied, such as an invalid phone number or bank account number.
3. Discrepancies between data supplied as part of the current credit application and data supplied as part of a previous application. If the applicant declares themselves to be 40 years of age, but on a previous application stated they were only 22, a possible case of fraud would be indicated. In order to be able to carry out this type of analysis, it is necessary to maintain detailed records of past applications, or to obtain information about previous credit applications from a shared industry resource such as a credit reference agency.

The other major type of fraud that can occur at application is identity theft, where an individual applies for credit using another person's details. In the UK the Credit Industry Fraud Avoidance Scheme (CIFAS) is a shared industry resource that maintains a database of known or suspected fraud cases reported to it by member organizations. CIFAS information can be obtained as part of a credit report from a credit reference agency, and if a lender receives an application from someone whose details match those recorded on the CIFAS database, the application will be flagged as a case of suspected fraud. If the application is subsequently declined the applicant's details will be added to the CIFAS database.

These methods of fraud identification are not particularly sophisticated and in cases of identity theft, do not stop fraud the first time it occurs because details can only be added to the CIFAS database after a suspected case of fraud has been identified. Nevertheless, these methods are widely quoted as preventing a considerable amount of fraudulent activity, with CIFAS claiming its database services prevented $1,976 million of fraud in 2007 (CIFAS 2008).

With both identity theft and first party fraud the lender is usually dealing with cases of suspected, rather than proven fraud. Therefore, the response that should be made when a suspected case of fraud is identified is to refer it for review by a fraud specialist, who should then attempt to confirm the identity and other details of the applicant before making a final decision about the application. However, in some organizations there is a tendency to decline any suspected fraud cases, rather than taking the time to investigate them thoroughly and incur the costs of investigation.

One of the interesting aspects of credit application fraud is that it is very unusual for any legal action to be taken against the suspected fraudster. This is because in detecting an attempted fraud the lender has not incurred any loss. Therefore there is no financial benefit to taking legal action via the courts.

9.2　Account management

Once a credit agreement has been created, details of the new agreement are passed to the account management system where an account record is created and maintained. Account management systems are complex – often costing several million dollars to install and several million dollars a year to maintain. This can mainly be attributed to the volume and type of processing required to maintain accounts on a day-to-day basis and the need to maintain links with external computer systems such as the VISA and MasterCard networks.

9.2.1　Account cycling and statement production

At the end of each statement period accounts are said to cycle as processing occurs to calculate interest and other charges arising, and to generate any additional information required to produce customers' statements of account. When processing is complete, statement details for all accounts cycling that day are produced and made available to the organization's print unit, responsible for the physical printing and dispatch of statements. For revolving credit products it is usual for accounts to be passed to a decision engine where credit scoring and policy rules are applied, possibly resulting in changes to the terms of business. It is also common to consult a credit reference agency at the cycle point to ascertain the status of the individual's credit commitments with other lenders. The types of decision that usually result from this are:

- To change the credit line and/or shadow limit.
- To change the interest rate(s).
- To issue one or more credit card cheques.
- To offer a payment holiday or other incentive.
- To offer other products or services.

The application of these decisions is similar to the way in which the original terms of business were assigned during the application process. So for a customer who has had a credit card for say 12 months, and who is still considered a good risk by having a high credit score, but whose spending has declined and is therefore suspected of making greater use of a rival product, the decision may be to raise the credit line and offer them a three month payment holiday. These changes can then be communicated with the customer's statement letter at little or no additional cost.

For products such as loans and mortgages, there is usually not a great deal to do once the account has been created other than to look for cross-sell opportunities. Therefore, there is less justification for regularly re-scoring accounts, or for paying for another credit report from a credit reference agency.

9.2.2 Transaction authorization and transaction fraud

For card systems, transactions are passed to the card issuer by the card network for authorization. In the vast majority of cases all this will involve is a simple check to ensure the customer has sufficient funds available and the card has not been reported lost or stolen. However, there are three situations where the transaction may be flagged for further attention:

1. Where the account is in serious breach of the terms of the agreement, such as the balance is well above the shadow limit or a state of serious delinquency exists. In this case the transaction will simply be declined and the account frozen – possibly leading to some attempt to contact the customer to try and bring the account back within the agreed terms.

2. Where things are more borderline the decision to authorize or decline the transaction will depend upon the customer's previous behaviour. If the customer had previously been a good customer of long standing, the transaction may be authorized. For customers with a history of arrears and/or breaching the terms of the agreement, the transaction is more likely to be declined.
3. The transaction is suspected of being fraudulent.

In identifying cases of suspected fraud, modern systems use policy rules or variations on credit scoring to identify transactions that display behaviour inconsistent with the historical behaviour of the account. If the odds of the transaction being fraudulent are higher than some threshold value (as defined by the fraud cut-off score if a fraud score is being used), it will not be authorized and further investigation will be undertaken to establish the true status of the account.

Fraud scores are usually based on information about the location, frequency, magnitude and type of transaction. If a credit card had been used occasionally for many years for small value purchases in the UK, then suddenly used many times in rapid succession to purchase high value items from jewellery stores in Mexico, this is likely to result in a high fraud score and flagged as a case of suspected fraud. The transaction will be held in a pending state and referred to a fraud expert who will attempt to contact the customer to see if the card is still in their possession, or the merchant to ask them to solicit further proof of identify from the customer. If contact cannot be established immediately, the transaction will be declined and the account frozen, preventing further transactions until the status of the account has been established.

One of the biggest problems in preventing fraudulent transactions is the false positive rate. On many occasions cases of suspected fraud turn out to be valid transactions and customers will find themselves having their card rejected or end up facing an embarrassing wait in front of a store full of people while manual authorization occurs. Therefore, relatively high thresholds tend to be set within most fraud systems resulting in relatively few referrals. The consequence of this strategy is that many actual cases of fraud are not identified when they occur because they are not sufficiently noteworthy or unusual. So if a stolen credit card was used to buy, for example, a few litres of petrol within a few miles of the card holder's address, the fraud would probably not be detected. However, card companies can hardly be blamed for this strategy as most people object (and hence end up defecting to a rival product) if they find themselves subject to frequent checks and delays whenever they attempt a card transaction that deviates slightly from the norm.

9.2.3   Customer or account level management?

If multiple credit products are managed within one system, or if a single customer is permitted to have more than one instance of the same type of product, a customer level identifier will be created within the account management system to allow all accounts held by each customer to be identified. This allows customer level as well as account level terms of business to be defined. So if a credit card provider, offering both Master-Card and VISA cards, decides that a customer is allowed a maximum credit line of $20,000, then if the customer has just one card, a credit line of $20,000 can be assigned. If the customer has both cards, the $20,000 can be split between the two accounts. Without a customer level view the lender would have to make the credit line decision independently on each account, which could result in a sub-optimal credit line assignment. For example, imagine that the aforementioned credit card provider decides to target all of its customers with a personal loan offer. If only an account level view is taken, customers with both cards will receive two personal loan offers – one for each of their accounts. This is a waste of a mailing and an annoyance for the customer. Also, if the customer applies for both loans, it is possible that only one would be accepted, with the other being treated as a repeat application, creating further customer dissatisfaction.

While customer level management is desirable, it requires a more complex and hence more costly system because each time a customer level decision is made information needs to be accumulated from across all of the customer's individual accounts.

9.3   Collections

When an individual fails to repay to the terms of an agreement, the account is said to be delinquent, in arrears or past due, leading the lender to initiate action in order to try and bring the account back to the terms of the agreement. While an account is in a state of mild delinquency, defined by many lenders as being less than three cycles in arrears (one to 90 days past due) it is subject to collections action. At this stage a lender is not looking to recover the entire debt, but to collect the amount of arrears owing so that the agreement is brought back up-to-date. If collections action fails and an account passes beyond the point where it is considered worthwhile trying to manage it back to a good paying status, it is transferred to debt recovery, where more specialist action will be taken to recover as much of the monies owed as possible before the agreement is terminated.

A typical mainstream provider of unsecured credit in the US/UK can expect to write-off between 3 and 6 percent of their loan book as bad debt, which can equate to hundreds of millions of dollars a year for a large organization. Therefore, any activity that can reduce this figure, even by just a few percent, can lead to significant improvements in profitability. Consequently, collections and debt recovery should be viewed as key operational areas, sufficiently resourced to be able to carry out substantial collections and debt recovery activity. However, within many organizations these functions have historically been undervalued and viewed as something of an afterthought within the overall design of the credit management infrastructure (Miller 2002, p.23). This is probably because collections and debt recovery functions have traditionally been seen as cost centres rather than as sources of revenue. However, this view is changing as more organizations have begun to acknowledge the contribution that can be made by their collections and debt recovery operations.

In many organizations collections activity is managed routinely and automatically within the main account management system, with standard communications sent to delinquent customers informing them of the status of their account and the necessity for them to deal with the situation. With the exception of some situations relating to secured loans and mortgages, hire-purchase and conditional sales agreements, a lender has no power to force a borrower to pay what they owe or to seize a borrower's assets, unless a court order has been obtained. Therefore, collections action is all about persuading the customer that it is in their interest to pay – if they are in a position do so. They may be sent one or more letters, or receive a reminder message printed on their next statement and possibly a phone call – all of which are relatively low cost activities. It is not normally the case for accounts in the early stages of delinquency to be singled out for specialist treatment, referred for manual processing or legal action taken unless the account falls into a high risk category – such as customers who fail to make a payment after receiving their first statement on a newly opened account. The customer may have simply forgotten to pay, but it is quite likely that this is either a case of fraud, or there has been some sort of problem setting up the account. Alternatively, the customer may be 'trying it on' to see what they can get away with before a lender takes action. All of these situations would benefit from prompt action that may need to be customized to individual cases to a greater extent than standard cases of mild delinquency.

9.3.1 Collections strategies

Many accounts in a mild state of delinquency are recoverable and can be persuaded to return to a good paying status, and lenders do not wish to alienate these customers. Therefore, the objective is to segment the delinquent population as best as possible into the following two groups:

1. Those customers with good intent and the financial means to bring the account back to a good paying status, but who have become delinquent for some trivial reason such as forgetting to pay the bill before they go on holiday, or where their statement was lost or destroyed unintentionally.
2. Those customers who do not intend to pay what they owe. Within this group there will be those who can't pay due to financial difficulty, and those who won't pay unless sufficient pressure is exerted in order to force them to do so.

In order to segment customers into these two groups, when an account first becomes delinquent it will be assessed for its likelihood of returning to a good paying status. This assessment will usually be via some type of credit score, a set of rules or a combination of the two. On the basis of this assessment a collections strategy will be assigned, defining the actions to be taken while the account remains delinquent. If by the conclusion of the collections strategy the customer has not brought the account back into line, the account will be suspended from normal account management activity and transferred to debt recovery. An example of a collections strategy is shown in Figure 9.5.

The form and content of the different communications with customers in relation to Figure 9.5 are as follows:

- **Letter 1.** A firm but polite letter, re-stating the terms of the agreement and requesting prompt payment. The customer is asked to call to discuss any problems or issues they may have with their account.
- **Letter 2.** A firm but polite letter, expressing concern over non-payment, stating further action will be taken if payment is not received within 7 days.
- **Letter 3.** A final no-nonsense written communication, requesting payment within 7 days or the account will be transferred to debt recovery where legal action may be taken.

Days past due date	Action path			
	Strategy 1	**Strategy 2**	**Strategy 3**	**Strategy 4**
0 (due date)				
1	Letter 1	Letter 1		
7	Statement message 1	Statement message 1	Statement message 3	Statement message 3
21	Phone call 1	Letter 2		
30 (due date)	**Transfer to debt recovery**	Phone call 2	Letter 4	
37		Statement message 2	Statement message 2	Statement message 3
42		Letter 3	Letter 2	Letter 4
49		Phone call 3	Phone call 2	
60 (due date)		**Transfer to debt recovery**	Letter 3	Letter 2
67			Statement message 2	Statement message 2
74				Letter 3
83			Phone call 3	Phone call 3
90 (due date)			**Transfer to debt recovery**	**Transfer to debt recovery**

Figure 9.5 Collections strategies and action paths

Note: The statement date is assumed to be 7 days after the payment due date and statements issued every 30 days. Therefore statement messages can be added to statements on day 7, 37, 67 etc.

- **Letter 4**. A polite reminder, gently prompting the customer to make a payment.
- **Statement message 1**. A short reminder, printed prominently on the borrower's monthly statement, stating that the payment date has been missed, asking the customer to contact the lender if they are experiencing any problems with their account.
- **Statement message 2**. Another reminder, using a different form of words from statement message 1, and warning of possible further action if payment is not received promptly.
- **Statement message 3**. A polite reminder message, gently prompting the customer to make a payment.

- **Phone call 1**. A specially scripted call where the customer services representative tries to establish if there is a genuine problem with the first statement, or if the account should be transferred to debt recovery.
- **Phone call 2**. A call designed to establish contact with the customer, determine the customer's situation and to discuss options for bringing the account back into line.
- **Phone call 3**. A final phone call made with the view of threatening transfer to debt recovery and legal action if the account is not brought back up-to-date within 7 days.

So, for example, if a customer does not make a payment by the due date, and if:

- This is not the customer's first statement AND
- The customer has not missed any other payments within the last 90 days AND
- The customer has a high collections score (a high likelihood of returning the account to a good paying status)

then in Figure 9.5 they will be assigned to strategy 4, designed for low risk customers with a good record of paying to the terms of the account. The first action of strategy 4 is to contact the customer via a polite statement message (statement message 3). This is printed on the customer's next statement, produced 7 days after the due date. Given that this is a low risk category, it can be expected that most customers will pay in response to this request. The lender then waits until the next statement date (37 days past the due date), at which point the statement message is repeated for anyone who has still not paid. If there is no response, this is followed by a polite reminder letter (letter 4) and then by a more firmly worded letter (Letter 2). If after 67 days payment has still not been made, then activity steps up a gear with a further statement message, followed by another letter and finally a phone call, all in quick succession. If on day 90 the account remains delinquent, it is transferred to the debt recovery department. The approach taken for someone who has a low collections score or has missed other payments within the last 90 days is somewhat different. They are assigned to strategy 2. With strategy 2 actions are taken more quickly, with firm demands for payment made much earlier, and transfer to debt recovery occurring after only 60 days if the account remains delinquent.

In practical situations, collections strategies also need to consider a range of additional factors. For example, what action to take if a partial payment is made. Sometimes the customer may take the initiative and contact the lender before delinquency has occurred because they know they will have difficulty making their next payment. Therefore, they may wish to negotiate to delay payment for a period of time, make a part payment or to write-off some of the debt. Alternatively, an account may be in arrears due to fraud committed by a third party. There will also be cases where people have died or have become seriously ill and these need to be identified and treated in an appropriate manner.

9.3.2   Designing collections strategies and action paths

Collections strategies are analogous to the terms of business in the way in which they are created and applied. They are usually implemented in the form of a decision tree within a decision engine, linked to the account management system, or in some cases, a specialized collections sub-system. Each collections strategy contains a different set of actions which, as with the terms of business, will have evolved over long experience of testing of many different champion/challenger strategies to find out which ones have the greatest impact on customer behaviour. As well as experimentation with the type of collections action and when it occurs, the text used in statement messages, telephone scripts and letters will also be varied to see how different ways of expressing the same information impacts customer response.

9.4   Debt recovery

When an account becomes more seriously delinquent, typically between three and four cycles past the due date (90–120 days past due), the focus shifts away from managing the account back to health and towards recovering as much of the total outstanding debt as possible. The types of action used in debt recovery are similar to those used in collections, with a heavy emphasis on the use of letters and phone calls to try and persuade the customer to pay. However, there is a move away from 'soft' actions designed not to upset the customer towards 'harsh' messages and threats of legal action. At this point accounts are routinely frozen and transferred to a specialist debt recovery function staffed by people trained to deal with delinquent accounts and to identify cases that may be fraudulent, or 'goneaways' where the customer has deliberately not informed the lender of a change of address.

Debt recovery is perhaps the most labour intensive area of credit management, requiring relatively large numbers of people to contact customers, negotiate repayments and manage the legal process should it prove necessary. One reason for maintaining a high level of human involvement is that people are far more effective than machines at picking out information about people's character and their ability and intent to repay from their mannerisms and speech patterns. However, most debt recovery departments do not have sufficient people available to pursue all delinquent accounts as fully as possible. Consequently, a key objective of debt recovery is to concentrate resources on those cases where the greatest amount of money is likely to be recovered with the minimum of effort. To do this, accounts undergo further assessment, often being ranked by some form of score to predict the likelihood of recovery, which is then considered along with the size of the debt. Those customers most likely to repay and with the largest outstanding debt are given the highest priority by the debt recovery team.

With a high volume of telephone activity, one of the most common tools employed within debt recovery departments are power dialers. These sophisticated telecommunications/work flow/computer systems can be loaded with lists of phone numbers and programmed to call customers *en-mass* based on known information about customer behaviour. For example, if in the past a customer had only ever been available to discus their debt situation after 6pm, the power dialer would not attempt to contact the customer until after that time. If the customer's phone is answered, the call is transferred to a human operator and the customer's details are made available on the operator's terminal. The tracking and monitoring of accounts can also be integrated within these systems, as can information from the account management system, to provide debt management platforms that allow all stages of collections and delinquency to be handled within a single integrated system.

In many organizations the debt recovery function will be branded as a different legal entity, with its own letter headings, contact details and office address, giving the impression the debt has been passed to a third party debt collector. In reality, the debt collection team will be just another function within the organization, with mail being forwarded from a PO box or other address. The advantages of doing this are twofold. First, it provides a clear message to the debtor that their delinquency has reached a new stage and that it is now being dealt with as a serious matter by a specialist team. Second, positioning debt recovery as a separate organization is perceived as isolating the main part of the lender's operations from the negative image many people associate with debt recovery practices.

9.4.1 Write-off, debt sale and legal action

If it has proved impossible to persuade a borrower to pay what they owe, or to come to some negotiated settlement, then four options are available:

1. Write-off the debt, taking no further action. This is a common strategy where the value of debt is small, often $100 or less.
2. Sell the debt. In the US around $100 billion of bad debt is traded every year (Cyrus 2006). Unsecured debt typically sells for between 7.5 and 10 percent of its face value, but can be anything up to 20 percent for good quality portfolios where there is a high chance of recovery (Legrady 2006).
3. Hire a specialist debt collector to collect on behalf of the lender. Usually, the debt collector will receive a commission on the funds recovered. Specialist debt collection agencies often resort to activities which are beyond the resources of the original lender, such as visiting an individual's home in an attempt to persuade the customer to repay the debt.
4. Take legal action to recover the debt through the courts. Although this often results in the court finding in favour of the lender, it does not necessarily mean the debt will be recovered. In many cases, the debtor does not repay what the court orders them to, and very little action can be taken if the debtor has no assets to possess in lieu of the debt. In other cases, the court's assessment of the debtor's ability to pay may result in a repayment schedule that lasts many years or even decades.

Legal issues are discussed in more detail in Chapter 5.

9.5 The business functions responsible for credit management

In order to deliver the services and systems required to run an effective credit operation across all stages of the credit lifecycle, mainstream lending organizations are structured around a number of different business functions. Each of these functions is tasked with applying a different set of skills and resources to ensure smooth delivery and management of their organization's products and services.

9.5.1 Marketing

The marketing department is responsible for acquiring new customers and maximizing the contribution of existing customers throughout the credit lifecycle. This includes the following tasks:

- Identifying appropriate customer groups to target for the product.
- Creating the product look and feel, in order to deliver the best possible brand image to the product's target audience.
- Formulating promotional campaigns to attract new customers to apply for the product.
- Formulating customer relationship management (CRM) strategies to target existing customers with the most appropriate cross-sell and up-sell opportunities in order to maximize the revenue generated from each customer.
- Delivering, tracking and monitoring the organization's promotional and CRM strategies in terms of response rates, volume of new customers, customer contribution to profits and so on.

Collections and debt recovery activities are not areas that usually come to mind in relation to marketing activity. However, knowledge of current or previous delinquency will impact on decisions about the type of marketing appropriate for these accounts. It may also be the case that for customers who are frequently delinquent, another of the company's products may be more appropriate, or that the relationship should be managed in a different way. As Miller (2001, p.28) notes, marketing has a role to play in reducing cases of mild delinquency by ensuring products are designed so that payments can be made as easily as possible; for example, encouraging customers to agree to make payments by direct debit which has been shown to result in a lower incidence of missed payments than other means of payment such as cash or cheque.

9.5.2 Credit

The credit department, sometimes referred to as the risk or credit strategy department, is responsible for making decisions about individual customer relationships on the basis of the risk profile of customers and their expected contribution to profit. Typical credit activities include:

- Working in conjunction with the marketing department to identify individuals who are potentially poor credit risks so that they can be excluded from direct marketing activity.
- Deciding the criteria under which applicants are accepted during the recruitment phase of the credit lifecycle, usually on the basis of credit scoring or judgemental decision rules.

- Designing the organization's credit granting strategy and setting the terms of business under which credit agreements will operate. For example, what credit line to grant a customer.
- Managing the terms of business on an ongoing basis as part of the account management phase of the credit lifecycle. For example, regular review of customers' credit lines.
- Implementing, tracking and monitoring of the organization's credit strategy in terms of revenues, write-off, provision estimates, overall contribution to profits and so on.
- Designing collections and debt recovery action plans to apply to accounts when they become delinquent. This will be undertaken in conjunction with the operational team(s) responsible for undertaking collections and debt recovery action.

The objectives of marketing and credit departments overlap considerably and in some organizations, particularly those based in the US, marketing and credit are a unified function with common business objectives set by senior management. In other countries this is less common because marketing activities have traditionally been volume led, with the goal of recruiting and retaining as many customers as possible, while the credit department is concerned with accepting and retaining only those customers who are likely to make a positive contribution to profit. One feature of consumer credit markets is the risk/response paradox. Those who are most credit hungry and most likely to respond to a promotional offer are those most likely to default in future, while those least likely to default are the worst in terms of response rates. Therefore, many of the individuals that the marketers judge to be 'good' prospects, end up being considered 'bad' by the credit function and vice versa. In practice, the best customers tend to be those somewhere in the middle; that is, those who have a moderate risk of defaulting and who also respond moderately well to promotional activity.

One reason why the cooperation between credit and marketing departments has a reputation for being somewhat better in the US than other countries is because both groups have access to very similar information about prospective customers at the time they are targeted and the time they apply. Therefore, it is possible to exclude from direct marketing activity potential applicants who would be likely to be rejected for the offer. In the UK this is not the case because of industry agreements that prevent the use of some data for marketing purposes. Therefore, regardless of the level of cooperation between departments, a significant proportion of those who are targeted for credit are declined due to the additional information that becomes available at the time the lending decision is made.

9.5.3 Operations

Operations deals with the physical side of the credit granting process and is responsible for implementing most of the actions and processes planned by other functions within the business. This includes:

- Producing and dispatching promotional materials created by the marketing department.
- Processing enquires and new applications for credit during the recruitment stage of the lifecycle.
- Maintaining and updating customer account records as part of the ongoing account management function. This may include management of a manual filing systems for paper based documentation such as signed credit agreements and customers' written correspondence.
- Dealing with customer enquiries and complaints.
- Producing and dispatching statements, promotional material and other communications via letter, e-mail, phone or any other channel.
- Undertaking collections and debt recovery activity to recover funds from delinquent customers. This will often be managed in conjunction with the credit department who will have overall responsibility for managing the volume of bad debt and write-off within the organization. The credit department will therefore have an interest in ensuring that the most efficient collections and debt recovery practices are being applied.

In most large organizations, operational functions are centered around branch networks and/or customer contact centres (call centres), dealing with outbound communications initiated by the credit provider and inbound communications from individuals seeking information, or requesting some action to be taken in relation to their account. Much of the communication with customers is carefully managed and monitored in order to maintain service levels, maximize revenues and keep costs to a minimum. Consequently, logistics forms a major part of operations management, ensuring that there are exactly the right amount of resources available to deal with customer demand patterns throughout the day, week, month and year. This includes dealing with fluctuations in demand due to promotional activity initiated by the marketing department and actions taken by the credit team to change the number or proportion of applicants being accepted for the product on the basis of their risk profile. Operations also needs to be flexible and able to respond to unforeseen events that may occur. If a product suddenly appears in best buy tables of the national press then a surge in customer enquiries and new applications can be expected. Alternatively, if there is a postal strike, there may be an increase in the number of telephone enquiries about the whereabouts of customer statements.

9.5.4   IT

IT plays an essential role in providing appropriate systems to meet the informational needs of all groups across the organization. Operationally, this covers things such as the account management system to process transactions and maintain account records, and work flow systems to match customer contacts with appropriate customer service staff, while at the same time supplying those members of staff with the information they require to deal with the customer in an efficient and timely manner.

From a managerial perspective, IT provides the reporting systems required to present a coherent view of the status of the business. This includes operational reporting of things such as daily transaction volumes, average call waiting times, staff performance levels and so on, as well as systems for the marketing, credit and finance departments to produce analysis of the current and historic status of the portfolio in terms of response rates, spending patterns, balances, payments, bad debt and the like.

9.5.5   Legal, and accounting and finance

Legal, and accounting and finance departments tend not to have a great deal of involvement in the day-to-day management of individual credit agreements. Operationally, there may be times when legal advice is sought about a particular situation, although this will be relatively rare for well run organizations where there should be a good working knowledge of common legal issues across all departments. The legal team will generally become involved when new legislation arises, requiring changes to the organization's systems and processes to comply with it.

Accounting and finance departments tend to be concerned with the cash flow within the business, and the income and expenditure figures required to produce company accounts, and to provide senior management with a coherent view of the financial status of the business. Accounting and finance departments will therefore liaise with other areas of the organization to obtain the information it needs to do this. They will also be responsible for managing the supply of funds needed to meet customer demand generated from the strategies created by the marketing and credit departments. Therefore, they will look to these departments to supply forecasts of expected demand for new credit and the expected income that will be generated from customer repayments.

9.6 Chapter summary

Credit management deals with the process of granting and managing credit throughout the life of a credit agreement. The credit lifecycle can be described as comprising four distinct stages:

1. Recruitment. When an application for credit is made, leading to the creation of a new credit agreement. At this stage the individual's suitability for the product is assessed, the terms of business under which credit will be offered are determined and the administrative duties required to create a new credit account are undertaken.
2. Account management. When a credit agreement already exists and is being managed on an ongoing basis.
3. Collections. When an account enters a state of mild delinquency. The objective at this stage is to encourage as many accounts as possible to return to a good paying status.
4. Debt recovery. When an account enters a state of serious delinquency. The primary objective when an account reaches this status is to secure the return of as much of the outstanding debt as possible, before terminating the agreement.

A number of different organizational functions work together to deliver the services required to manage customers across these areas. Marketing focuses on identifying the best products and services to offer and the best way to present these to the customer. The credit department decides with whom to enter into a credit agreement and the terms of business under which the credit agreement will operate. Operations has wide over-arching responsibilities to ensure that the organization has the resources available to physically manage the business. The IT department provides computer systems to deal with the operational day-to-day management of customer accounts, and management reporting systems upon which the organization's performance is measured and new strategies formulated.

9.7 Suggested sources of further information

McNab, H. and A. Wynn (2004). *Principles and Practice of Consumer Credit Risk Management*. Financial World Publishing. Written by two industry practitioners from the UK to complement The Chartered Institute of Bankers' Diploma in

Financial Services Management. It is practically focused and well suited to credit and marketing professionals who are looking to gain a broad understanding of the practical day-to-day requirements of managing a consumer credit portfolio.

Finlay, S. (2008). The *Management of Consumer Credit: Theory and Practice*. Palgrave Macmillan. This is one of my other books, which looks at the way in which major lending institutions such as banks and building societies manage their consumer credit portfolios throughout the credit lifecycle.

Appendix A: The Calculation of Interest and APR

The objective of this appendix is to explain how the annual percentage rate of charge (APR) is calculated. We begin with a review of the formulae by which simple and compound interest are calculated.

A.1   Simple and compound interest

Simple interest is where the total interest charge is based only on the initial amount borrowed, the length of the loan and the interest rate charged. If the following symbols are used:

S = The sum borrowed, known as the principal.
t = The time over which the money is borrowed, known as the term.
r = The interest rate expressed as a percentage (so a rate of 0.05 used for calculations is the same as 5 percent)
I = The total amount of interest that must be paid.

Then the interest payable on a loan can be calculated using the following formula:

$$I = S * r * t \tag{1}$$

For example, for $1,000 borrowed for a term of two years at an interest rate of 10 percent per annum, the total interest payable at the end of two years would be:

$1,000 * 0.1 * 2 = $200.

Where compound interest is applied, the term is divided up into a number of intervals of equal length. At the end of each interval, interest is calculated and added to the outstanding debt. In the next interval interest is calculated on the total sum outstanding; that is, the original sum, plus the interest that has already accrued from previous intervals. If n is used to represent the number of intervals over which interest is to be applied, then the following formula can be used to calculate the total compound interest accruing over the term of the loan:

$$I = S * [(1 + r)^n - 1] \tag{2}$$

Using the same example as before, but this time with compound interest applied at the end of each year (so the loan comprises of two intervals, each of one year); then the total interest payable will be:

$$1,000 * [(1 + 0.1)^2 - 1) = \$210.$$

Compound interest is often quoted over one interval of time, such as a year, but calculated and applied to the outstanding debt over shorter intervals; such as a day or month. In this case, the interest rate for each sub-interval is calculated as:

$$r_n = (1 + r)^{t/n} - 1 \tag{3}$$

Where:

r = The interest rate over time t.
n = The number of intervals within t, for which interest is to be calculated.
r_n = The interest rate over time t/n.

For example, if a lender quotes an annual interest rate of 9.9 percent, but applies compound interest to accounts on a monthly basis, the monthly equivalent rate is:

$$(1 + 0.099)^{1/12} - 1 = 0.7898 \text{ percent per month.}$$

For the reverse situation, where the interest rate for one interval is known, but you want to know what the equivalent rate is over a term equal to some multiple of this interval, the appropriate formula is:

$$r = (1 + r_n)^t - 1 \tag{4}$$

So if the monthly interest rate, r_n is 1.0 percent per month then the equivalent annual rate of interest is:

$(1.01)^{12} - 1 = 12.68$ percent per year.

Note that simply multiplying the monthly rate by 12 leads to an underestimate of the equivalent annual rate.

A.2   Calculating interest for fixed term amortizing loans and mortgages

For fixed term amortizing loans, such as a repayment mortgage, the outstanding debt decreases over time. Consequently, the interest charged each interval decreases, reflecting the reduced debt. With each subsequent payment the borrower is paying off more of the principal and less interest. What people normally want to know is; given an initial sum to be repaid over a fixed term and at a fixed rate of interest, what will the monthly payments be? In this situation the value of each payment can be calculated as:

$$P = S* \left[\frac{r*(1+r)^t}{(1+r)^t - 1} \right] \tag{5}$$

Where:

P = The payment each interval, with the first payment made at the end of the first interval.
S = The principal (the loan amount).
r = The interest rate charged over each interval (e.g. each day, month or year).
t = The term of the loan; that is, number of intervals over which the agreement runs.

The total amount payable over the entire term of the loan is then simply $P * t$, and the total interest charge over the term can be calculated as:

$$I = (P * t) - S. \tag{6}$$

So for a $50,000 mortgage repaid over 240 months (20 years) at a monthly interest rate of 0.4789 percent (5.9 percent per annum using formula 4) the regular monthly payment (using formula 5) will be:

$$P = \$50,000 * \left[\frac{0.04789 * (1 + 0.004789)^{240}}{(1 + 0.04789)^{240} - 1} \right] = \$350.950518$$

and the total amount payable will be:

$350.950518 * 240 = \$84,228.10.$

and the total interest payable over the lifetime of the agreement can be calculated using (6):

$(\$350.950518 * 240) - \$50,000.00 = \$34,228.10.$

In practice, the standard payment would be rounded down to $350.95 and the first payment adjusted to include the outstanding $0.10; that is, $351.05. Also note that calculations should be made using at least six decimal places to ensure a suitable level of accuracy is maintained.

For balloon loans, such as interest only mortgages, interest is the same for each interval and calculated using the simple method defined in (1). For the $50,000 loan, the interest paid each month would be:

$\$50,000 * 0.004789 = \$239.45.$

Therefore, the total sum repaid over the term of the agreement would be:

$240 * \$239.45 + \$50,000 = \$107,468.$

Of which $57,468 ($107,468 – $50,000) is interest.

A.3   Calculating interest for credit cards

In theory, interest on a credit card is calculated in exactly the same way as any other type of credit agreement. What makes credit card charges so difficult for people to understand is that different interest rates are applied to different parts of the balance at different times. The result is that two credit cards that technically charge the same rate of interest can result in different amounts being charged for the same amount of debt. Some of the differences in the way that card providers calculate interest are as follows:

- Some lenders will start charging interest from the date that the card was used to make a purchase. Others will only begin to charge interest on the date that the transaction registers on the account. This can be one to two days after the transaction occurred, due to the time it takes for it to be processed by the card network.
- Some lenders calculate interest separately for each transaction. If the balance is not settled in full by the due date, then interest is charged on each transaction from the day it occurred to the statement date following the due date. Others choose to apply the average balance method. An average daily balance is calculated for the entire statement period and interest is calculated on this average figure. With the average balance method the date that payments are made to the account are important because the earlier a payment is made the lower the average balance will be, resulting in a lower interest charge.
- When someone makes a part payment, leaving part of their balance to revolve, interest can be charged on the entire balance or only on the amount outstanding after a payment has been made. If a customer receives a statement showing a balance of $1,200 and then pays $900 by the due date, a balance of $300 will revolve to the next statement. Interest can be charged on $1,200 or $300.
- When a balance has revolved from a previous statement, but is then settled in full by the next due date, three options are available. The first is to charge no interest because the balance has been paid in full. The second is to charge interest only on the sum that revolved. The third is to charge interest on the full statement balance. For example, a balance of $500 revolves from the previous statement period (this includes any interest from the previous period that would have been charged because the balance revolved). Another $100 is spent using the card so that the total balance appearing on the new statement is $600. The $600 is then paid in full by the due date. Some lenders would charge no interest because the balance was paid in full. Some would charge interest on the $500 that revolved, others on the full $600.

A secondary issue is payment hierarchies. Many revolving credit products allow different types of transaction to be charged at different interest rates. A customer may have part of their balance on an introductory rate, part on a balance transfer rate, part on the lender's standard rate and so on. When the customer makes a payment, which part of the balance will it be used to pay? The most common strategy is for the lowest interest rate part of the balance to be paid first. So if someone has made use of a zero rate balance transfer option to transfer debt from another card, then this part of the balance will be paid first, before any new transactions attracting the lender's standard rate of interest.

A.4   Calculating APR

The method of calculating APR presented here is based on UK legislation as described in the UK government publication: 'Credit Charges and APR' (Office of Fair Trading 2001) – which is based on EU Directive 98/7/EC. A similar method is also used in the US and many other countries. However, while the mathematical formula used to calculate APR is very similar to the one described here, the actual APR calculation can vary from country to country because different definitions/ assumptions are applied to the values that are used as inputs to the formula. Consequently, non-UK readers should consult appropriate material from their home country in addition to that presented here.

The calculation of the APR is based on the schedule of advances made to the borrower and payments made to the lender over the term of the agreement. It is defined as the value at which the two sides of the borrower-lender agreement 'balance,' as represented by the following formula:

$$\sum_{k=1}^{m} \frac{S_k}{(1+r)^{t_k}} = \sum_{j=1}^{n} \frac{P_j}{(1+r)^{t_j}} \tag{7}$$

Where:

S_k is the advance made to the borrower at time t_k.
t_k is the time of advance S_k in years, after the start of the agreement.
P_j is the payment made by the borrower at time t_j in years.
t_j is the time of the payment P_j in years.
m is the total number of advances made to borrower over the term of the agreement.

n is the total number of payments made by the borrower over the term of the agreement.

r is the as yet unknown APR – the derivation of which will be discussed in due course.

This is known as the net present value method for calculating APR. The payments, P_j must be based on the Total Charge for Credit (TCC). The TCC is the sum of all mandatory charges incurred over the term of the agreement that the borrower must pay. In the UK this includes:

- Interest.
- Administration, documentation or arrangement fees.
- Mandatory payment protection insurance fees.
- Mandatory maintenance or product guarantee fees.
- Credit brokerage fees paid by the borrower.
- Option to purchase fees (for hire-purchase agreements).
- Charges for linked transactions which only exist because of the credit agreement. For example, a mandatory servicing contract on a washing machine, which was bought under a hire-purchase agreement.
- Any other fees for services charged as part of the agreement.

In the UK the following exemptions to the TCC are allowed:

- Charges for breaking the terms of the agreement, for example, missing or being late with a repayment.
- Early settlement fees, for repaying the outstanding balance on a loan before the agreed date.
- Optional payment protection insurance.
- Optional guarantees or maintenance contracts.
- Fees which would also be charged to cash customers. For example, a delivery charge on a sofa, which applies regardless of whether it is bought on cash or credit terms.
- Incidental charges, not directly linked to the credit agreement. For example, if a customer is a fee paying member of a club, which begins offering goods or services on credit terms, the membership fee can be excluded, if club membership is not solely for the purposes of obtaining credit.
- Bank charges. For example, fees for processing payments made by cheque.
- Charges for the transfer of funds, unless the borrower has no choice, or the charges are 'abnormally high'.

In the UK a number of assumptions about the TCC are also allowed for situations where the exact term or amount of lending is unknown:

- If the amount of the loan is not known, then where a credit limit is granted (such as for a credit card), it is assumed the loan is for $3,000. The exception to this is if the credit limit is less than $3,000, in which case the value of the credit limit is used in calculations.
- Where the credit limit is not known, charges are based on a nominal value of $3,000.
- If the term of the loan is not known, interest charges are based on a period of one year.
- If different interest rates apply to different parts of the agreement at different times (such as a discount rate mortgage or an introductory rate on a credit card), each rate should be used for the appropriate part of the agreement for which it applies, and the APR quoted for each time period. For the case where the exact term is not known and the interest rate changes within a year, the highest interest rate charged during the year should be used.
- If the interest rate is potentially variable over the course of the agreement, the TCC should be calculated on the basis of the interest rate at the start of the agreement.
- If repayments are variable (as with most credit cards), it is assumed the borrower repays the balance in full over a period of one year, via 12 equal monthly installments.

Once the schedule of advances and repayments are known, the goal is to find the value of the APR; that is, r in equation (7). This is not a trivial exercise and is difficult to calculate precisely. The usual practice is to use an iterative method, such as Binary Partitioning or the Newton-Raphson algorithm to generate an estimate of r to a required level of accuracy. If one has access to Microsoft Excel it is not necessary to know the logic for such algorithms as the Solver add-in, selected from the tools menu, can be used. Figure A.1 shows how to set up Excel for this purpose.

Consider a credit agreement with the following features:

- A loan $15,000 is advanced for a term of 12 months.
- The loan is amortizing in nature, with the borrower making 12 equal monthly payments covering both interest and capital so that the entire debt has been repaid after 12 months.
- The regular monthly payment is $1,350.

	A	B	C	D	E
	File Edit View Insert Format Tools Data Window Help				
	E20 ▼ f_x 0				
1	APR (r) =	0.154489			
2					
3	Time in years (t)	Advances at time t (S_k)	Repayments at time t (P_j)	$S_k/(1+r)^t$	$P_j/(1+r)^t$
4	0.0000	$15,000.00	$0.00	15000	0
5	0.0833	$0.00	$1,350.00	0	1333.93
6	0.1667	$0.00	$1,350.00	0	1318.06
7	0.2500	$0.00	$1,350.00	0	1302.38
8	0.3333	$0.00	$1,350.00	0	1286.88
9	0.4167	$0.00	$1,350.00	0	1271.56
10	0.5000	$0.00	$1,350.00	0	1256.43
11	0.5833	$0.00	$1,350.00	0	1241.48
12	0.6667	$0.00	$1,350.00	0	1226.71
13	0.7500	$0.00	$1,350.00	0	1212.11
14	0.8333	$0.00	$1,350.00	0	1197.68
15	0.9167	$0.00	$1,350.00	0	1183.43
16	1.0000	$0.00	$1,350.00	0	1169.35
17					
18	Totals		$16,200.00	15000.00	15000.00
19					
20	Difference between sum of $S_k/(1+r)^t$ and sum of $P_j/(1+r)^t$				0.000000

Solver Parameters

Set Target Cell: E20

Equal To: ○ Max ○ Min ● Value of: 0

By Changing Cells:

B1

Guess

Subject to the Constraints:

Add   Change   Delete

Solve   Close   Options   Reset All   Help

Figure A.1   Calculating the APR using the Excel Solver

- The first repayment is made one month after the start of the agreement.

Note that because the lender has quoted the value of monthly payments the interest rate is immaterial to the APR calculation.

In column A is *t*, the time in years. Column B and C contain the advances and payments made at time each *t*. Columns D and E contain the two sides of equation (7) with the summations performed at the bottom of each column in row 18. Cell E20 is the difference between the two summations (D18 – E18). The correct APR value is the one that results in both summations being equal; that is, where the difference (E20) is zero. Once the spreadsheet has been created the APR is calculated using the following steps:

1. Entering a 'seed value' for the APR in cell B1. Any value is suitable to initialize the process, for example, a value of 1.0.
2. Launch the solver from the tools menu.[1]
3. In the solver parameters dialog box set the target cell to E20.
4. Select the 'equal to: value of:' option and enter a value of zero.
5 Set the 'by changing cells' dialog to B1.
6. Click 'Solve'.

The solver will automatically adjust the value in the APR field (B1) until the difference (field E20) is zero. In this example the APR is 15.4 percent.

Under UK legislation, the APR presented to the customer, may be rounded to within one decimal place of its actual value. So if the APR is 15.4489 percent, 15.4 percent may be quoted. The legislation also defines a year as either 365 days or 365.25 days, to take into account leap years – the lender may choose which figure to use. A month is defined as 1/12 of a year, regardless of the actual length of the month, and a week as 1/52 of a year.

A.5   Example interest and APR calculations

Example 1. A credit provider offers an unsecured personal loan with the following features:

- $7,500 is advanced over a term of 36 months.
- Interest is charged at an annual rate of 8.9 percent.
- Interest is applied monthly to the outstanding balance.

- There is a three month repayment holiday at the start of the agreement. Therefore, the first repayment is due four months after the start of the agreement.
- The loan is amortizing in nature, with the borrower making equal monthly repayments over the period of the loan, once the payment holiday period is over.
- The lender charges an arrangement fee of $65, payable when the agreement is made.

To calculate the total repayments made by the borrower (the TCC), the first step is to calculate the interest charged over the period of the loan and the monthly repayments, as follows:

1. The monthly equivalent interest rate, is calculated using equation (3):

   $(1 + 0.089)^{1/12} - 1 = 0.713029$ percent per month.

2. For the first three months, no payments are made and interest accrues on a compound basis as calculated using equation (2):

   $$\$7,500 * [(1 + 0.00713029)^3 - 1] = \$161.1578$$

   Resulting in a total balance of $7616.1578 by the end of month 3.

3. For the remaining 33 months, repayments can be calculated using equation (5):

   $$P = \$7616.1578 * \left[\frac{0.00713029 * (1 + 0.00713029)^{33}}{(1 + 0.00713029)^{33} - 1} \right] = \$259.8273$$

Therefore, the standard repayment is rounded down to $259.82, resulting in an initial repayment of $260.06. The TCC is then calculated as the sum of the monthly repayments plus the arrangement fee:

$$\$260.06 + (\$259.82 * 32) + \$65 = \$8639.30$$

and the total interest payable is:

$$\$8,639.30 - \$7,500.00 - \$65 = \$1074.30$$

The APR is then calculated based on the schedule of advances and repayments as summarized in Table A.1.

Table A.1 Schedule of advances and repayments

Time (months)	Time (years)	Advances $	Repayments $
0	0.000	7,500	65.00
1	0.833	0	0.00
2	1.667	0	0.00
3	0.250	0	0.00
4	0.333	0	260.06
5	0.417	0	259.82
...	...	...	...
35	2.917	0	259.82
36	3.000	0	259.82
Total		**7,500**	**8,639.30**

Using Excel Solver gives the APR to be 0.090862 or 9.1 percent, rounded to the first decimal place.

Example 2. A credit provider offers a credit card with the following product features:

- Interest is charged at 14.9 percent per annum on all transactions (1.1642 percent per month).
- Interest is applied to the outstanding balance on the same day each month (the statement date).
- The first statement is issued one month after the start of the agreement, with the due date 20 days after the statement date (note that the same calculation would result for any due date within one month of the statement date).
- The credit limit is $8,000. As the credit limit is above the $3,000, for the purposes of calculating the TCC and the APR, it is assumed that the borrower is advanced a sum of $3,000 at the start of the agreement.
- There is a $100 annual fee, which appears on the first statement and then every twelfth statement.

As discussed in Section A.4, for credit cards in the UK, the APR must be based on the assumption that the outstanding balance is paid in full over a period of 12 months, by 12 equal monthly installments. Therefore, the first step is to calculate what each of the 12 payments

	A	B	C	D	E	F
1	Annual interest rate		14.90%			
2	Monthy interest Rate		1.16%			
3						
4	Monthly repayment		$278.19			
5						
6	Month	Time in years (t)	Advances	Repayments	Interest charge this month	Outstanding balance
7	0	0.0000	$3,000	$0	$0.00	$3,000.00
8	1	0.0833	$100	$278.19	$34.92	$2,856.73
9	2	0.1667	$0	$278.19	$33.26	$2,611.80
10	3	0.2500	$0	$278.19	$30.41	$2,364.01
11	4	0.3333	$0	$278.19	$27.52	$2,113.34
12	5	0.4167	$0	$278.19	$24.60	$1,859.75
13	6	0.5000	$0	$278.19	$21.65	$1,603.20
14	7	0.5833	$0	$278.19	$18.66	$1,343.67
15	8	0.6667	$0	$278.19	$15.64	$1,081.12
16	9	0.7500	$0	$278.19	$12.59	$815.52
17	10	0.8333	$0	$278.19	$9.49	$546.82
18	11	0.9167	$0	$278.19	$6.37	$274.99
19	12	1.0000	$0	$278.19	$3.20	$0.00
20						
21	Totals		$3,100.00	$3,338.31	$238.31	

Figure A.2   Calculating monthly credit card repayments

should be. We can again use Excel Solver to do this, as illustrated in Figure A.2.

The solver is used to vary the monthly repayment (Cell C4) so that the outstanding balance after 12 months is zero (Cell F19). This gives a monthly repayment figure of $278.19. Once the monthly payment is known, solver can be applied again to calculate the APR as shown in Figure A.3.

	A	B	C	D	E	F
1	APR (r) =	0.2218096				
2						
3	Month	Time in years (t)	Advances at time t (S_k)	Repayments at time t (P_j)	$S_k/(1+r)^t$	$P_j/(1+r)^t$
4	0	0.0000	$3,000.00	$0.00	3000.00	0.00
5	1	0.0833	$0.00	£278.19	0.00	273.59
6	2	0.1667	$0.00	£278.19	0.00	269.06
7	3	0.2500	$0.00	£278.19	0.00	264.60
8	4	0.3333	$0.00	£278.19	0.00	260.22
9	5	0.4167	$0.00	£278.19	0.00	255.91
10	6	0.5000	$0.00	£278.19	0.00	251.68
11	7	0.5833	$0.00	£278.19	0.00	247.51
12	8	0.6667	$0.00	£278.19	0.00	243.41
13	9	0.7500	$0.00	£278.19	0.00	239.38
14	10	0.8333	$0.00	£278.19	0.00	235.42
15	11	0.9167	$0.00	£278.19	0.00	231.52
16	12	1.0000	$0.00	£278.19	0.00	227.69
17						
18	Totals		$3,000.00	$3,338.31	3000.00	3000.00
19						
20	Difference between sum of $S_k/(1+r)^t$ and sum of $P_j/(1+r)^t$					0.00
21						

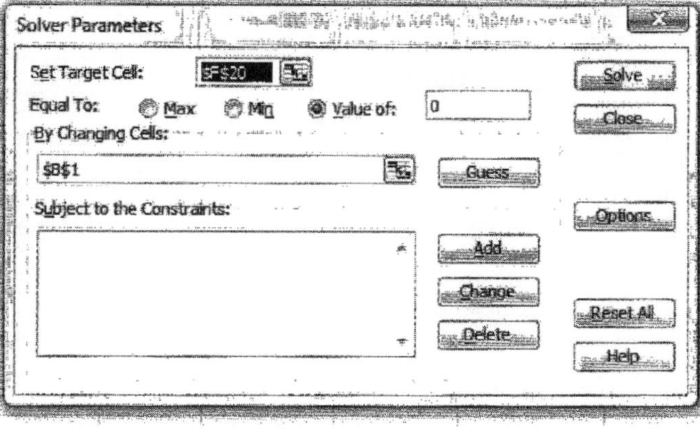

Solver Parameters

Set Target Cell: F20

Equal To: ○ Max ○ Min ● Value of: 0

By Changing Cells:

B1

Subject to the Constraints:

Solve
Close
Guess
Options
Add
Change
Delete
Reset All
Help

Figure A.3 Calculating credit card APR

Note that this time the $100 annual charge no longer features in the advances column. This is because for the purposes of the APR calculation it is considered to be a fee, not an advance, and therefore has been included within the standard monthly repayments. This gives an APR of 22.18 percent.

Notes

Chapter 1

1   Under this definition debts incurred from a partnership would be classified as consumer credit because the partners have individual liability.

Chapter 2

1   With a standard agreement this will be after all required payments have been made, but other conditions could apply.
2   The hirer always has the choice not to exercise their option to buy and hence withdraw from the agreement – although there may be penalty charges specified in the agreement if this occurs. With most hire-purchase agreements the option to buy is exercised automatically when the final rental installment is paid resulting in the title (ownership) of the goods transferring to the hirer.
3   The term 'merchant' encompasses retailers and service providers, such as hairdressers and dentists.
4   Based on the simple method of calculating interest as described in Appendix A.
5   There can be exceptions to this. If someone obtained a loan to purchase a car and the lender paid the car dealer directly then the credit would be restricted.
6   This was based on the rates charged by a single large pawnshop. A more recent 'ad hoc' review of pawnshop rates that I found quoted on the internet was broadly in agreement with these figures.
7   Note that 'musharaka' and 'murabaha' are alternative English spellings of musharakah and murabahah respectively, which are used in some texts.
8   Restrictions on credit union lending vary by country. In some, credit unions can only lend funds that have been provided by members. In others, they can borrow from and lend to other credit unions, and in some, they can also obtain funds from other financial institutions to support of their lending.
9   Estimate provided by the National Pawnbrokers Association in 2004.

Chapter 3

1   Today, usury is generally used to describe an excessive or extortionate level of interest.
2   Although they could be productive. So it was, for example, natural for a mill to be productive in turning grain into flour.
3   Homer and Sylla report that it was only in the first half of the nineteenth century that the Catholic Church accepted that it was acceptable to borrow at an interest rate defined by (secular) law, and it wasn't until 1950 that the

Church formally accepted that banking was an honest way for someone to earn their livelihood (Homer and Sylla 1996, p.81).

4   A 48 percent per annum interest rate cap was reintroduced in England between 1927 and 1974.

5   This was equivalent to $4 at the time. In 2008 the equivalent value was about $172 (The National Archive 2008).

6   In 1861 this was a considerable sum, equal to about $860 in 2008 (The National Archive 2008).

Chapter 4

1   This report identifies three measures for literacy. The 34 percent figure is for document literacy. This measures the ability of the reader to identify and understand information from different parts of a text, where the information may be presented in a number of different formats.

Chapter 5

1   In 2008 this was $970.

2   In 2008 this was $1040.

3   In 2008 the fee was $20 for data held by credit reference agencies and financial services organizations.

4   The Fair and Accurate Credit Transactions Act 2003 extended the rights of individuals to review any other information that credit reference agencies hold about them, in addition to that which is contained in their credit report.

5   There is a few dollars difference between the fees for Chapter 7 and Chapter 13 respectively.

Chapter 6

1   At the time of writing the OFTs investigation is still ongoing, and a decision has yet to be reached as to whether such fees can continue to be charged.

2   Kempson reports that 75 percent of households have access to some type of credit facility and 6 percent of all households are currently in arrears with a credit commitment. Therefore, the number of credit enabled households in arrears is $6.0/0.75 = 8$ percent.

3   In the article a Barclays spokesperson was reported to have claimed that the 10 percent figure quoted was over-inflated and untrue, but declined to provide any alternative figures.

4   In most cases merchant acquirers also charge a one-off fee to cover the installation of the equipment required to process transactions. For a small store with a single terminal, this cost will typically be several hundred dollars.

5   In May 2008 the average interchange fee was limited to 0.55 percent of a transaction's value. This figure is subject to regular review by the Reserve Bank of Australia.

6 One of the main reasons for making this change was to remove liability from member organizations in the event that legal action was taken against the networks in respect of the merchant and interchange fees they charge.

7 After write-off has occurred it is still possible to recover some of the outstanding debt. This may be as a result of litigation or further debt recovery action. Alternatively, the debt may be sold to a third party debt collector for a proportion of its original value. Any monies recovered after write-off have occurred are treated as a positive contribution to profits.

8 Between the end of 2004 and start of 2008 write-off rates increased significantly. For credit card debt write-offs rose from around 3.5 percent to over 7 percent. For other unsecured lending write-off rates increased from around 2.75 percent to 3.75 percent.

9 IAS standards are not universally applied. In the US for example, US GAAP (Generally Accepted Accounting Principles) are widely used in the production of company accounts.

10 In practice, this figure varies from less than 10 percent to more than 70 percent depending on the lender, the product and the target audience.

11 The 0.35 risk weight for mortgages and the 0.75 risk weight for other types of consumer borrowing apply only if the organization satisfies certain regulatory requirements regarding the stability and quality of their portfolio. Different weights also apply for impaired loans. If the regulatory requirements are not met then higher risk weights are applied. For reasons of expediency a more detailed discussion of standardized risk weights is not entered into here.

12 There is a specific equation defined within the accord for calculating the stressed value – for simplicity a factor is used in the text as a proxy for the full formulation.

13 In most cases these will be existing models of customer repayment behaviour, used by the business to manage accounts during the customer management phase of the credit lifecycle.

14 Organizations can define as many different risk grades as they like, but it is usually to have somewhere between 10 and 20.

Chapter 7

1 In real lending situations most people who default on a credit agreement will have made a number of repayments before defaulting. Therefore, the amount a lender will actually write-off will only be a proportion of the original loan amount.

2 Although this was clearly very unethical, in the country where the scorecard was intended for use it would have been legal.

3 Some lenders will use two or more different brands for the same credit product. Therefore, the situation can arise where an applicant unknowingly applies for the same product twice.

4 Note that there may operational reasons for estimating numbers of default cases, for example staffing levels within debt recovery departments or as input to capital requirements calculations.

5 For decision making purposes, lenders are often more interested in the relative ranking of individuals within a population, rather than absolute measures of behaviour (Thomas *et al.* 2001).

Chapter 8

1 There is not a consistent definition of the term 'thin credit file' across the industry. Therefore, individual interpretations of the level of data that constitutes a thin file may vary from lender to lender.
2 It is not suggested that credit reference agencies deliberately bias bureau scores in any way that would be illegal under US, UK or European law. In my experience great care is taken to ensure that all legal requirements are met.
3 A gigabyte is approximately one billion bytes.
4 This is a rather simplistic representation based on an 18 hour operating window each day. In practice some searches occur in real time as a credit application is made and some within batch processes performed overnight.
5 A terabyte is 1,000 gigabytes.

Chapter 9

1 In many regions a credit agreement must contain full details of the credit offered, including the amount, term and APR. If any of these details are unknown when a credit application is made, the credit agreement can only be signed after the application has been processed and the full terms of the offer have been agreed in principle. However, if the full terms of the credit agreement are known prior to the applicant applying, then a credit agreement can be signed by the applicant as part of the application form that they complete – if the form contains all of the relevant terms and conditions.

Appendix

1 Before Solver can be used for the first time it needs to be installed via the add-ins option on the Excel tools menu.

Bibliography

Andreau, J. (1999). *Banking and Business in the Roman World*, 1st edn, Cambridge University Press.

APACS (2007). *Card Fraud the Facts 2007*, APACS.

Avery, R. B., Bostic, R. W., Calem, P. S. and Canner, G. B. (2000). Credit scoring: statistical issues and evidence from credit-bureau files. *Real Estate Economics* 28(3): 523–47.

Balmer, N., Pleasence, P., Buck, A. and Walker, H. C. (2005). Worried sick: the experience of debt problems and their relationship with health, illness and disability. *Social Policy & Society* 5(1): 39–51.

Bank of England (2008). *Financial Stability Review. April 2008. Issue 23*, Bank of England.

Bank for International Settlements (2005). *An Explanatory Note on the BASEL II IRB Risk Weight Functions*. Bank of International Settlements.

Barclaycard (2008). Credit cards. *http://www.barclaycard.co.uk/personal-home/cards/index.html*. 27/03/2008.

Barron, J. M. and Staten, M. (2000). *The Value of Comprehensive Credit Reports: Lessons from the U.S. Experience*, Credit Research Centre, McDonough School of Business, Georgetown University.

Beaver, P. (1981*). A Pedlar's Legacy*, 1st edn, Henry Melland Limited.

Bentham, J. (1787). *Defence of Usury*. Kessinger Publishing.

Blaxton (1974). *The English Usurer or, Usury Condemned*, Theatrum Orbis Terrarum Ltd. & Walter J. Johnson, Inc.

Boatright, J. (1999). *Ethics in Finance*, 1st edn, Blackwell.

British Bankers' Association (2008). March 2008 – Credit card statistics. *http://www.bba.org.uk/bba/jsp/polopoly.jsp?d=470&a=13557*. 08/04/2008.

Brown, R. E. and Collins, R. F. (1995). Canonicity. *The New Jerome Biblical Commentary*. R. E. Brown, J. A. Fitzmyer and R. E. Murphy. London, Chapman: 1034–54.

Brumby, F., McTear, A., Williams, C. and Border, R. (2004). *Personal Insolvency*, 1st edn, Cavendish Publishing.

Butler, B., Butler, D. and Isaacs, A. (eds) (1997). *Oxford Dictionary of Finance and Banking*, 2nd edn, Oxford University Press.

Burton, D. (2007). *Credit and Consumer Society*, 1st edn, Routledge.

Calder, L. (1999). *Financing the American Dream*, 1st edn, Princeton University Press.

Callcredit (2001). Fair Isaac and Callcredit issue 'wake up call' to U.K. consumer credit agencies. http://www.callcredit.plc.uk/corporate_scripts/press_ view-story.asp?ID=7. 04/01/2005.

Capon, N. (1982). Credit scoring systems – a critical analysis. *Journal of Marketing* 46(2): 82–91.

Carter, H. (2004). Widow hits at lenders after debt suicide. *The Guardian*: 12/03/2004.

Cate, F. H., Litan, R. E., Staten, M. and Wallison, P. (2003). *Financial Privacy, Consumer Prosperity and the Public Good*, 1st edn, AEI Brookings.

Chandler, G. G. and Coffman, J. Y. (1979). A comparative analysis of empirical vs. judgemental credit evaluation. *Journal of Retail Banking* 2: 15–26.

Chilton, B. (2000). *Rabbi Jesus: An Intimate Biography*, 1st edn, Doubleday.

Chryssides, G. D. and Kaler, J. H. (1993). *An Introduction to Business Ethics*, 1st edn, Chapman and Hall.

CIFAS (2008). 2007 Fraud facts. CIFAS. *http://www.cifas.org.uk/default.asp?edit_id=790–57* 23/07/2008.

Cole, R. and Mishler, L. (1998). *Consumer and Business Credit Management*, 11th edn, McGraw Hill.

Collard, S. and Kempson, E. (2005). *Affordable Credit. The Way Forward*, The Policy Press.

Collin, P. H. (2003). *Dictionary of Banking & Finance*, 3rd edn, Bloomsbury.

Competition Commission (1997). *The Littlewoods Organization Plc and Freemans Plc (a subsidiary of Sears Plc): A report on the proposed merger*, Competition Commission.

Consumer Affairs Directorate (2001). *Report by the Task Force on Tackling Over-indebtedness*, Department of Trade and Industry.

Consumer Affairs Directorate (2003). *Second Report by the Task Force on Tackling Over-indebtedness*, Department of Trade and Industry.

Consumer Credit (Rebate on Early Settlement) Regulations 1983 (1983). The Stationary Office Ltd.

Consumer Credit (Advertisements) Regulations 2004 (2004a). The Stationery Office Ltd.

Consumer Credit (Early Settlement) Regulations 2004 (2004b). The Stationery Office Ltd.

Cooperative Bank (2008). *http://www.co-operativebank.co.uk*. 24/02/2008.

Corby, R. (2004). Don't be afraid of throwing down the gauntlet to banks. *The Guardian*: 25/09/2004.

Cotell, C. (2004). Barclays exposed over huge insurance rip-off. *The Guardian*: 06/03/2004.

Cox, S. (2003). *Industry Information on Household Debt Levels and Debt Recovery Costs*, OFWAT.

Crisp, R. (ed.) (2000). *Nicomachean Ethics*, 1st edn, Cambridge University Press.

Crowder, M., Hand, D. J. and Krzanowski, W. J. (2005). On customer lifetime value. *Credit Scoring and Credit Control IX*, Edinburgh, Credit Research Centre. University of Edinburgh School of Management.

Cyrus, W. (2006). *It's a sellers' market, for now*. Credit today: debt sale & purchase. October 2006.

Department of Trade and Industry (2004). *The Effect of Interest Rate Controls in Other Countries*, Department of Trade and Industry.

Dobson, P. (1996). *Sale of Goods and Consumer Credit*, 5th edn, Sweet & Maxwell.

Dobson, P. (2003). *Sale of Goods and Consumer Credit*, 6th edn, Sweet & Maxwell.

Drentea, P. and Lavrakas, P. J. (2000). Over the limit: the association among health, race and debt. *Social Science & Medicine* 50(4): 517–29.

Durand, D. (1941). *Risk Elements in Consumer Instatement Financing*, 1st edn, National Bureau of Economic Research.

Einzig, P. (1966). *Primitive Money In its Ethnological, Historical and Economic Aspects*, 2nd edn, Pergamon Press.

Eisenbeis, R. A. (1977). Pitfalls in the application of discriminant analysis in business, finance and economics. *Journal of the American Statistical Association* 72: 557–65.

Eisenbeis, R. A. (1978). Problems in applying discriminant analysis in credit scoring models. *Journal of Banking & Finance* **2**(3): 205–19.

Ellison, A., Collard, S. and Forster, R. (2006). *Illegal Lending in the UK*, Department of Trade and Industry.

Emmet, B. and Jeuck, J. E. (1950). *Catalogues and Counters. A History of Sears, Roebuck and Company*, 1st edn, The University of Chicago Press.

Evans, D. and Schmalensee, R. (1999). *Paying With Plastic. The Digital Revolution in Buying and Borrowing*, 1st edn, The MIT Press.

Evans, D. and Schmalensee, R. (2005). *Paying With Plastic. The Digital Revolution in Buying and Borrowing*, 2nd edn, The MIT Press.

Everson, S. (ed.) (1988). *Aristotle: The Politics*, Cambridge University Press.

Experian (2004). UK companies record first increase in profitability for five years Experian. *http://press.experian.com/press_releases.cfm*. 03/12/2004.

Experian (2005). *http://experian.magnitude.co.uk/index.htm*. 04/01/2005.

Experian (2007). Explaining Experian. *http://www.investis.com/corporate/financial/ reports/2007/expexperian/explaining_070807.pdf*. 04/09/2007.

Experian. (2008). History. *http://www.experiangroup.com/corporate/about/history*. 22/04/2008.

Fair Isaac Corporation (2003). *A Written Statement of Fair Isaac Corporation on Consumer Understanding and Awareness of the Credit Granting Process Before the United States Senate Committee on Banking, Housing, and Urban Affairs*. Washington D.C., Fair Isaac Corporation: 24.

Fernandez, G. (2003). *Data Mining Using SAS Applications*, 1st edn, Chapman & Hall/CRC.

Finance and Leasing Association (2000). *Guide to Credit Scoring 2000*, Finance and Leasing Association.

Financial Services (Distance Marketing) Regulations 2004 (2004c). The Stationery Office Ltd.

Finlay, P. (2000). *Strategic Management. An Introduction to Business and Corporate Strategy*, 1st edn, Pearson Education Limited.

Finlay, S. M. (2006a). Predictive models of expenditure and indebtedness for assessing the affordability of new consumer credit applications. *Journal of the Operational Research Society* **57**(6).

Finlay, S. M. (2006b). *Modelling Issues in Credit Scoring*, PhD Thesis, Lancaster University, Lancaster, UK.

Finlay, S. M. (2008). Towards profitability. A utility approach to the credit scoring problem. Journal *of the Operational Research Society* **59**(7): 921–31.

Finlay, S. (2005). *Consumer Credit Fundamentals*, 1st edn, Palgrave Macmillan.

Finlay, S. (2008). *The Management of Consumer Credit. Theory and Practice*, 1st edn, Palgrave Macmillan.

Finley, M. I. (1973). *The Ancient Economy*, 1st edn, Chatto & Windus.

Finn, M. C. (2003). *The Character of Credit. Personal Debt in English Culture, 1740–1914*, 1st edn, Cambridge University Press.

Gelpi, R. and Julien-Labruyere, F. (2000). *The History of Consumer Credit: Doctrines and Practice*, 1st edn, St. Martin's Press.

Goth, P., McKillop, D. and Ferguson, C. (2006). *Building Better Credit Unions*, 1st edn, The Policy Press.

Grant, T. (ed.) (2007). *International Directory of Company Histories: 90*, 1st edn, St James Press.

Greig, C. M. (1992). *The Growth of Credit Information*, 1st edn. Blackwell. Cambridge.

Gup, B. E. (2004). *The New Basel Capital Accord*, 1st edn, Thomson.

Hamilton, C. (2004). *Growth Fetish*, 1st edn, Pluto Press Ltd.

Hand, D. J. and Henley, W. E. (1997). Statistical classification methods in consumer credit scoring: a review. *Journal of the Royal Statistical Society Series a-Statistics in Society* **160**: 523–41.

Hand, D. J., Mannila, H. and Smith, P. (2001). *Principles of Data Mining*, 1st edn, MIT Press.

Harter, T. R. (1974). Potentials of credit scoring: myth or fact. *Credit and Financial Management* **76**: 27–8.

Haurant, S. (2007). Pawn star in the ascendancy. *The Guardian. http://www.guardian. co.uk/business/2007/feb/13/loans.* 26/02/2008.

Holland, T. (2004). *Rubicon*, 1st edn, Abacus.

Homer, S. and Sylla, R. (1996). *A History of Interest Rates*, 3rd edn, Rutgers.

Homer, S. and Sylla, R. (2005). *A History of Interest Rates*, 4th edn, Rutgers.

Hopper, M. A. and Lewis, E. M. (1992). Development and use of credit profit measures for account management. *IMA Journal of Mathematics Applied to Business and Industry* **4**: 3–17.

Horan, R. D., Bulte, E. and Shogren, J. F. (2005). How trade saved humanity from biological exclusion: an economic theory of Neanderthal extinction. *Journal of Economic Behavior & Organization* **58**(1).

Houlden, J. L. (1992). Lord's Prayer. *The Anchor Bible Dictionary Volume 4 K-N.* D. N. Freeman. Doubleday. **4**: 356–62.

House of Commons Treasury Committee (2003). *Transparency: Increasing Clarity in Credit Card Charges: First Report of Session 2003–4*, House of Commons.

Howells, P. and Bain, K. (2004). *Financial Markets and Institutions*, 4th edition, Pearson Education.

Ingham, G. (2004). *The Nature of Money*, 1st edn, Polity Press.

Jacoby, M. B. (2002). Does indebtedness influence health? A preliminary inquiry. *Journal of Law Medicine & Ethics* **30**(4): 560–71.

Jasper, M. C. (2006). Consumer Rights Law. 2nd edn. Oceana.

Jentzsch, N. (2007). *Financial Privacy: An International Comparison of Credit Reporting Systems*, 2nd edn, Springer.

Johnson, P. (1985). *The Working Class Economy in Britain 1870–1939*, 1st edn, Clarendon Press.

Jones, P. and Skinner, A. (eds) (1992). *Adam Smith Reviewed*, 1st edn, Edinburgh University Press.

Kellison, B., Brockett, P., Shin, S. and Li, S. (2003). *A Statistical Analysis of the Relationship Between Credit History and Insurance Losses*, Bureau of Business Research.

Kempson, E. (2002). *Over-indebtedness in Britain*, Department of Trade and Industry.

Kempson, E. and Whyley, C. (1999). *Extortionate Credit in the UK – A Report to the Department of Trade and Industry*, Department of Trade and Industry.

Kempson, E., Whyley, C., Caskey, J. and Collard, S. (2000). *In or Out? Financial Exclusion: A Literature and Research Review*, Financial Services Authority.

Kerridge, E. (2002). *Usury, Interest and the Reformation*, 1st edn, Ashgate Publishing Limited.

Klein, P. A. (1971). *The Cyclical Timing of Consumer Credit, 1920–67*, 1st edn, National Bureau of Economic Research.

Knight, J. (2004). BBC News Online. 'Retired and £111,000 in debt' *http:/news. bbc.co.uk/1/hi/business/3188679.stm*. 11/06/2004.

Kutner, M., Greenberg, E. and Baer, J. (2005). *A First Look at the Literacy of America's Adults in the 21st Century*, US Department of Education: Institute of Education Sciences.

Layard, R. (2006). *Happiness: Lessons from a New Science*, 1st edn, Penguin Books Ltd.

Lee, J. and Hogarth, J. M. (1999). The price of money: consumers' understanding of APRs and contract interest rates. *Journal of Public Policy & Marketing* **18**(1): 66–76.

Lee, W. A. (2003). Sallie, Bureaus end a dispute over disclosure. *American Banker* **168**(214): 1–2.

Leenders, E. (2005). Stay calm all of you lenders. *Credit Today*. **August 2005**: 11.

Legrady, P. (2006). *The Debt Buying Marketplace: The UK and Worldwide. Credit Today: Debt Sale & Purchase*. **October 2006**.

Leonard, K. J. (1998). Credit scoring and quality management. *Statistics in Finance*. D. J. Hand and S. D. Jacka. London, Edward Arnold.

Levene, T. (2004). MP Urges inquiry into bank profits from payment protection. *The Guardian*: 10/04/2004.

Lewis, M. (1990). *The Credit Card Industry: A History*, 1st edn, Twayne Publishers.

Lewis, E. M. (1992). *An Introduction to Credit Scoring*, 2nd edn, Athena Press.

Lucas, A. (2001). Statistical challenges in credit card issuing. *Applied Stochastic Models in Business and Industry* **17**(1): 83–92.

Makridakis, S., Wheelwright, S. C. and Hyndman, R. J. (1998). *Forecasting Methods and Applications*, 3rd edn, John Wiley & Sons.

Mandell, L. (1990). *The Credit Card Industry: A History*, 1st edn, Twayne Publishers.

McNab, H. and Wynn, A. (2004). *Principles and Practice of Consumer Risk Management*, 2nd edn, Financial World Publishing.

Miller, M. J. (2001). *Credit Reporting Systems Around the Globe: The State of the Art in Public Credit Registries and Private Credit Reporting Firms*, World Bank: 70.

Miller, M. J. (ed.) (2003). *Credit Reporting Systems and the International Economy*, 1st edn, MIT Press.

Miller, R. (2002). Attitudes towards debt collection. *Consumer Collections & Recoveries: Operations and Strategies*. M. Bailey, White Box: 23–30.

Mills, P. S. and Presley, J. R. (1999). *Islamic Finance: Theory and Practice*, 1st edn, Macmillan Press Ltd.

Moneyfacts. (2007). Double The Trouble From Mortgage Fees. *http://www.money-facts.co.uk/Mortgages/articles/mortgage-fees-double-trouble.aspx*. 01/03/2008

Morbin, T. (2003). Would you credit it? *Financial World* (October 2003).

MORI Market Dynamics (2004). "Credit card debt 'overstated, over reported and largely a myth'. MORI market dynamics. *http://www.morimarketdynamics.com/ news_credit-card-myth-pr.php*. 08/11/2004.

Myers, J. H. and Forgy, E. W. (1963). The development of numerical credit evaluation systems. *Journal of the American Statistical Association* **50**: 799–806.

Nettleton, S. and Burrows, R. (1998). Mortgage debt, insecure home ownership and health: an exploratory analysis. *Sociology of Health & Illness* **20**(5): 731–53.

Norris, J. D. (1978). *R.G. Dun & Co. 1841–1900*, 1st edn, London, Greenwood Press.

Office of Fair Trading (2001). Credit charges and APR. Office of Fair Trading. *http://www.oft.gov.uk/NR/rdonlyres/19342C6E-BB3E-41E9-AA15–29054CD31D77/0/oft144.pdf.* 16/01/2005.

Office of Fair Trading (2003). *MasterCard Interchange Fees: Preliminary Conclusions*, Office of Fair Trading.

Office of Fair Trading (2006). *Calculating Fair Default Charges in Credit Card Contracts. A Statement of the OFT's Position*, Office of Fair Trading.

Olen, J. and Barry, V. (1989). *Applying Ethics*, 3rd edn, Wadsworth Publishing Company.

Pederson, J. P. (ed.) (2002). *International Directory of Company Histories*: 47, 1st edn, St James Press.

Perfect, D. and Hurrell, K. (2003). *Pay and Income*, Equal Opportunities Commission.

Peterson, C. L. (2004). *Taming The Sharks. Towards a Cure for the High-Cost Credit Market*, 1st edn, The University of Akron Press.

Price, S. J. (1959). *Building Societies. Their Origin and History*, 2nd edn, Franey & Co. London.

Provident Personal Credit (2008). Provident personal credit. Loan calculator. *http://www.providentpersonalcredit.com//products/loancalculator.aspx?&red=1.* 15/02/2008.

Reading, R. and Reynolds, S. (2001). Debt, Social disadvantage and maternal depression. *Social Science & Medicine* 53(4): 441–53.

Reichheld, F. F. (2001). *The Loyalty Effect*, 1st edn, Harvard Business School Publishing.

Reserve Bank of Australia (2001). *Reform of Credit Card Schemes in Australia*, Reserve Bank of Australia.

Reserve Bank of Australia (2006). *Payment Systems (Regulation) Regulations 2006*. Reserve Bank of Australia.

Rosenberg, E. and Gleit, A. (1994). Quantitative methods in credit management: a survey. *Operations Research* 42: 589–613.

Savery, J. (1977). Numerical points systems in credit screening. *Management Decisions* 15: 36–50.

Shaffer, S. (1998). The winner's curse in banking. *Journal of Financial Intermediation* 7(4): 359–92.

Siddiqi, N. (2005). *Credit Risk Scorecards*, 1st edn, John Wiley & Sons.

Singer, P. (ed.) (1994). *Ethics*, 1st edn, Oxford University Press.

Skipworth, G. and Dyson, D. (1997). *Consumer Credit Law*, 1st edn, LAG Education and Service Trust Limited.

Smullen, J. and Hand, N. (eds) (2008). *Oxford Dictionary of Finance and Banking*. 4th edn. Oxford, Oxford University Press.

Stark, W. (1952). *Defence of Usury*, 1st edn, George Allen and Unwin.

Staten, M. and Johnson, R. W. (1995). *The Case for Deregulating Interest Rates on Consumer Credit*, Credit Research Centre, Krannert Graduate School of Management, Purdue University.

Tapp, A. (2004). *Principles of Direct and Database Marketing*, 3rd edn, FT Prentice Hall.

Taylor, A. (2002). *Working Class Credit and Community Since 1918*, 1st edn, Palgrave Macmillan.

Tebbutt, M. (1983). *Making Ends Meet. Pawnbroking & Working Class Credit*, 1st edn, St. Martin's Press Inc.

The Advertising Association (2007). *The Advertising Statistics Yearbook 2007*, 25th edn, WARC.

The American Bar Association (2006). *Guide to Credit and Bankruptcy*, 1st edn, Random House.

The Federal Reserve Board (2005). *Federal Reserve Statistical Release: Charge-off and Delinquency Rates on Loans and Leases at Commercial Banks*, The Federal Reserve Board.

The Federal Reserve Board (2008) Federal reserve statistical release Z.1. Flow of Funds Accounts of the United States. Flows and Outstandings Fourth Quarter 2007. *http://www.federalreserve.gov/releases/z1*. 16/05/2008.

The National Archive. (2008). Currency converter. *http://www.nationalarchives.gov.uk/currency/results.asp#mid*. 22/05/2008.

Thomas, L. C., Banasik, J. and Crook, J. N. (2001). Recalibrating scorecards. *Journal of the Operational Research Society* 52(9): 981–8.

Thomas, L. C., Edelman, D. B. and Crook, J. N. (2002). *Credit Scoring and Its Applications*, 1st edn, Siam.

Thomas, L. C., Oliver R. W. and Hand, D. J. (2005). A survey of the issues in consumer credit modelling research. *Journal of the Operational Research Society* 56(9): 1006–15.

TransUnion. (2008). Company History. *http://www.transunion.com/corporate/aboutUs/whoWeAre/history.page*. 28/04/2008.

U.S. Supreme Court (1978). Marquette National Bank of Minneapolis v. First of Omaha Service Corp *et al.*, 439 U.S. 299 (1978), *U.S. Supreme Court*.

U.S. Senate (1979). *Credit card redlining*. Sub-committee on Consumer Affairs of the Committee on Banking, Housing and Urban Affairs, U.S. Government Printing Office.

Usmani, M. T. (2002). *An introduction to Islamic Finance*, 1st edn, Kluwer Law International.

Viviano, B. T. (1995). The Gospel According to Matthew. *The New Jerome Biblical Commentary*. R. E. Brown, J. A. Fitzmyer and R. Murphy. Chapman: 630–74.

Ward, D. (2004). Judge says home improvement agreement with credit company was extortionate. *The Guardian*: 29/10/2004.

Watt, N. (1999). 'Babies get NI numbers in welfare fraud clampdown'. *The Guardian*: 3 July 1999.

Webley, S. and More, E. (2003). *Does Business Ethics Pay?*, Institute of Business Ethics.

Whyley, C. and Brooker, S. (2004). *Home Credit: An Investigation into the Home Credit Market*, National Consumer Council.

Williams, J., Clemens, S., Oleinikova, K. and Tarvin, K. (2003). *The Skills for Life Survey*, Department of Education and Skills.

Wonderlic, E. F. (1952). An analysis of factors in granting credit. *Indiana University Bulletin* 50: 163–76.

Wood, F. and Sangster, A. (1999). *Business Accounting 1*, 8th edn, Financial Times Professional Limited.

Index